INTRODUCTION

TO THE

SCIENCE OF RELIGION,

FOUR LECTURES

DELIVERED AT THE ROYAL INSTITUTION,

IN FEBRUARY AND MAY, 1870.

BY

F. MAX MÜLLER, M.A.

Foreign Member of the French Institute, etc.

New Edition.

"QUOD UBIQUE, QUOD SEMPER, QUOD AB OMNIBUS."

London:

LONGMANS, GREEN, AND CO.

1882.

OXFORD:

BY E. PICKARD HALL, M.A., AND J. H. STACY,

PRINTERS TO THE UNIVERSITY.

DEDICATED

TO RALPH WALDO EMERSON

IN MEMORY OF HIS VISIT TO OXFORD

IN MAY, M DCCC LXXIII,

AND IN ACKNOWLEDGMENT OF CONSTANT REFRESHMENT

OF HEAD AND HEART

DERIVED FROM HIS WRITINGS

DURING THE LAST TWENTY-FIVE YEARS.

PREFACE.

THESE Lectures, intended as an introduction to a comparative study of the principal religions of the world, were delivered at the Royal Institution in London, in February and March 1870, and printed in Fraser's Magazine of February, March, April, and May of the same year. I declined at that time to publish them in a separate form, hoping that I might find leisure to work up more fully the materials which I had collected for many years. I thought that I should thus be enabled to make these lectures more instructive and more complete, and at the same time meet several objections that had been raised by some critics against the very possibility of a scientific study of religions, and against the views which I ventured to put forward on the origin, the growth, and the real value of the ancient systems of faith, elaborated by different branches of the human race. A small edition only of these lectures was printed privately,. and sent to some of my friends, whose remarks have proved in many cases most valuable and instructive.

If now I have decided on republishing these Lectures, I have done so because I fear that as during the three years that have elapsed since their delivery, so again during the years to come I shall find little leisure for these researches. I have just finished a new edition of the text of the Rig-veda, and I now feel bound to print the last volume of my large edition of the Rig-veda with the commentary of Sâyana. When that is done, the translation of the hymns of the Rig-veda, of which the first volume was published in 1869, will have to be continued, and I see but little chance that, with these tasks before me, I shall be able to devote much time to my favourite study of ancient language, mythology, and religion.

I should gladly have left these Lectures to their ephemeral fate; but as they have been republished in America, and translated in France and Italy, they have become the subject of friendly and unfriendly remarks in several works on Comparative Theology. A German translation also being on the eve of publication, I at last determined to publish them in their original form, and to render them at least as perfect as I could at the present moment. The Lectures, as now printed, contain considerable portions which were written in 1870, but had to be left out in the course of delivery, and therefore also in Fraser's Magazine. I have inserted such corrections and supplementary notes as I had made from time to time in the course of my reading, and a few remarks were added at the last moment, whilst seeing these sheets through the Press.

For more complete information on many points

touched upon in these Lectures, I must refer my
readers to my Essays on the Science of Religion,
and the Essays on Mythology, Traditions and Customs, published in 1867 under the title of 'Chips from
a German Workshop[1].'

The literature of Comparative Theology is growing
rapidly, particularly in America. The works of James
F. Clarke, Samuel Johnson, O. B. Frothingham, the
lectures of T. W. Higginson, W. C. Gannett, and J. W.
Chadwick, the philosophical papers by F. E. Abbot,
all show that the New World, in spite of all its pre-
occupations, has not ceased to feel at one with the
Old World; all bear witness to a deep conviction
that the study of the ancient religions of mankind
will not remain without momentous practical results.
That study, I feel convinced, if carried on in a bold,
but scholar-like, careful, and reverent spirit, will
remove many doubts and difficulties which are due
entirely to the narrowness of our religious horizon;
it will enlarge our sympathies, it will raise our
thoughts above the small controversies of the day,
and at no distant future evoke in the very heart of
Christianity a fresh spirit, and a new life.

F. M. M.

Oxford, May 12, 1873.

[1] Since republished with additions in 'Selected Essays,' 2 vols.
Longmans, 1881.

CONTENTS.

FIRST LECTURE.

DELIVERED AT THE ROYAL INSTITUTION,
FEBRUARY 19, 1870.

WHEN I undertook for the first time to deliver a course of lectures in this Institution, I chose for my subject the *Science of Language*. What I then had at heart was to show to you, and to the world at large, that the comparative study of the principal languages of mankind was based on sound and truly scientific principles, and that it had brought to light results which deserved a larger share of public interest than they had as yet received. I tried to convince not only scholars by profession, but historians, theologians, and philosophers, nay everybody who had once felt the charm of gazing inwardly upon the secret workings of his own mind, veiled and revealed as they are in the flowing folds of language, that the discoveries made by comparative philologists could no longer be ignored with impunity; and I submitted that after the progress achieved in a scientific study of the principal branches of the vast realm of human speech, our new science, the Science of Language, might claim by right its seat at the Round-table of the intellectual chivalry of our age.

Such was the goodness of the cause I had then to defend that, however imperfect my own pleading, the verdict of the public has been immediate and almost unanimous. During the years that have elapsed since

B

the delivery of my first course of lectures, the Science of Language has had its full share of public recognition. Whether we look at the number of books that have been published for the advancement and elucidation of our science, or at the excellent articles in the daily, weekly, fortnightly, monthly, and quarterly reviews, or at the frequent notices of its results scattered about in works on philosophy, theology, and ancient history, we may well rest satisfied. The example set by France and Germany in founding chairs of Sanskrit and Comparative Philology, has been followed of late in nearly all the universities of England, Ireland, and Scotland. We need not fear for the future of the Science of Language. A career so auspiciously begun, in spite of strong prejudices that had to be encountered, will lead on from year to year to greater triumphs. Our best public schools, if they have not done so already, will soon have to follow the example set by the universities. It is but fair that schoolboys who are made to devote so many hours every day to the laborious acquisition of languages, should now and then be taken by a safe guide to enjoy from a higher point of view that living panorama of human speech which has been surveyed and carefully mapped out by patient explorers and bold discoverers: nor is there any longer an excuse why, even in the most elementary lessons, nay I should say, why more particularly in these elementary lessons, the dark and dreary passages of Greek and Latin, of French and German grammar, should not be brightened by the electric light of Comparative Philology.

When last year I travelled in Germany I found

that lectures on Comparative Philology were attended in the universities by nearly all who study Greek and Latin. At Leipzig there were hundreds of students who crowded the lecture room of the Professor of Comparative Philology, and the classes of the Professor of Sanskrit consisted of more than fifty undergraduates, most of them wishing to acquire that amount of knowledge of Sanskrit which is absolutely necessary before entering upon a study of Comparative Grammar.

The introduction of Greek into the universities of Europe in the fifteenth century could hardly have caused a greater revolution than the discovery of Sanskrit and the study of Comparative Philology in the nineteenth. Very few indeed now take their degree of Master of Arts in Germany or would be allowed to teach at a public school, without having been examined in the principles of Comparative Philology, nay in the elements of Sanskrit grammar. Why should it be different in England? The intellectual fibre, I know, is not different in the youth of England and in the youth of Germany, and if there is but a fair field and no favour, Comparative Philology, I feel convinced, will soon hold in England too, that place which it ought to hold at every public school, in every university, and in every classical examination[1].

In beginning to-day a course of lectures on the

---

[1] Since this was written, Comparative Philology has been admitted to its rightful place in the University of Oxford. In the first Public Examination candidates for Honours in Greek or Latin Literature will be examined in the elements of Comparative Philology as illustrating the Greek and Latin languages. In the final Public Examination, Comparative Philology will form a special subject, by the side of the history of Ancient Literature.

Science of Religion,—or I should rather say on some preliminary points that have to be settled before we can enter upon a truly scientific study of the religions of the world,—I feel as I felt when first pleading in this very place for the Science of Language.

I know that I shall have to meet determined antagonists who will deny the very possibility of a scientific treatment of religions, as formerly they denied the possibility of a scientific treatment of languages. I foresee even far more serious conflicts with familiar prejudices and deep-rooted convictions; but I feel at the same time that I am prepared to meet my antagonists, and I have such faith in their honesty and love of truth, that I doubt not of a patient and impartial hearing on their part, and of a verdict influenced by nothing but by the evidence that I shall have to place before them.

In these our days it is almost impossible to speak of religion at all, without giving offence either on the right or on the left. With some, religion seems too sacred a subject for scientific treatment; with others it stands on a level with alchemy and astrology, as a mere tissue of errors or halucinations, far beneath the notice of the man of science.

In a certain sense, I accept both these views. Religion *is* a sacred subject, and whether in its most perfect or in its most imperfect form, it has a right to our highest reverence. In this respect we might learn something from those whom we are so ready to teach. I quote from the 'Declaration of Principles' by which the church founded by Keshub Chunder Sen professes to be guided. After stating that no created object shall ever be worshipped, nor any man or inferior being

or material object be treated as identical with God, or
like unto God, or as an incarnation of God, and that
no prayer or hymn shall be said unto or in the name
of any one except God, the declaration continues:

'No created being or object that has been or may
hereafter be worshipped by any sect shall be ridiculed
or contemned in the course of the divine service to be
conducted here.'

'No book shall be acknowledged or received as the
infallible Word of God: yet no book which has been
or may hereafter be acknowledged by any sect to be
infallible shall be ridiculed or contemned.'

'No sect shall be vilified, ridiculed, or hated.'

It might be thought, perhaps, that these broad
sentiments of religious toleration were borrowed by
Keshub Chunder Sen, or rather by the founder of
the Brahma-Samâj, Rammohun Roy, from Christian
writers. That may be so. But they need not have
gone to Europe for these truly Christian principles.
They might have found them inscribed on the very
rocks of India, placed there more than 2000 years
ago by Asoka, who ruled from 259 to 222 B.C.
Asoka, who had left the old Vedic religion, and
had embraced the essential principles of Buddha's
teaching, says in one of his Edicts: 'The King Piyadasi wishes that all sects should dwell everywhere
(unmolested); for all of them approve of restraint (of
the senses) and purification of the soul.' And again,
'The King Piyadasi honours all sects, monks and house-
holders; he honours them by liberality and various
kinds of favours. . . . But there is a fundamental law
for every sect, namely moderation in speech, that one
should not exalt one's own sect in decrying others,

and not depreciate them lightly, but that one ought on the contrary to show always to other sects the honour due to them.   In this manner one exalts one's own sect, and benefits others, while in acting otherwise one injures one's own sect, and does not benefit others. He who exalts his own sect and decries others, does it from devotion to his own sect in order to make it illustrious, but really in acting thus he only damages his own sect.   Therefore peace alone is good, so that all should hear and listen gladly to the opinions of others[1].'

The Students of the Science of Religion should at all events endeavour not to be outdone in impartiality by this ancient king. And, as for myself, I can promise that no one who attends these lectures, be he Christian or Jew, Hindu or Mohammedan, shall hear his own way of serving God spoken of irreverently[2]. But true reverence does not consist in declaring a subject, because it is dear to us, to be unfit for free and honest inquiry: far from it! True reverence is shown in treating every subject, however sacred, however dear to us, with perfect confidence; without fear and without favour; with tenderness and love, by all means, but, before all, with an unflinching and uncompromising loyalty to truth.

On the other hand, I fully admit that religion has

---

[1] 'Les Inscriptions de Piyadasi,' par E. Senart, 1881, p. 174; Septième Edit; p. 249, Douzième Edit.

[2] My attention has been directed to a curious instance of real atavism. My great grand-father, Basedow, the founder of the *Philanthropinum*, at Dessau, wrote almost *totidem verbis* ' that in the general divine service at his school nothing should happen by word or deed, that could not be approved of by every worshipper of God, be he Christian, Jew, Mohammedan, or De'st.' See 'Archiv fur Lebensbeschreibung,' p. 63; Raumer, 'Geschichte der Pädagogik,' ii. p. 274.

stood in former ages, and stands also in our own age, if we look abroad, and if we look into some of the highest and some of the lowest places at home, on a level with alchemy and astrology. There exist superstitions, little short of fetishism; and, what is worse, there exists hypocrisy, as bad as that of the Roman augurs.

In practical life it would be wrong to assume a neutral position between such conflicting views. Where we see that the reverence due to religion is violated, we are bound to protest; where we see that superstition saps the roots of faith, and hypocrisy poisons the springs of morality, we must take sides. But as students of the Science of Religion we move in a higher and more serene atmosphere. We study error, as the physiologist studies a disease, looking for its causes, tracing its influence, speculating on possible remedies of this ἱερὸς νοῦσος, but leaving the application of such remedies to a different class of men, to the surgeon and the practical physician. *Diversos diversa juvant* applies here as everywhere else, and a division of labour, according to the peculiar abilities and tastes of different individuals, will always yield the best results. The student of the history of the physical sciences is not angry with the alchemists, nor does he argue with the astrologists: he rather tries to enter into their view of things, and to discover in the errors of alchemy the seeds of chemistry, and in the halucinations of astrology a yearning and groping after a true knowledge of the heavenly bodies. It is the same with the student of the Science of Religion. He wants to find out what religion is, what foundation it has in the soul of man, and what laws it follows in its historical growth. For that purpose the study of errors is to him more instructive than the study of that religion which he considers the true one, and the smiling augur as interesting a subject as the Roman suppliant who veiled his face in prayer, that he might be alone with his God.

The very title of the Science of Religion will jar, I know, on the ears of many persons, and a comparison of all the religions of the world, in which none can claim a privileged position, will no doubt seem to many dangerous and reprehensible[1], because ignoring that peculiar reverence which everybody, down to the mere fetish worshipper, feels for his *own* religion and for his *own* God. Let me say then at once that I myself have shared these misgivings, but that I have tried to overcome them, because I would not and could not allow myself to surrender either what I hold to be the truth, or what I hold still dearer than the truth, the right of testing truth. Nor do I regret it. I do not say that the Science of Religion is all gain. No, it entails losses, and losses of many things which we hold dear. But this I will say, that, as far as my humble judgment goes, it does not entail the loss of anything that is essential to true religion, and that if we strike the balance honestly, the gain is immeasurably greater than the loss.

One of the first questions that was asked by classical scholars when invited to consider the value of the Science of Language, was, 'What shall we gain by a comparative study of languages?' Languages, it was said, are wanted for practical purposes, for speaking

---

[1] 'The so-called "Science of Religion" of the present day, with its attempts to put into competition the sacred books of India and the Holy Scriptures, is deeply to be deprecated.' Bishop of Gloucester.

and reading; and by studying too many languages at once, we run the risk of losing the firm grasp which we ought to have on the few that are really important. Our knowledge, by becoming wider, must needs, it was thought, become shallower, and the gain, if there is any, in knowing the structure of dialects which have never produced any literature at all, would certainly be outweighed by the loss in accurate and practical scholarship.

If this could be said of a comparative study of languages, with how much greater force will it be urged against a comparative study of religions! Though I do not expect that those who study the religious books of Brahmans and Buddhists, of Confucius and Laotse, of Mohammed and Nânak, will be accused of cherishing in their secret heart the doctrines of those ancient masters, or of having lost the firm hold on their own religious convictions, yet I doubt whether the practical utility of wider studies in the vast field of the religions of the world will be admitted with greater readiness by professed theologians than the value of a knowledge of Sanskrit, Zend, Gothic, or Celtic for a thorough mastery of Greek and Latin, and for a real appreciation of the nature, the purpose, the laws, the growth and decay of language was admitted, or is even now admitted, by some of our most eminent professors and teachers.

People ask, What is gained by comparison?—Why, all higher knowledge is acquired by comparison, and rests on comparison. If it is said that the character of scientific research in our age is pre-eminently comparative, this really means that our researches are now based on the widest evidence that can be obtained, on the broadest inductions that can be grasped by the human mind.

What can be gained by comparison?—Why, look at the study of languages. If you go back but a hundred years and examine the folios of the most learned writers on questions connected with language, and then open a book written by the merest tiro in Comparative Philology, you will see what can be gained, what has been gained, by the comparative method. A few hundred years ago, the idea that Hebrew was the original language of mankind was accepted as a matter of course, even as a matter of faith, the only problem being to find out by what process Greek, or Latin, or any other language could have been developed out of Hebrew. The idea, too, that language was revealed, in the scholastic sense of the word, was generally accepted, although, as early as the fourth century, St. Gregory, the learned bishop of Nyssa, had strongly protested against it[1]. The grammatical framework of a language was either considered as the result of a conventional agreement, or the terminations of nouns and verbs were supposed to have sprouted forth like buds from the roots and stems of language; and the vaguest similarity in the sound and meaning of words was taken to be a sufficient criterion for testing their origin and their relationship. Of all this philological somnambulism we hardly find a trace in works published since the days of Humboldt, Bopp, and Grimm.

Has there been any loss here? Has it not been pure gain? Does language excite our imagination less, because we know that, though the faculty of

[1] 'Lectures on the Science of Language,' vol. i. p. 32.

speaking is the work of Him who works in all
things, the invention of words for · naming each
object was left to man, and was achieved through
the working of the human mind? Is Hebrew less
carefully studied, because it is no longer believed to
be a revealed language, sent down from heaven, but a
language closely allied to Arabic, Syriac and ancient
Babylonian, and receiving light from these cognate,
and in some respects more primitive, languages, for
the explanation of many of its grammatical forms,
and for the exact interpretation of many of its
obscure and difficult words? Is the grammatical
articulation of Greek and Latin less instructive,
because instead of seeing in the terminations of nouns
and verbs merely arbitrary signs to distinguish the
plural from the singular, or the future from the
present, we can now perceive an intelligible principle
in the gradual production of formal out of the
material elements of language? And are our ety-
mologies less important, because, instead of being
suggested by superficial similarities, they are now
based on honest historical and physiological research?
Lastly, has our own language ceased to hold its own
peculiar place? Is our love for our own native
tongue at all impaired? Do men speak less boldly
or pray less fervently in their own mother tongue,
because they know its true origin and its unadorned
history; because they know that everything in
language that goes beyond the objects of sense, is and
must be pure metaphor? Or does any one deplore
the fact that there is in all languages, even in the
jargons of the lowest savages, order and wisdom;
nay, something that makes the world akin?

Why, then, should we hesitate to apply the comparative method, which has produced such great results in other spheres of knowledge, to a study of religion? That it will change many of the views commonly held about the origin, the character, the growth, and decay of the religions of the world, I do not deny; but unless we hold that fearless progression in new inquiries, which is our bounden duty and our honest pride in all other branches of knowledge, is dangerous in the study of religions, unless we allow ourselves to be frightened by the once famous dictum, that whatever is new in theology is false, this ought to be the very reason why a comparative study of religions should no longer be neglected or delayed.

When the students of Comparative Philology boldly adapted Goethe's paradox, '*He who knows one language knows none*,' people were startled at first; but they soon began to feel the truth which was hidden beneath the paradox. Could Goethe have meant that Homer did not know Greek, or that Shakespeare did not know English, because neither of them knew more than his own mother tongue? No! what was meant was that neither Homer nor Shakespeare knew what that language really was which he handled with so much power and cunning. Unfortunately the old verb 'to can,' from which 'canny' and 'cunning,' is lost in English, otherwise we should be able in two words to express our meaning, and to keep apart the two kinds of knowledge of which we are here speaking. As we say in German *können* is not *kennen*, we might say in English, *to can*, that is to be cunning, is not *to ken*, that is to know; and it would then become clear at once, that the most eloquent speaker and the most gifted poet, with all their cunning of words and skilful mastery of expression, would have but little to say if asked, what really is language ? The same applies to religion. *He who knows one, knows none.* There are thousands of people whose faith is such that it could move mountains, and who yet, if they were asked what religion really is, would remain silent, or would speak of outward tokens rather than of the inward nature, or of the faculty of faith.

It will be easily perceived that religion means at least two very different things. When we speak of the Jewish, or the Christian, or the Hindu religion, we mean a body of doctrines handed down by tradition, or in canonical books, and containing all that constitutes the faith of Jew, Christian, or Hindu. Using religion in that sense, we may say that a man has changed his religion, that is, that he has adopted the Christian instead of the Brahmanical body of religious doctrines, just as a man may learn to speak English instead of Hindustani.

But religion is also used in a different sense. As there is a faculty of speech, independent of all the historical forms of language, there is a faculty of faith in man, independent of all historical religions. If we say that it is religion which distinguishes man from the animal, we do not mean the Christian or Jewish religion; we do not mean any special religion; but we mean a mental faculty or disposition, which, independent of, nay in spite of sense and reason, enables man to apprehend the Infinite under different names, and under varying disguises. Without that faculty, no religion, not even the lowest worship of idols and fetishes, would be possible; and if we will but listen attentively, we can hear in all religions a groaning of the spirit, a struggle to conceive the inconceivable, to utter the unutterable, a longing after the Infinite, a love of God. Whether the etymology which the ancients gave of the Greek word ἄνθρωπος, man, be true or not (they derived it from ὁ ἄνω ἀθρῶν, he who looks upward), certain it is that what makes man man, is that he alone can turn his face to heaven; certain it is that he alone yearns for something that neither sense nor reason can supply, nay for something which both sense and reason by themselves are bound to deny.

If then there is a philosophical discipline which examines into the conditions of sensuous or intuitional knowledge, and if there is another philosophical discipline which examines into the conditions of rational or conceptual knowledge, there is clearly a place for a third philosophical discipline that has to examine into the existence and the conditions of that third faculty of man, co-ordinate with, yet independent of, sense and reason, the faculty of the Infinite[1], which is at the root of all religions. In German we can distinguish that third faculty by the name of *Vernunft*, as opposed to *Verstand*, reason, and *Sinn*, sense. In English I know no better name for it, than the faculty of faith, though it will have to be guarded by careful definition, in order to confine it to those objects only, which cannot be supplied either by the evidence of the senses, or by the evidence of reason, and the existence of which is nevertheless postulated by something without us

---

[1] I use the word Infinite, because it is less liable to be misunderstood than the Absolute, or the Unconditioned, or the Unknowable. On the distinction between the Infinite and the Indefinite, see Kant, 'Critique of Pure Reason,' translated by M. M., vol. ii. p. 442.

which we cannot resist. No simply historical fact can ever fall under the cognisance of faith, in our sense of the word.

If we look at the history of modern thought, we find that the dominant school of philosophy, previous to Kant, had reduced all intellectual activity to *one* faculty, that of the senses, '*Nihil in intellectu quod non ante fuerit in sensu*'—'Nothing exists in the intellect but what has before existed in the senses,' was their watchword; and Leibniz answered epigrammatically, but most profoundly, '*Nihil—nisi intellectus*,' 'Yes, nothing but the intellect.' Then followed Kant, who, in his 'Criticism of Pure Reason,' written ninety years ago, but not yet antiquated, proved that our knowledge requires, besides the data of sensation, the admission of the intuitions of space and time, and the categories, or, as we might call them, the laws and necessities of the understanding. Satisfied with having established the *a priori* character of the categories and the intuitions of space and time, or, to use his own technical language, satisfied with having proved the possibility of synthetic judgments *a priori*, Kant declined to go further, and he most energetically denied to the human intellect the power of transcending the finite, or the faculty of approaching the Infinite. He closed the ancient gates through which man had gazed into Infinity; but, in spite of himself, he was driven in his 'Criticism of Practical Reason,' to open a side-door through which to admit the sense of duty, and with it the sense of the Divine. This has always seemed to me the vulnerable point in Kant's philosophy, for if philosophy has to explain what is, not what ought to be, there will be and can be no rest till we admit that there is in man a third faculty, which I call simply the faculty of apprehending the Infinite, not only in religion, but in all things; a power independent of sense and reason, a power in a certain sense contradicted by sense and reason, but yet a very real power, which has held its own from the beginning of the world, neither sense nor reason being able to overcome it, while it alone is able to overcome in many cases both reason and sense[1].

According to the two meanings of the word religion, then, the science of religion is divided into two parts; the former, which has to deal with the historical forms of religion, is called *Comparative Theo-*

[1] As this passage has given rise to strange misunderstandings, I quote a passage from another lecture of mine, not yet published: 'It is difficult at present to speak of the human mind in any technical language whatsoever, without being called to order by some philosopher or other. According to some, the mind is one and indivisible, and it is the subject-matter only of our consciousness which gives to the acts of the mind the different appearances of feeling, remembering, imagining, knowing, willing or believing. According to others, mind, as a subject, has no existence whatever, and nothing ought to be spoken of except states of consciousness, some passive, some active, some mixed. I myself have been sharply taken to task for venturing to speak, in this enlightened 19th century of ours, of different faculties of the mind,— faculties being purely imaginary creations, the illegitimate offspring of mediaeval scholasticism. Now I confess I am amused rather than frightened by such pedantry. Faculty, *facultas*, seems to me so good a word that, if it did not exist, it ought to be invented in order to express the different modes of action of what we may still be allowed to call our mind. It does not commit us to more than if we were to speak of the *facilities* or *agilities* of the mind, and those only who change the forces of nature into gods or demons, would be frightened by the faculties as green-eyed monsters seated in the dark recesses of our Self. I shall therefore retain the name of faculty,' &c.

On the necessity of admitting a faculty of perceiving the Infinite I have treated more fully in my 'Lectures on the Science of Language,' vol. ii. pp. 625–632. The subject is ably discussed by Nicotra Sangiacomo, in *L'Infinito di Max-Müller*, Catania, 1882.

logy; the latter, which has to explain the conditions under which religion, whether in its highest or its lowest form, is possible, is called *Theoretic Theology.*

We shall at present have to deal with the former only; nay it will be my object to show that the problems which chiefly occupy theoretic theology, ought not to be taken up till all the evidence that can possibly be gained from a comparative study of the religions of the world has been fully collected, classified, and analysed. I feel certain that the time will come when all that is now written on theology, whether from an ecclesiastical or philosophical point of view, will seem as antiquated, as strange, as unaccountable as the works of Vossius, Hemsterhuys, Valckenaer, and Lennep, by the side of Bopp's Comparative Grammar.

It may seem strange that while theoretical theology, or the analysis of the inward and outward conditions under which faith is possible, has occupied so many thinkers, the study of comparative theology has never as yet been seriously taken in hand. But the explanation is very simple. The materials on which alone a comparative study of the religions of mankind could have been founded were not accessible in former days, while in our own days they have come to light in such profusion that it is almost impossible for any individual to master them all.

It is well known that the Emperor Akbar (1542–1605)[1] had a passion for the study of religions, and that he invited to his court Jews, Christians, Mohammedans, Brahmans, and Zoroastrians, and had as many of their sacred books as he could get access to, trans-

[1] See Note A, On Akbar.

C

lated for his own study[1]. Yet, how small was the collection of sacred books that even an Emperor of India could command not more than 300 years ago, compared to what may now be found in the library of any poor scholar! We have the original text of the Veda, which neither the bribes nor the threats of Akbar could extort from the Brahmans. The translation of the Veda which he is said to have obtained, was a translation of the so-called Atharva-veda, and comprised most likely the Upanishads only, mystic and philosophical treatises, very interesting, very important in themselves, but as far removed from the ancient poetry of the Veda as the Talmud is from the Old Testament, as Sufiism is from the Koran. We have the Zendavesta, the sacred writings of the so-called fire-worshippers, and we possess translations of it, far more complete and far more correct than any that the Emperor Akbar obtained from Ardsher, a wise Zoroastrian whom he invited from Kirman to India[2]. The religion of Buddha, certainly in many respects more important than either Brahmanism, or Zoroastrianism, or Mohammedanism, is never mentioned in the religious discussions that took place every Thursday evening[3] at the imperial court of Delhi. Abulfazl, it is said, the minister of Akbar, could find no one to assist him in his inquiries respecting Buddhism. We possess the whole sacred canon of the Buddhists in various languages, in Pâli, Burmese, and Siamese, in Sanskrit, Tibetan, Mongolian, and Chinese,

[1] Elphinstone's 'History of India,' ed. Cowell, book ix. cap. 3.
[2] See 'Journal of the Asiatic Society of Bengal,' 1868, p. 14.
[3] See 'Aini Akbari,' transl. by Blochmann, p. 171, note 3.

and it is our fault entirely, if as yet there is no complete translation in any European tongue of this important collection of sacred books. The ancient religions of China again, that of Confucius and that of Laotse, may now be studied in excellent translations of their sacred books by anybody interested in the ancient faiths of mankind.

But this is not all. We owe to missionaries particularly, careful accounts of the religious belief and worship among tribes far lower in the scale of civilisation than the poets of the Vedic hymns, or the followers of Confucius. Though the belief of African and Melanesian savages is more recent in point of time, it may or may not represent an earlier and far more primitive phase in point of growth, and is therefore as instructive to the student of religion as the study of uncultivated dialects has proved to the student of language[1].

Lastly, and this, I believe, is the most important advantage which we enjoy as students of the history of religion, we have been taught the rules of critical scholarship. No one would venture, now-a-days, to quote from any book, whether sacred or profane, without having asked these simple and yet momentous questions: When was it written? Where? and by whom? Was the author an eye-witness, or does he only relate what he has heard from others? And if the latter, were his authorities at least contemporaneous with the events which they relate, and were they

[1] See Tiele, 'De Plaats van de Godsdiensten der Naturvolken in de Godsdienstgeschiedenis,' Amsterdam, 1873. E. B. Tylor, 'Fortnightly Review,' 1866, p. 71.

under the sway of party feeling or any other disturbing influence? Was the whole book written at once, or does it contain portions of an earlier date; and if so, is it possible for us to separate these earlier documents from the body of the book?

A study of the original documents on which the principal religions of the world profess to be founded, carried on in this spirit, has enabled some of our best living scholars to distinguish in each religion between what is really ancient and what is comparatively modern; between what was the doctrine of the founders and their immediate disciples, and what were the afterthoughts and, generally, the corruptions of later ages. A study of these later developments, of these later corruptions, or, it may be, improvements, is not without its own peculiar charm, and is full of practical lessons; yet, as it is essential that we should know the most ancient forms of every language, before we proceed to any comparisons, it is indispensable also that we should have a clear conception of the most primitive form of every religion, before we proceed to determine its own value, and to compare it with other forms of religious faith. Many an orthodox Mohammedan, for instance, will relate miracles wrought by Mohammed; but in the Koran Mohammed says distinctly, that he is a man like other men. He disdains to work miracles, and appeals to the great works of Allah, the rising and setting of the sun, the rain that fructifies the earth, the plants that grow, and the living souls that are born into the world— who can tell whence?—as the real signs and wonders in the eyes of a true believer. 'I am only a warner,' he says; 'I cannot show you a sign—a miracle—

except what ye see every day and night. Signs are with God[1].'

The Buddhist legends teem with miserable miracles attributed to Buddha and his disciples—miracles which in wonderfulness certainly surpass the miracles of any other religion: yet in their own sacred canon a saying of Buddha's is recorded, prohibiting his disciples from working miracles, though challenged to do so by the multitudes, who required a sign that they might believe. And what is the miracle that Buddha commands his disciples to perform? 'Hide your good deeds,' he says, 'and confess before the world the sins you have committed.' That is the true miracle of Buddha.

Modern Hinduism rests on the system of caste as on a rock which no arguments can shake: but in the Veda, the highest authority of the religious belief of the Hindus, no mention occurs of the complicated system of castes, such as we find it in Manu: nay, in one place, where the ordinary classes of the Indian, or any other society, are alluded to, viz. the priests, the warriors, the citizens, and the slaves, all are represented as sprung alike from Brahman, the source of all being.

It would be too much to say that the critical sifting of the authorities for a study of each religion has been already fully carried out. There is work enough still to be done. But a beginning, and a very successful beginning, has been made, and the results thus brought to light will serve as a wholesome caution to everybody who is engaged in religious researches. Thus,

[1] 'The Speeches and Table-talk of the Prophet Mohammad,' by Stanley Lane-Poole, 1882, Introd. p. xxxvi and xli.

if we study the primitive religion of the Veda, we
have to distinguish most carefully, not only between
the hymns of the Rig-veda on one side, and the
hymns collected in the Sâma-veda, Yagur-veda, and
Atharva-veda on the other, but critical scholars distinguish with equal care between the more ancient
and the more modern hymns of the Rig-veda itself,
so far as even the faintest indications of language, of
grammar, or metre enable them to do so.

In order to gain a clear insight into the motives
and impulses of the founder of the worship of Ahuramazda, we must chiefly, if not entirely, depend on
those portions of the Zendavesta which are written in
the Gâthâ dialect, a more primitive dialect than that
of the rest of the sacred code of the Zoroastrians.

In order to do justice to Buddha, we must not mix
the practical portions of the Tripitaka, the Dharma,
with the metaphysical portions, the Abhidharma.
Both, it is true, belong to the sacred canon of the
Buddhists; but their original sources lie in very different latitudes of religious thought.

We have in the history of Buddhism an excellent
opportunity for watching the process by which a
canon of sacred books is called into existence. We
see here, as elsewhere, that during the lifetime of the
teacher, no record of events, no sacred code containing
the sayings of the master was wanted. His presence
was enough, and thoughts of the future, and more
particularly, of future greatness, seldom entered the
minds of those who followed him. It was only after
Buddha had left the world, that his disciples attempted
to recall the sayings and doings of their departed friend
and master. At that time everything that seemed to

redound to the glory of Buddha, however extraordinary and incredible, was eagerly welcomed, while witnesses who would have ventured to criticise or reject unsupported statements, or to detract in any way from the holy character of Buddha, had no chance of even being listened to[1]. And when, in spite of all this, differences of opinion arose, they were not brought to the test by a careful weighing of evidence, but the names of 'unbeliever' and 'heretic' (nâstika, pâshanda) were quickly invented in India as elsewhere, and bandied backwards and forwards between contending parties, till at last, when the doctors disagreed, the help of the secular power had to be invoked, and kings and emperors assembled councils for the suppression of schism, for the settlement of an orthodox creed, and for the completion of a sacred canon. We know of King Asoka, the contemporary of Seleucus, sending his royal missive to the assembled elders, and telling them what to do, and what to avoid, warning them also in his own name of the apocryphal or heretical character of certain books which, as he thinks, ought not to be admitted into the sacred canon[2].

---

[1] 'Mahâvansa,' p. 12, Nâññehi tatha vatthabbam iti, 'it cannot be allowed to other priests to be present.'

[2] The following is Professor Kern's translation of the Second Bairat Rock Inscription, containing the rescript which Asoka addressed to the Council of Magadha: 'King Priyadarsin of Magadha greets the Assembly (of Clerics) and wishes them welfare and happiness. Ye know, Sirs, how great is our reverence and affection for the Triad which is called *Buddha* (the Master), *Faith*, and *Assembly*. All that our Lord Buddha has spoken, my Lords, is well spoken. Wherefore, Sirs, it must indeed be regarded as having indisputable authority, so the true faith shall last long. Thus, my Lords, I honour in the first place these religious works :—Summary of the Discipline, The Supernatural Powers of the Master (or of the Masters), The Terrors of the Future, The Song of the Hermit, The Sûtra on Asceticism, The Question of Upatishya, and the Admonition of Râhula concerning Falsehood,

We here learn a lesson, which is confirmed by the study of other religions, that canonical books, though they furnish in most cases the most ancient and most authentic information within the reach of the student of religion, are not to be trusted implicitly, nay, that they must be submitted to a more searching criticism and to more stringent tests than any other historical books. For that purpose the Science of Language has proved in many cases a most valuable auxiliary. It is not easy to imitate ancient language so as to deceive the practised eye of the grammarian, even if it were possible to imitate ancient thought that should not betray to the historian its modern origin. A forged book, like the Ezour-veda, which deceived even Voltaire, and was published by him as 'the most precious gift for which the West was indebted to the East,' could hardly impose again on any Sanskrit scholar of the present day. This most precious gift from the East to the West, is about the silliest book that can be read by the student of religion, and all one can say in its defence is that the original writer never meant it as a forgery, never intended it for the purpose for which it was used by Voltaire.

I may add that a book which has lately attracted considerable attention, *La Bible dans l'Inde*, by M. Jacolliot, belongs to the same class of books. Though the passages from the sacred books of the Brahmans

uttered by our Lord Buddha. These religious works, Sirs, I wish that the monks and nuns, for the advancement of their good name, should uninterruptedly study and remember, as also the laics of the male and female sex. For this end, my Lords, I cause this to be written, and have made my wish evident.' See Indian Antiquary, vol. v. p. 257; Cunningham, 'Corpus Inscript. Indic.,' p. 132; Oldenberg, 'Vinaya-pitaka,' vol. i., Introd. p. xl.

are not given in the original, but only in a very poetical
French translation, no Sanskrit scholar would hesitate
for one moment to say that they are forgeries, and
that M. Jacolliot, the President of the Court of Justice
at Chandernagore, has been deceived by his native
teacher. We find many childish and foolish things in
the Veda, but when we read the following line, as an
extract from the Veda:

'La femme c'est l'âme de l'humanité,—'

it is not difficult to see that this is the folly of the
nineteenth century, and not of the childhood of the
human race. M. Jacolliot's conclusions and theories
are such as might be expected from his materials[1].

With all the genuine documents for studying the
history of the religions of mankind that have lately
been brought to light, and with the great facilities
which a more extensive study of Oriental languages
has afforded to scholars at large for investigating the
deepest springs of religious thought all over the
world, a comparative study of religions has become
a necessity. If we were to shrink from it, other
nations and other creeds would take up the work. A
lecture was lately delivered at Calcutta, by the
minister of the Âdi-Samâj (i.e. the Old Church), 'On
the Superiority of Hinduism to every other existing
Religion.' The lecturer held that Hinduism was
superior to all other religions, 'because it owed its
name to no man; because it acknowledged no mediator between God and man; because the Hindu
worships God, in the intensely devotional sense, as
the soul of the soul; because the Hindu alone can

---

[1] See Selected Essays, vol. ii., p. 468 sq.

worship God at all times, in business and pleasure, and everything; because, while other Scriptures inculcate the practice of piety and virtue for the sake of eternal happiness, the Hindu Scriptures alone maintain that God should be worshipped for the sake of God alone, and virtue practised for the sake of virtue alone ; because Hinduism inculcates universal benevolence, while other faiths merely refer to man ; because Hinduism is non-sectarian (believing that all faiths are good if the men who hold them are good), non-proselytizing, pre-eminently tolerant, devotional to an entire abstraction of the mind from time and sense, and the concentration of it on the Divine; of an antiquity running back to the infancy of the human race, and from that time till now influencing in all particulars the greatest affairs of the State and the most minute affairs of domestic life[1].'

A Science of Religion, based on an impartial and truly scientific comparison of all, or at all events, of the most important, religions of mankind, is now only a question of time.   It is demanded by those whose voice cannot be disregarded.   Its title, though implying as yet a promise rather than a fulfilment, has become more or less familiar in Germany, France, and America; its great problems have attracted the eyes of many inquirers, and its results have been anticipated either with fear or with delight.   It becomes therefore the duty of those who have devoted their life to the study of the principal religions of the world in their original documents, and who value religion and reverence it in whatever form it may present itself, to take possession of this new territory in

[1] See 'Times,' Oct. 27, 1872.

the name of true science, and thus to protect its sacred precincts from the inroads of those who think that they have a right to speak on the ancient religions of mankind, whether those of the Brahmans, the Zoroastrians, or Buddhists, or those of the Jews and Christians, without ever having taken the trouble of learning the languages in which their sacred books are written. What should we think of philosophers writing on the religion of Homer, without knowing Greek, or on the religion of Moses, without knowing Hebrew?

I do not wonder at Mr. Matthew Arnold[1] speaking scornfully of *La Science des Religions*, and I fully agree with him that such statements as he quotes would take away the breath of a mere man of letters. But are these statements supported by the authority of any scholars? Has anybody who can read either the Vedas or the Old and New Testaments in the original ever maintained that ' the sacred theory of the Aryas passed into Palestine from Persia and India, and got possession of the founder of Christianity and of his greatest apostles, St. Paul and St. John; becoming more perfect, and returning more and more to its true character of a " transcendent metaphysic," as the doctors of the Christian Church developed it?' Has Colebrooke, or Lassen, or Bournouf, ever suggested 'that we Christians, who are Aryas, may have the satisfaction of thinking that the religion of Christ has not come to us from the Semites, and that it is in the hymns of the Veda and not in the Bible that we are to look for the primordial source of any religion; that the theory of Christ is the theory of the

[1] 'Literature and Dogma,' p. 117.

Vedic Agni, or *fire*; that the Incarnation represents the Vedic solemnity of the production of *fire*, symbol of fire of every kind, of all movement, life, and thought; that the Trinity of Father, Son, and Spirit is the Vedic Trinity of Sun, Fire, and Wind; and God finally a cosmic unity.' Mr. Arnold quotes indeed the name of Burnouf, but he ought to have known that Eugène Burnouf has left no son and no successor.

Those who would use a comparative study of religions as a means for lowering Christianity by exalting the other religions of mankind, are to my mind as dangerous allies as those who think it necessary to lower all other religions in order to exalt Christianity. Science wants no partisans. I make no secret that true Christianity, I mean the religion of Christ, seems to me to become more and more exalted the more we know and the more we appreciate the treasures of truth hidden in the despised religions of the world. But no one can honestly arrive at that conviction, unless he uses honestly the same measure for all religions. It would be fatal for any religion to claim an exceptional treatment, most of all for Christianity. Christianity enjoyed no privileges and claimed no immunities when it boldly confronted and confounded the most ancient and the most powerful religions of the world. Even at present it craves no mercy, and it receives no mercy from those whom our missionaries have to meet face to face in every part of the world. Unless Christianity has ceased to be what it was, its defenders should not shrink from this new trial of strength, but should encourage rather than depreciate the study of comparative theology.

And let me remark this, in the very beginning, that no other religion, with the exception, perhaps, of early Buddhism, would have favoured the idea of an impartial comparison of the principal religions of the world—would ever have tolerated our science. Nearly every religion seems to adopt the language of the Pharisee rather than that of the Publican. It is Christianity alone which, as the religion of humanity, as the religion of no caste, of no chosen people, has taught us to study the history of mankind, as our own, to discover the traces of a divine wisdom and love in the development of all the races of the world, and to recognise, if possible, even in the lowest and crudest forms of religious belief, not the work of the devil, but something that indicates a divine guidance, something that makes us perceive, with St. Peter, 'that God is no respecter of persons, but that in every nation he that feareth him and worketh righteousness is accepted with him.'

In no religion was there a soil so well prepared for the cultivation of Comparative Theology as in our own. The position which Christianity from the very beginning took up with regard to Judaism, served as the first lesson in comparative theology, and directed the attention even of the unlearned to a comparison of two religions, differing in their conception of the Deity, in their estimate of humanity, in their motives of morality, and in their hope of immortality, yet sharing so much in common that there are but few of the psalms and prayers in the Old Testament in which a Christian cannot heartily join even now, and but few rules of morality which he ought not even now to obey. If we have once learnt to see in the exclusive religion of the Jews a preparation of what was to be the all-embracing religion of humanity, we shall feel much less difficulty in recognising in the mazes of other religions a hidden purpose; a wandering in the desert, it may be, but a preparation also for the land of promise.

A study of these two religions, the Jewish and the Christian, such as it has long been carried on by some of our most learned divines, simultaneously with the study of Greek and Roman mythology, has, in fact, served as a most useful preparation for wider inquiries. Even the mistakes that have been committed by earlier scholars have proved useful to those who followed after; and, once corrected, they are not likely to be committed again. The opinion, for instance, that the pagan religions were mere corruptions of the religion of the Old Testament, once supported by men of high authority and great learning, is now as completely surrendered as the attempts of explaining Greek and Latin as corruptions of Hebrew[1].

The theory again, that there was a primeval preternatural revelation granted to the fathers of the human race, and that the grains of truth which catch our eye when exploring the temples of heathen idols, are the scattered fragments of that sacred heirloom,—the seeds that fell by the wayside or upon stony places—would find but few supporters at present; no more, in fact, than the theory that there was in the beginning one complete and perfect primeval language,

---

[1] Tertullian, 'Apolog.' xlvii: 'Unde haec, oro vos, philosophis aut poetis tam consimilia? Nonnisi de nostris sacramentis: si de nostris sacramentis, ut de prioribus, ergo fideliora sunt nostra magisque credenda, quorum imagines quoque fidem inveniunt.' See Hardwick, 'Christ and other Masters,' vol. i. p. 17.

broken up in later times into the numberless languages
of the world.

Some other principles, too, have been established
within this limited sphere by a comparison of Judaism
and Christianity with the religions of Greece and
Rome, which will prove extremely useful in guiding
us in our own researches. It has been proved, for
instance, that the language of antiquity is not like
the language of our own times; that the language of
the East is not like the language of the West; and
that, unless we make allowance for this, we cannot
but misinterpret the utterances of the most ancient
teachers and poets of the human race. The same
words do not mean the same thing in Anglo-Saxon
and English, in Latin and French: much less can we
expect that the words of any modern language should
be the exact equivalents of words belonging to an
ancient Semitic language, such as the Hebrew of the
Old Testament.

Ancient words and ancient thoughts, for both go
together, have in the Old Testament not yet arrived
at that stage of abstraction in which, for instance,
active powers, whether natural or supernatural, can
be represented in any but a personal and more or
less human form. When we speak of a temptation
from within or from without, it was more natural for
the ancients to speak of a tempter, whether in a
human or in an animal form; when we speak of the
ever-present help of God, they call the Lord their
rock, and their fortress, their buckler, and their high
tower. They even speak of 'the Rock that begat
them' (Deut. xxxii. 18), though in a very different
sense from that in which Homer speaks of the rock

from whence man has sprung. What with us is a heavenly message, or a godsend, was to them a winged messenger; what we call divine guidance, they speak of as a pillar of a cloud, to lead them the way, and a pillar of light to give them light; a refuge from the storm, and a shadow from the heat. What is really meant is no doubt the same, and the fault is ours, not theirs, if we wilfully misinterpret the language of ancient prophets, if we persist in understanding their words in their outward and material aspect only, and forget that before language had sanctioned a distinction between the concrete and the abstract, between the purely spiritual as opposed to the coarsely material, the intention of the speakers comprehended both the concrete and the abstract, both the material and the spiritual, in a manner which has become quite strange to us, though it lives on in the language of every true poet. Unless we make allowance for this mental parallax, all our readings in the ancient skies will be, and must be, erroneous. Nay, I believe it can be proved that more than half of the difficulties in the history of religion owe their origin to this constant misinterpretation of ancient language by modern language, of ancient thought by modern thought, particularly whenever the word has become more sacred than the spirit.

That much of what seems to us, and seemed to the best among the ancients, irrational and irreverent in the mythologies of India, Greece, and Italy can thus be removed, and that many of their childish fables can thus be read again in their original child-like sense, has been proved by the researches of Comparative Mythologists. The phase of language which gives rise, inevitably, we may say, to these misunderstandings, is earlier than the earliest literary documents. Its work in the Aryan languages was done before the time of the Veda, before the time of Homer, though its influence continues to be felt to a much later period.

Is it likely that the Semitic languages, and, more particularly, Hebrew, should, as by a miracle, have escaped altogether the influence of a process which is inherent in the very nature and growth of language, and which, in fact, may rightly be called an infantine disease, against which no precautions can be of any avail?

I hold indeed that the Semitic languages, for reasons which I explained on a former occasion, have suffered less from mythology than the Aryan languages; yet we have only to read the first chapters of Genesis in order to convince ourselves, that we shall never understand its ancient language rightly, unless we make allowance for the influence of ancient language on ancient thought. If we read, for instance, that after the first man was created, one of his ribs was taken out, and that rib made into a woman, every student of ancient language sees at once that this account must not be taken in its bare, literal sense. We need not dwell on the fact that in the first chapter of Genesis a far less startling account of the creation of man and woman had been given. What could be simpler, and therefore truer, than: 'So God created man in his own image, in the image of God created he him; male and female created he them. And God blessed them, and God said unto them, Be fruitful, and multiply, and replenish the earth, and subdue it?' The question then is, how, after this account of the creation of

man and woman, could there be a second account
of the creation of man, of his lone estate in the garden
of Eden, and of the removal of one of his ribs, which
was to be made into a help meet for him?

Those who are familiar with the genius of ancient
Hebrew, can hardly hesitate as to the original intention of such traditions.   Let us remember that
when we, in our modern languages, speak of the selfsame thing, the Hebrews speak of the bone (עֶצֶם), the
Arabs of the eye of a thing.   This is a well known
Semitic idiom, and it is not without analogies in other
languages.   'Bone' seemed a telling expression for
what we should call the innermost essence; 'eye' for
what we should call the soul or self of a thing.   In
the ancient hymns of the Veda, too, a poet asks:
'Who has seen the first-born, when he who had no
bones, i.e. no form, bore him that had *bones?*' i.e. when
that which was formless assumed form, or, it may be,
when that which had no essence, received an essence?
And he goes on to ask: 'Where was the life, the
blood, the soul of the world? Who sent to ask this
from any that knew it?'   In the ancient language of
the Veda, bone, blood, breath, are all meant to convey
more than what we should call their material meaning;
but in course of time, the Sanskrit *âtman*, meaning
originally breath, dwindled away into a mere pro-
noun, and came to mean self.   The same applies to
the Hebrew *'etzem*.   Originally meaning bone, it came
to be used at last as a mere pronominal adjective, in
the sense of self or same.

After these preliminary explanations, we can well
understand that, while if speaking and thinking in a
modern language Adam might have been made to say

to Eve, 'Thou art the same as I am,' such a thought would in ancient Hebrew be expressed by: 'Thou art bone of my bone, and flesh of my flesh.' Let such an expression be repeated for a few generations only, and a literal, that is to say, a material and deceptive interpretation, would soon spring up, and people would at last bring themselves to believe that the first woman was formed from the bone of the first man, or from a rib, for the simple reason, it may be, because it could better be spared than any other bone. Such a misunderstanding, once established, retained its place on account of its very strangeness, for a taste for the unintelligible springs up at a very early time, and threatens to destroy among ancient nations the power of appreciating whatever is simple, natural, and wholesome. Thus only can it be explained that the account of the creation of the woman obtained its place in the second chapter, though in clear opposition to what had been said in the first chapter of Genesis[1].

It is not always possible to solve these ancient riddles, nor are the interpretations which have been attempted by various scholars always right. The only principle I stand up for is this, that misunderstandings of this kind are inevitable in ancient languages, and that we must be prepared to meet with them in the religions of the Semitic as well as of the Aryan nations.

Let us take another Semitic religion, the ancient religion of Babylon, as described to us in the fragments of Berosus. The similarities between that religion and the religion of the Jews are not to be mistaken, but such is the contrast between the sim-

[1] See 'Selected Essays,' vol. ii. p. 456.

plicity of the Bible language and the wild extra-
vagance of the Babylonian theogonies, that it requires
some courage to guess at the original outlines behind
the distorted features of a hideous caricature[1].

We have no reason to doubt the accuracy of
Berosus in describing the religion of the Babylonians,
at least for the time in which he lived. He was a
Babylonian by birth, a priest of the temple of Belus,
a contemporary of Alexander the Great. He wrote
the History of the Chaldæans, in Greek, evidently
intending it to be read by the Greek conquerors,
and he states in his first book that he composed it
from the registers, astronomical and chronological,
which were preserved at Babylon, and which comprised a period of 200,000 years (150,000, according
to the Syncellus). The history of Berosus is lost.
Extracts from it had been made by Alexander Poly-
histor, in the first century before our era; but his
work too is lost. It still existed, however, at the
time when Eusebius (270–340) wrote his Chronicon,
and was used by him in describing the ancient history
of Babylon. But the Chronicle of Eusebius, too, is
lost, at least in Greek, and it is only in an Armenian
translation of Eusebius that many of the passages
have been preserved to us, which refer to the history
of Babylon, as originally described by Berosus. This
Armenian translation was published in 1818, and its
importance was first pointed out by Niebuhr[2]. As
we possess large extracts from Eusebius, preserved

---

[1] Bunsen, 'Egypt,' iv. p. 364.
[2] Eusebii Pamphili Caesariensis Episcopi Chronicon Bipartitum,
nunc primum ex Armeniaco textu in Latinum conversum, opera P. Jo.
B. Aucher; Venetiis, 1818.

by Georgius the Syncellus, i. e. the concellaneus, or cell-companion, the Vice-patriarch of Constantinople, who wrote a Chronography about 800 A.D., it is possible in several places to compare the original Greek text with the Armenian, and thus to establish the trustworthiness of the Armenian translation.

Berosus thus describes the Babylonian traditions of the creation [1]:

'There was a time in which all was darkness and water, and in these were generated monstrous creatures, having mixed forms; men were born with two and some with four wings, with two faces, having one body, but two heads, a man's and a woman's, and bearing the marks of male and female nature; and other men with the legs and horns of goats, or with horses' feet, and having the hind quarters of horses, but the fore part of men, being in fact like Hippocentaurs. Bulls also were produced having human heads, and dogs with four bodies, having fishes' tails springing from their hinder parts; and horses with dogs' heads, and men and other creatures, having heads and bodies of horses, but tails of fishes; and other creatures having the shape of all sorts of beasts. Besides these, fishes, and reptiles, and snakes and many other wonderful and strange beings, one having the appearance of the other, the images of which are to be seen in the temple of Belus. At the head of all was a woman, called Omorka [2] (Armen. Marcaja), which

---

[1] Eusebii Chronicon, vol. i. p. 22. 'Fragmenta Historicorum,' vol. ii. p. 497.

[2] According to Lenormant ('Deluge,' p. 30) Betit Um-Uruk. In modern Armenian, Am-argā is said to mean mother-earth. Prof. Dietrich explained the word as homer-kai, the matter of the egg. See Bunsen's 'Egypt,' iv. p. 150.

is said to be *Thalatth*[1] in Chaldean, and translated
in Greek, *Thalassa* (or sea). When all these were
thus together, *Belus* came and cut the woman in two:
and one half of her he made the earth, and the other
half the sky; and he destroyed all the creatures that
were in her.   But this account of nature is to be understood allegorically.   For when all was still moist,
and creatures were born in it, then the god (Belus)
cut off his own head, and the gods mixed the blood
that flowed from it with the earth, and formed men;
wherefore men are rational, and participate in the
divine intelligence.'

'And Belus, whom they explain as Zeus (and the
Armenians as Aramazd), cut the darkness in two, and
separated earth and heaven from each other, and
ordered the world.   And animals which could not
bear the power of the light, perished.   And Belus,
when he saw the desert and fertile land, commanded
one of the gods to cut off his head, to mix the earth
with the blood flowing from it, and to form men and
beasts that could bear the air.   And Belus established
also the stars, and the sun, and the moon, and the five
planets.'

---

[1] Mr. Sayce writes to me: 'Perhaps Lenormant is right in correcting
Θαλάτθ (when compared with the Ταυθέ or Ταυθή of Damascius) into
Θαυάτθ, that is, the Assyrian *Tihamtu* or *Tamtu*, the sea, the Heb.
תהום.   In this case the correspondence of the Babylonian account
with Genesis i. 2 will be even greater.'   Bunsen explained Taládeth
from the Hebrew yalad, as meaning 'laying eggs.'   Bunsen's 'Egypt,'
vol. iv. p. 150.   Dr. Haupt ('Die Sumerische-akkadische Sprache,'
p. 276) points out that *m* in Sumero-Accadian dwindled down to v, and
that the same change may be observed in Assyrian also.   Thus the
Assyrian *Támdu*, sea (= tahmatu, or ti 'âmdu, ti'âmtu, stat. constr.
t' âmat; cf. Hebrew tehom) is represented as Ταυθέ by Damascius,
'Questiones de primis principiis,' ed. Kopp. p. 384), and Damkina, the
wife of Éa, as Δαύκη.

Nothing can be at first sight more senseless and confused than this Babylonian version of the genesis of the earth and of man; yet, if we examine it more carefully, we can still distinguish the following elements:

1. In the beginning there was darkness and water.

In Hebrew: Darkness was upon the face of the deep.

2. The heaven was divided from the earth.

In Hebrew: Let there be a firmament in the midst of the waters, and let it divide the waters from the waters ..... And God called the firmament Heaven; ..... and God called the dry land Earth.

3. The stars were made, and the sun and the moon, and the five planets.

In Hebrew: And God made two great lights; the greater light to rule the day, and the lesser light to rule the night; he made the stars also.

4. Animals of various kinds were created.

5. Men were created.

It is in the creation of animals in particular that the extravagant imagination of the Babylonians finds its widest scope. It is said that the images of these creatures are to be seen in the temple of Belus, and as their description certainly agrees with some of the figures of gods and heroes that may now be seen in the British Museum, it is not unlikely that the Babylonian story of the creation of these monsters may have arisen from the contemplation of the ancient idols in the temples of Babylon. But this would still leave the original conception of such monsters unexplained.

The most important point, however, is this, that

the Babylonians represented man as participating in divine intelligence. The symbolical language in which they express this idea is no doubt horrible and disgusting, but let us recollect that the Hebrew symbol, too, 'that God breathed into man's nostrils the breath of life,' is after all but another weak attempt at expressing the same idea,—an idea so exalted that no language can ever express it without loss or injury.

In order to guess with some hope of success at the original meaning of ancient traditions, it is absolutely necessary that we should be familiar with the genius of the language in which such traditions took their origin. Languages, for instance, which do not denote grammatical gender, will be free from many mythological stories which in Sanskrit, Greek, and Latin are inevitable. Dr. Bleek, the indefatigable student of African languages, has frequently dwelt on this fact. In the Preface to his Comparative Grammar of the South-African Languages, published in 1862, he says:

'The forms of a language may be said to constitute in some degree the skeleton frame of the human mind whose thoughts they express . . . . How dependent, for example, the highest products of the human mind, the religious ideas and conceptions of even highly civilized nations, may be upon this manner of speaking has been shown by Max-Müller, in his essay on Comparative Mythology (Oxford Essays, 1856)[1]. This will become still more evident from our African researches. The primary cause of the ancestor worship of the one race (Kafirs, Negroes, and Polynesians), and of the sidereal worship, or of those forms

[1] 'Chips from a German Workshop,' vol. ii. pp. 1-146.

of religion which have sprung from the veneration of heavenly bodies, of the other (Hottentots, North-African, Semitic, and Aryan nations), is supplied by the very forms of their languages. The nations speaking Sex-denoting languages are distinguished by a higher poetical conception, by which human agency is transferred to other beings, and even to inanimate things, in consequence of which their personification takes place, forming the origin of almost all mythological legends. This faculty is not developed in the Kafir mind, because not suggested by the form of their language, in which the nouns of persons are not (as in the Sex-denoting languages) thrown together with those of inanimate beings into the same classes or genders, but are in separate classes, without any grammatical distinction of sex[1].'

If therefore, without possessing a knowledge of the Zulu language, I venture on an interpretation of an account of creation that has sprung up in the thought and language of the Zulus, I do so with great hesitation, and only in order to show, by one instance at least, that the religions of savages, too, will have to

[1] See also his Preface to the second volume of the Comparative Grammar, published 1869. Mr. E. B. Tylor has some valuable remarks on the same subject, in his article on the Religion of Savages, in the Fortnightly Review, 1866, p. 80. Looked at from a higher point of view, it is, of course, not language, as such, which dominates the mind, but thought and language are only two manifestations of the same energy, mutually determining each other. Failing to perceive this, one has to take refuge, like Tylor, with the old so-called anthropomorphism, as the apparent source of all mythology. But this gives us only a tautological, not a genetic explanation of mythology. There is an important difference between the inevitable and the evitable affections of the genius of language. The deepest source of mythology lies in the former, and must be carefully distinguished from the later sporadic diseases of language.

submit hereafter to the same treatment which we apply to the sacred traditions of the Semitic and Aryan nations. I should not be at all surprised if the tentative interpretation which I venture to propose, were proved to be untenable by those who have studied the Zulu dialects, but I shall be much more ready to surrender my interpretation, than to lose the conviction that there is no solid foundation for the study of the religions of savages except the study of their languages.

How impossible it is to arrive at anything like a correct understanding of the religious sentiments of savage tribes without an accurate and scholarlike knowledge of their dialects, is best shown by the old controversy whether there are any tribes of human beings entirely devoid of religious sentiments or no. Those who, for some reason or other, hold that religious sentiments are not essential to human nature, find little difficulty in collecting statements of travellers and missionaries in support of their theory. Those who hold the opposite opinion find no more difficulty in rebutting such statements[1]. Now the real point to settle before we adopt the one or the other view is, what kind of authority can be claimed by those whose opinions we quote; did they really know the language, and did they know it, not only sufficiently well to converse on ordinary subjects, but to enter into a friendly and unreserved conversation on topics on which even highly educated people are so apt to misunderstand each other? We want informants, in fact, like Dr. Callaway, Dr. Bleek, men

---

[1] See Schelling, Werke, vol. i. p. 72; and Mr. E. B. Tylor's reply to Sir John Lubbock, 'Primitive Culture,' vol. i. p. 381.

who are both scholars and philosophers. Savages
are shy and silent in the presence of white men, and
they have a superstitious reluctance against mention-
ing even the names of their gods and heroes. Not
many years ago it was supposed, on what would seem
to be good authority, that the Zulus had no religious
ideas at all; at present our very Bishops have been
silenced by their theological inquiries.

Captain Gardiner, in his Narrative of a Journey to
the Zoolu Country undertaken in 1835, gives the
following dialogue:

'Have you any knowledge of the power by whom
the world was made? When you see the sun rising
and setting, and the trees growing, do you know who
made them and who governs them?'

TPAI, a Zulu (after a little pause, apparently deep
in thought),—'No; we see them, but cannot tell how
they come; we suppose that they come of themselves.'

A. 'To whom then do you attribute your success
or failure in war?'

TPAI. 'When we are not successful, and do not
take cattle, we think our father (*Itongo*) has not
looked upon us.'

A. 'Do you think your father's spirits (*Amatongo*)
made the world?'

TPAI. 'No.'

A. 'Where do you suppose the spirit of man goes
after it leaves the body?'

TPAI. 'We cannot tell.'

A. 'Do you think it lives for ever?'

TPAI. 'That we cannot tell; we believe that the
spirit of our forefathers looks upon us when we go

to war; but we do not think about it at any other time.'

A. 'You admit that you cannot control the sun or the moon, or even make a hair of your head to grow. Have you no idea of any power capable of doing this?'

TPAI. 'No; we know of none: we know that we cannot do these things, and we suppose that they come of themselves.'

It may seem difficult to find a deeper shade of religious darkness than is pictured in this dialogue. But now let us hear the account which the Rev. Dr. Callaway[1] gives of the fundamental religious notions which he, after a long residence among the various clans of the Zulus, after acquiring an intimate knowledge of their language, and, what is still more important, after gaining their confidence, was able to extract from their old men and women. They all believe, first of all, in an ancestor of each particular family and clan, and also in a common ancestor of the whole race of man. That ancestor is generally called the Unkulunkulu, which means the great-great-grandfather[2]. When

---

[1] Dr. Callaway, 'Unkulunkulu,' p. 54.

[2] Ibid. p. 48. *Unkulunkulu*, the word by which God is rendered in Zulu, is derived, according to Bleek, by reduplication of a (nasalised) form of the 9th class from the adjective stem -kulu (great, large, old, u-ku-kula, to grow, etc.), and seems to mean originally a great-great-grandfather, or the first ancestor of a family or tribe, though perhaps the unnasalised form *u-kulukulu* is at present more usual in this signification. Then it was applied by metaphor to that being from whom everything was derived, who according to the Zulu tradition has created all men, animals, and other things to whom life and death are due, &c. In Inhambane the word for God, derived from the same root is *Mulungulu*; in Ki-hiáu, Ki-kamba, and Kinika it is *Mulungu*; in Ki-suáheli, *Mlungu*; in Makua, *Mulingo* or *Muluko*; in Sofala, *Murungu*; in Tette, *Murungo* or *Morungo*; in the Ku-suáheli dialect

pressed as to the father of this great-great-grandfather, the general answer of the Zulus seems to be that he 'branched off from a reed,' or that he 'came from a bed of reeds.'

Here, I cannot help suspecting that language has been at work spinning mythology. In Sanskrit the word (parvan) which means originally a knot or joint in a cane, comes to mean a link, a member; and, transferred to a family, it expresses the different shoots and scions that spring from the original stem. The name for stem or race and lineage in Sanskrit is vamsa, which originally means a reed, a bamboo-cane. In the Zulu language a reed is called uthlanga, strictly speaking a reed which is capable of throwing out off-shoots[1]. It comes thus metaphorically to mean a source of being. A father is the uthlanga of his children, who are supposed to have branched off from him. Whatever notions at the present day the ignorant among the natives may have of the meaning of this tradition, so much seems to be generally admitted, even among Zulus, that originally it could not have been intended to teach that men sprang from a real reed[2]. 'It cannot be doubted,' Dr. Callaway writes, 'that the word alone has come down to the people, whilst the meaning has been lost.'

of Mombas, *Múñgu*; in the Ki-pokómo, *Muñgo*; in Otyi-Hereró, o *Mukuru*; see Bleek, 'Comparative Grammar,' §§ 389-394. In Hereró *tate Mukuru* is our father *Mukuru*; see Kolbe's 'English-Hererv Dictionary,' s. v. God.

[1] Dr. Callaway, 'Unkulunkulu,' p. 2, note.

[2] In Herero, 'tua memva i Mukuru' means, we have been created, i. e. broken out of the omumborombonga (creation-tree) in Herero fashion by Mukuru; see Kolbe's 'English-Herero Dictionary,' s. v. God.

The interpretation which I venture to propose of this Zulu myth is this:—The Zulus may have said originally that they were all offshoots of a reed, using reed in the same sense in which vamsa is used in Sanskrit, and meaning therefore no more than that they all were children of one father, members of one race. As the word uthlanga, which came to mean race, retained also its original meaning, viz. reed, people, unaccustomed to metaphorical language and thought, would soon say that men came from a reed, or were fetched from a bed of reeds, while others would take Uthlanga for a proper name and make him the ancestor of the human race. Among some Zulu tribes we actually find that while Unkulunkulu is the first man, Uthlanga is represented as the first woman[1]. Among other tribes where Unkulunkulu was the first man, Uthlanga became the first woman (p. 58).

Every nation, every clan, every family requires sooner or later an ancestor. Even in comparatively modern times the Britons, or the inhabitants of Great Britain, were persuaded that it was not good to be without an ancestor, and they were assured by Geoffrey of Monmouth that they might claim descent from Brutus. In the same manner the Hellenes, or the ancient inhabitants of Hellas, claimed descent from Hellen. The name of Hellenes, originally restricted to a tribe living in Thessaly[2], became in time the name of the whole nation[3], and hence it was but natural that *Æolos*, the ancestor of the Æolians,

---

[1] Dr. Callaway, 'Unkulunkulu,' p. 58. According to the Popol Vuh the first woman was created from the marrow of a reed   see 'Selected Essays,' ii. p. 394.

[2] Hom. Il. 2. 684.   [3] Thucyd. i. 3.

Doros, the ancestor of the Dorians, and *Xuthos*, the father of Achæos and Ion, should all be represented as the sons of Hellen. So far all is intelligible, if we will only remember that this is the technical language of the heraldic office of ancient Greece.

But very soon the question arose, who was the father of Hellen, the ancestor of the Greeks, or, according to the intellectual horizon of the ancient Greeks, of the whole human race? If he was the ancestor of the whole human race, or the first man, he could only be the son of Zeus, the supreme god, and thus we find that Hellen is by some authorities actually called the son of Zeus. Others, however, give a different account. There was in Greece, as in many countries, the tradition of a general deluge by which every living being had been destroyed, except a few who escaped in a boat, and who, after the flood had subsided, repeopled the earth. The person thus saved, according to Greek traditions, was called *Deukalion*, the ruler of Thessaly, the son of Prometheus. Prometheus had told him to build a ship and furnish it with provisions, and when the flood came, he and his wife Pyrrha were the only people who escaped.

Thus it will be seen that the Greeks had really two ancestors of the human race, Hellen and Deukalion, and in order to remove this difficulty, nothing remained but to make Hellen the son of Deukalion. All this is perfectly natural and intelligible, if only we will learn to speak, and not only to speak, but also to think the language of the ancient world.

The story then goes on to explain how Deukalion

became the father of all the people on earth; that he and his wife Pyrrha were told to throw stones (or the bones of the earth) backward behind them, and that these stones became men and women.   Now here we have clearly a myth or a miracle,—a miracle, too, without any justification, for if Pyrrha was the wife of Deukalion, why should not Hellen be their son? All becomes clear, if we look at the language in which the story is told.   Pyrrha means the Red, and was originally a name for the red earth.   As the Hellenes claimed to be indigenous or autochthonic, born of the earth where they lived, Pyrrha, the red Earth, was naturally called their mother, and being the mother of the Hellenes, she must needs be made the wife of Deukalion, the father of the Hellenes.   Originally, however, Deukalion, like Manu in India, was represented as having alone escaped from the deluge, and hence the new problem how, without a wife, he could have become the father of the people? It was in this perplexity, no doubt, that the myth arose of his throwing stones behind him, and these stones becoming the new population of the earth.   The Greek word for people was λαός, that for stones λᾶες;—hence what could be more natural, when children asked, whence the λαός or the people of Deukalion came, than to say that they came from λᾶες or stones [1]?

I might give many more instances of the same kind, all showing that there was a meaning in the

---

[1] The North American Indians told Roger Williams, that 'they had it from their fathers, that *Kautantowwit* made one man and woman of a stone, which disliking, he broke them in pieces, and made another man and woman of a tree, which were the fountain of all mankind.' 'Publications of Narragansett Club,' vol. i. p. 158.

most meaningless traditions of antiquity, all showing, what is still more important, that these traditions, many of them in their present state absurd
and repulsive, regain a simple, intelligible, and even
beautiful character if we divest them of the crust
which language in its inevitable decay has formed
around them.

We never lose, we always gain, when we discover
the most ancient intention of sacred traditions, instead
of being satisfied with their later aspect, and their
modern misinterpretations. Have we lost anything
if, while reading the story of Hephæstos splitting open
with his axe the head of Zeus, and Athene springing
from it, full armed, we perceive behind this savage
imagery, Zeus as the bright Sky, his forehead as
the East, Hephæstos as the young, not yet risen Sun,
and Athene as the Dawn, the daughter of the Sky,
stepping forth from the fountain-head of light—

Γλαυκῶπις, with eyes like an owl (and beautiful they
are);

Παρθένος, pure as a virgin;

Χρύσεα, the golden;

’Ακρία, lighting up the tops of the mountains, and
her own glorious Parthenon in her own favourite town
of Athens;

Παλλάς, whirling the shafts of light;

’Αλέα, the genial warmth of the morning;

Πρόμαχος, the foremost champion in the battle
between night and day;

Πάνοπλος, in full armour, in her panoply of light,
driving away the darkness of night, and rousing men
to a bright life, to bright thoughts, to bright endeavours?

E

Would the Greek gods lose in our eyes if, instead of believing that Apollon and Artemis murdered the twelve children of Niobe, we perceived that Niobe was, in a former period of language, a name of snow and winter, and that no more was intended by the ancient poet than that Apollon and Artemis, the vernal deities, must slay every year with their darts the brilliant and beautiful, but doomed children of the Snow? Is it not something worth knowing, worth knowing even to us after the lapse of four or five thousand years, that before the separation of the Aryan race, before the existence of Sanskrit, Greek, or Latin, before the gods of the Veda had been worshipped, and before there was a sanctuary of Zeus among the sacred oaks of Dodona, one supreme Deity had been found, had been named, had been invoked by the ancestors of our race, and had been invoked by a name which has never been excelled by any other name, Dyaus, Zeus, Jupiter, Tyr,—all meaning originally light and brightness, a concept which on one side became materialized as sky, morning, and day, while on the other it developed into a name of the bright and heavenly beings, the Devas, as one of the first expressions of the Divine?

No, if a critical examination of the ancient language of our own religion leads to no worse results than those which have followed from a careful interpretation of the petrified language of ancient India and Greece, we need not fear; we shall be gainers, not losers. Like an old precious metal, the ancient religion, after the rust of ages has been removed, will come out in all its purity and brightness: and the image which it discloses will be the image of the

Father, the Father of all the nations upon earth;
and the superscription, when we can read it again,
will be, not in Judæa only, but in the languages of
all the races of the world, the Word of God, revealed, where alone it can be revealed,—revealed in
the heart of man.

SECOND LECTURE.

DELIVERED AT THE ROYAL INSTITUTION,
FEBRUARY 26, 1870.

THERE is no lack of materials for the student of the Science of Religion. It is true that, compared with the number of languages which the comparative philologist has to deal with, the number of religions is small. In a comparative study of languages, however, we find most of our materials ready for use; we possess grammars and dictionaries, while it is difficult to say, where we are to look for the grammars and dictionaries of the principal religions of the world. Not in the catechisms, or the articles, not even in the so-called creeds[1] or confessions of faith which, if they do not give us an actual misrepresentation of the doctrines which they profess to epitomise, give us always the shadow only, and never the soul and substance of a religion. But how seldom do we find even such helps!

Among Eastern nations it is not unusual to distinguish between religions that are founded on a book, and others that have no such vouchers to produce.

---

[1] 'What are creeds? Skeletons, freezing abstractions, metaphysical expressions of unintelligible dogmas; and these I am to regard as the expositions of the fresh, living, infinite truth which came from Jesus! I might with equal propriety be required to hear and receive the lispings of infancy as the expressions of wisdom. Creeds are to the Scriptures, what rushlights are to the sun.'—Dr. Channing, 'On Creeds.'

The former are considered more respectable, and, though they may contain false doctrine, they are looked upon as a kind of aristocracy among the vulgar and nondescript crowd of bookless or illiterate religions [1].

To the student of religion canonical books are, no doubt, of the utmost importance, but he ought never to forget that canonical books too give the reflected image only of the real doctrines of the founder of a new religion, an image always blurred and distorted by the medium through which it had to pass. And how few are the religions which possess a sacred canon! how small is the aristocracy of real book-religions in the history of the world!

Let us look at the two races that have been the principal actors in that great drama which we call the history of the world, the *Aryan* and the *Semitic*, and we shall find that two members only of each race can claim the possession of a sacred code. Among the *Aryans*, the *Hindus* and the *Persians;* among the *Shemites*, the *Hebrews* and the *Arabs*. In the Aryan family the Hindus, in the Semitic family the Hebrews, have each produced two book-religions; the Hindus have given rise to Brahmanism and Buddhism; the Hebrews to Mosaism and Christianity. Nay, it is important to observe that in each family the third book-religion can hardly lay claim to an independent origin, but is only a weaker repetition of the first. Zoroastrianism has its sources in the same stratum

---

[1] Even before Mohammed, the people in possession of a book (ahl i kitáb) were in Arabic distinguished from the ummiyun, the heathen. The name ahl i kitáb was, however, properly restricted to Jews, Christians, and Mohammedans; see Note A.

which fed the deeper and broader stream of Vedic religion; Mohammedanism springs, as far as its most vital doctrines are concerned, from the ancient fountain-head of the religion of Abraham, the worshipper and the friend of the one true God.

If you keep before your mind the following simple outline, you can see at one glance the river-system in which the religious thought of the Aryan and the Semitic nations has been running for centuries—of those, at least, who are in possession of sacred and canonical books.

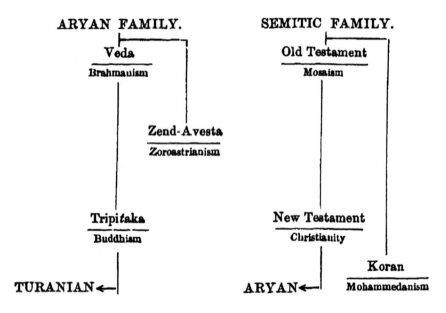

While Buddhism is the direct offspring, and, at the same time, the antagonist of Brahmanism, Zoroastrianism is rather a deviation from the straight course of ancient Vedic faith, though it likewise contains a protest against some of the doctrines of the earliest worshippers of the Vedic gods. The same, or nearly the same relationship holds together the three prin-

cipal religions of the Semitic stock, only that, chrono-
logically, Mohammedanism is later than Christianity,
while Zoroastrianism is earlier than Buddhism.

Observe also another, and, as we shall see, by no
means accidental coincidence in the parallel ramifica-
tions of these two religious stems.

Buddhism, which is the offspring of, but at the
same time marks a reaction against, the ancient Brahmanism of India, withered away after a time on the
soil from which it had sprung, and assumed its real
importance only after it had been transplanted from
India, and struck root among Turanian nations in the
very centre of the Asiatic continent. Buddhism,
being at its birth an Aryan religion, ended by becoming the principal religion of the Turanian world.

The same transference took place in the second
stem. Christianity, being the offspring of Mosaism,
was rejected by the Jews as Buddhism was by the
Brahmans. It failed to fulfil its purpose as a mere
reform of the ancient Jewish faith, and not till it
had been transferred from Semitic to Aryan ground,
from the Jews to the Gentiles, did it develope its real
nature and assume its world-wide importance. Having
been at its birth a Semitic religion, it became the
principal religion of the Aryan world.

There is one other nation only, outside the pale of
the Aryan and Semitic families, which can claim one,
or even two book-religions as its own. China is the
mother of two religions, each founded on a sacred
code—the religion of Confucius, (Kung Fu-tze, i. e.
Kung, the Master,) and the religion of Lao-tse, the
former resting on the Five King and the Four Shu,
the latter on the Tao-te-king.

With these eight religions the library of the Sacred
Books of the whole human race is complete, and an
accurate study of these eight codes, written in Sanskrit, Pâli, and Zend, in Hebrew, Greek, and Arabic,
lastly in Chinese, might in itself not seem too formidable an undertaking for a single scholar.   Yet, let us
begin at home, and look at the enormous literature
devoted to the interpretation of the Old Testament,
and the number of books published every year on
controverted points in the doctrine or the history of
the Gospels, and you may then form an idea of what
a theological library would be that should contain
the necessary materials for an accurate and scholarlike interpretation of the eight sacred codes.   The
Tao-te-king, the canonical book of the followers of
Lao-tse, contains only about 5,320 words, the commentaries written to explain its meaning are endless[1].
Even in so modern, and, in the beginning, at least, so
illiterate a religion as that of Mohammed, the sources
that have to be consulted for the history of the faith
during the early centuries of its growth are so abund-
ant, that few critical scholars could master them in
their completeness[2].

If we turn our eyes to the Aryan religions, the

---

[1] Julien, ' Tao-te-king,' p. xxxv ; see infra, p. 62.

[2] Sprenger, ' Das Leben des Mohammed,' vol. i. p. 9 :—'Die Quellen,
die ich benutzt habe, sind so zahlreich, und der Zustand der Gelehr-
samkeit war unter den Moslimen in ihrer Urzeit von dem unsrigen so
verschieden, dass die Materialien, die ich über die Quellen gesammelt
habe, ein ziemlich beleibtes Bändchen bilden werden.   Es ist in der
That nothwendig, die Literaturgeschichte des Islâm der ersten zwei
Jahrhunderte zu schreiben, um den Leser in den Stand zu setzen, den
hier gesammelten kritischen Apparat zu benutzen.   Ich gedenke die
Resultate meiner Forschungen als eins separates Werkchen nach der
Prophetenbiographie herauszugeben.'

sacred writings of the Brahmans, in the narrowest
acceptation of the word, might seem within easy
grasp. The hymns of the Rig-veda, which are the
real bible of the ancient faith of the Vedic Rishis, are
only 1,028 in number, consisting of about 10,580
verses [1]. The commentary, however, on these hymns,
of which I have published six good-sized quarto
volumes, is estimated at 100,000 lines consisting of
32 syllables each, that is at 3,200,000 syllables [2].
There are, besides, the three minor Vedas, the Yagur-
veda, the Sâma-veda, the Atharva-veda, which, though
of less importance for religious doctrines, are indispensable for a right appreciation of the sacrificial
and ceremonial system of the worshippers of the
ancient Vedic gods.

To each of these four Vedas belong collections of
so-called Brâhmaṇas, scholastic treatises of a later
time, it is true, but nevertheless written in archaic
Sanskrit, and reckoned by every orthodox Hindu as
part of his revealed literature. Their bulk is much
larger than that of the ancient Vedic hymn-books.

And all this constitutes the text only for numberless treatises, essays, manuals, glosses, &c., forming an
uninterrupted chain of theological literature, extending over more than three thousand years, and receiving new links even at the present time. There are,
besides, the inevitable parasites of theological literature, the controversial writings of different schools of
thought and faith, all claiming to be orthodox, yet
differing from each other like day and night; and
lastly, the compositions of writers, professedly at

[1] Max Müller, 'History of Ancient Sanskrit Literature,' p. 220.
[2] See Note B.

variance with the opinions of the majority, declared
enemies of the Brahmanic faith and the Brahmanic
priesthood, whose accusations and insinuations, whose
sledge-hammer arguments, and whose poisoned arrows
of invective need fear no comparison with the weapons
of theological warfare in any other country.

Nor can we exclude the sacred law-books, nor the
ancient epic poems, the Mahâbhârata and Râmâya*n*a,
nor the more modern, yet sacred literature of India,
the Purâ*n*as and Tantras, if we wish to gain an insight
into the religious belief of millions of human beings,
who, though they all acknowledge the Veda as their
supreme authority in matters of faith, are yet unable
to understand one single line of it, and in their daily
life depend entirely for spiritual food on the teaching
conveyed to them by these more recent and more
popular books.

And even then our eye would not have reached
many of the sacred recesses in which the Hindu
mind has taken refuge, either to meditate on the
great problems of life, or to free itself from the
temptations and fetters of worldly existence by
penances and mortifications of the most exquisite
cruelty. India has always been teeming with religious sects, and as far as we can look back into
the history of that marvellous country, its religious
life has been broken up into countless local centres
which it required all the ingenuity and perseverance
of a priestly caste to hold together with a semblance
of dogmatic uniformity. Some of these sects may
almost claim the title of independent religions, as,
for instance, the once famous sect of the Sikhs,
possessing their own sacred code and their own

priesthood, and threatening for a time to become a
formidable rival of Brahmanism and Mohammedanism
in India. Political circumstances gave to the sect of
Nânak its historical prominence and more lasting
fame. To the student of religion it is but one out
of many sects which took their origin in the fifteenth
and sixteenth centuries, and attempted to replace the
corruptions of Hinduism and Mohammedanism by a
purer and more spiritual worship. The Granth, i. e.
the Volume, the sacred book of the Sikhs, though
tedious as a whole, contains here and there treasures
of really deep and poetical thought: and we may
soon hope to have a complete translation of it by
Dr. Trumpp[1]. But there are other collections of
religious poetry, more ancient and more original than
the stanzas of Nânak; nay, many of the most beautiful verses of the Granth were borrowed from these
earlier authorities, particularly from Kabir, the pupil
of Râmânand. Here there is enough to occupy the
students of religion: an intellectual flora of greater
variety and profuseness than even the natural flora of
that fertile country.

And yet we have not said a word as yet of the
second book-religion of India — of the religion of
Buddha, originally one only out of numberless sects,
but possessing a vitality which has made its branches
to overshadow the largest portion of the inhabited
globe. Who can say—I do not speak of European
scholars only, but of the most learned members of
the Buddhist fraternities—who can say that he has

---

[1] This translation has since been published, 'The Adi Granth, or the
Holy Scriptures of the Sikhs,' translated from the original Gurmukhi
by Dr. E. Trumpp, London, 1877.

read the whole of the canonical books of the Buddhist Church, to say nothing of their commentaries or later treatises?

According to a tradition preserved by the Buddhist schools of the South and of the North, the sacred canon comprised originally 80,000 or 84,000 tracts, but most of them were lost, so that there remained only 6,000[1]. According to a statement in the Saddharmâlaṅkâra, the text and commentary of the Buddhist canon contain together 29,368,000 letters, while the English translation of the Bible is said to contain 3,567,180 letters, vowels being here counted as separate from the consonants.

At present there exist two sacred canons of Buddhist writings, that of the South, in Pâli, and that of the North, in Sanskrit. The Buddhist canon in Pâli has been estimated as twice as large as the Bible, though in an English translation it would probably be four times as large[2]. Spence Hardy gave the number of stanzas as 275,250 for the Pâli canon, and as 361,550 for its commentary, and by stanza he meant a line of 32 syllables.

The Buddhist canon in Sanskrit consists of what is called the 'Nine Dharmas[3].' In its Tibetan translation that canon, divided into two collections, the Kanjur and Tanjur, numbers 325 volumes folio, each weighing in the Pekin edition from four to five pounds.

Besides these two canons, there is another collateral branch, the canon of the Gainas. The Gainas trace

---

[1] See Burnouf, 'Introduction à l'histoire du Buddhisme indien,' p. 37. 'Selected Essays,' ii. p. 170.
[2] 'Selected Essays,' ii. p. 179.
[3] Ibid. p. 183.

the origin of their religion back to Mahâvîra, who was believed, however, to have been preceded by 23 Tîrthakara, the 23rd being Pârsva (250 before Mahâvîra). Mahâvîra is called also Gñâtaputra[1] or Gñâtriputra or Gñâtiputra by both Gainas and Bauddhas (Nâtaputta in Pâli, Nâyaputta in Gaina Prâkrit), and is reported by both sects to have died at Pâpâ. The date of his death, as given by the Gainas, 527 B.C., would make him older than Buddha. The true relation, however, of the Gainas to the Bauddhas, or followers of Sâkyamuni, remains still to be determined. Their sacred books are written in a Prâkrit dialect, commonly called Ardhamâgadhî, while the dialect of the Pâli scriptures is called Mâgadhî. According to the Siddhânta-dharma-sâra these Gaina scriptures are collectively called Sûtras or Siddhântas, and classed, first, under two heads of Kalpa-sûtra and Âgama, five works coming under the former, and forty-five under the latter head; and secondly, under eight different heads, viz. 1, eleven Angas; 2, twelve Upângas; 3, four Mûla-sûtras; 4, five Kalpa-sûtras; 5, six Khedas; 6, ten Payannas; 7, Nandi-sûtra; 8, Anuyogadvârasûtra. The total extent of these fifty works together with their commentaries is, according to Gaina belief, 600,000 slokas[2]. In the form in which we now possess them, the Gainas Sûtras are not older than the fifth century A.D. (See 'Indian Antiquary,' ix. p. 161.)

Within a smaller compass lies the sacred literature of the third of the Aryan book-religions, the so-called

---

[1] See Bühler, 'Indian Antiquary,' vii. p. 143; H. Jacobi, 'On Mahâvîra and his predecessors,' Indian Antiquary, ix. 158; also his preface to the Kalpasûtra of Bhadrabâhu, 1879.

[2] Rajendralala Mitra, 'Notices of Sanskrit MSS.' vol. iii. p. 67.

Zend-Avesta. But here the very scantiness of the ancient texts increases the difficulty of its successful interpretation, and the absence of native commentaries has thrown nearly the whole burden of deciphering on the patience and ingenuity of European scholars.

If lastly we turn to China, we find that the religion of Confucius is founded on the Five King and the Four Shu—books in themselves of considerable extent, and surrounded by voluminous commentaries, without which even the most learned scholars would not venture to fathom the depth of their sacred canon [1].

Lao-tse, the contemporary, or rather the senior, of Confucius, is reported to have written a large number of books [2]: no less than 930 on different questions of faith, morality, and worship, and 70 on magic. His principal work, however, the Tao-te-king, which represents the real scripture of his followers, the Tao-sse, consists only of about 5,000 words [3], and fills no more than thirty pages. But here again we find that for that very reason the text is unintelligible without copious commentaries, so that M. Julien had to consult more than sixty commentators for the purpose of his translation, the earliest going back as far as the year 163 B.C.

There is a third established religion in China, that of Fo; but Fo is only the Chinese corruption of

[1] 'The Chinese Classics, with a Translation, Notes, Prolegomena, and Indexes.' By James Legge, D.D. 7 vols. See also 'Sacred Books of the East,' vols. iii, xvi.

[2] Stan. Julien, 'Tao-te-king,' p. xxvii.

[3] Ibid. pp. xxxi. xxxv. The texts vary from 5,610, 5,630, 5,688 to 5,722 words. The text published by M. Stan. Julien consists of 5,320 words. A new translation of the 'Tao-te-king' has been published at Leipzig by Dr. Victor von Strauss, 1870.

Buddha, and though the religion of Buddha, as transferred from India to China, has assumed a peculiar character and produced an enormous literature of its own, yet Chinese Buddhism cannot be called an independent religion. We must distinguish between the Buddhism of Ceylon, Burmah, and Siam, on one side, and that of Nepal, Tibet, Mongolia, China, Corea, and Japan on the other. In China, however, although the prevailing form of Buddhism is that of the Sanskrit canon, commonly called the Northern canon, some of the books belonging to the Pâli or Southern canon have been translated and are held in reverence by certain schools.

But even after we have collected this enormous library of the sacred books of the world, with their indispensable commentaries, we are by no means in possession of all the requisite materials for studying the growth and decay of the religious convictions of mankind at large. The largest portion of mankind, —ay, and some of the most valiant champions in the religious and intellectual struggles of the world, would still be unrepresented in our theological library. Think only of the Greeks and the Romans! think of the Teutonic, the Celtic, and Slavonic nations! Where are we to gain an insight into what we may call their real religious convictions, previous to the comparatively recent period when their ancient temples were levelled to the ground to make room for new cathedrals, and their sacred oaks were felled to be changed into crosses, planted along every mountain pass and forest lane? Homer and Hesiod do not tell us what was the religion, the real heart-religion, of the Greeks, nor were their own poems ever considered as sacred,

or even as authoritative and binding, by the highest
intellects among the Greeks. In Rome we have not
even an Iliad or Odyssey; and when we ask for the
religious worship of the Teutonic, the Celtic, or the
Slavonic tribes, the very names of many of the deities
in whom they believed are forgotten and lost for ever,
and the scattered notices of their faith have to be
picked up and put together like the small stones of a
broken mosaic that once formed the pavement in the
ruined temples of Rome.

The same gaps, the same want of representative
authorities, which we witness among the Aryan, we
meet again among the Semitic nations, as soon as we
step out of the circle of their book-religions. The
Babylonians, Assyrians, the Phenicians and Carthaginians, the Arabs before their conversion to Mohammedanism, all are without canonical books, and a
knowledge of their religion has to be gathered, as
well as may be, from monuments, inscriptions, traditions, from proper names, from proverbs, from curses,
and other stray notices which require the greatest
care before they can be properly sifted and successfully fitted together[1].

But now let us go on further. The two beds in
which the stream of Aryan and Semitic thought has
been rolling on for centuries from south-east to north-

[1] It has been pointed out by Professor Nöldeke that not only the
great religions, but mere sects also are sometimes in possession of Sacred
Books. Such are the Mandæans (representing the Aramæan nationality), the Druses, the Yezidis, Nosairis, and, it may be, some more
half-pagan sects under a Muslim garb. Even some of the Manichæan
writings, of which fragments exist, might be added to this class, and
would throw much light on the independent growth of gnosticism,
which can be by no means fully explained as a mere mixture of Christian
and Iranian ideas.

west, from the Indus to the Thames, from the Euphrates to the Jordan and the Mediterranean, cover but a narrow tract of country compared with the vastness of our globe. As we rise higher, our horizon expands on every side, and wherever there are traces of human life, there are traces also of religion. Along the shores of the ancient Nile we see still standing the Pyramids, and the ruins of temples and labyrinths, their walls covered with hieroglyphic inscriptions, and with the strange pictures of gods and goddesses. On rolls of papyrus, which have defied the ravages of time, we have even fragments of what may be in a certain sense called the sacred books of the Egyptians. Yet, though much has been deciphered in the ancient records of that mysterious race, the main spring of the religion of Egypt and the original intention of its ceremonial worship are far, as yet, from being fully disclosed to us.

As we follow the sacred stream to its distant sources, the whole continent of Africa opens before us, and wherever we see kraals and cattle-pens, depend upon it there was to be seen once, or there is to be seen even now, the smoke of sacrifices rising up from earth to heaven. The relics of the ancient African faith are rapidly disappearing; but what has been preserved is full of interest to the student of religion with its strange worship of snakes and ancestors, its vague hope of a future life, and its not altogether faded reminiscence of a Supreme God, the Father of the black as well as of the white man[1].

[1] Dr. Callaway, 'Unkulunkulu,' p. 45: 'It is as though we sprang from Uthlanga; we do not know where we were made. We black men had the same origin as you, white men.'

F

From the eastern coast of Africa our eye is carried across the sea where, from Madagascar to Hawaii, island after island stands out like so many pillars of a sunken bridge that once spanned the Indian and Pacific oceans. Everywhere, whether among the dark Papuan or the yellowish Malay, or the brown Polynesian races scattered on these islands, even among the lowest of the low in the scale of humanity, there are, if we will but listen, whisperings about divine beings, imaginings of a future life; there are prayers and sacrifices which, even in their most degraded and degrading form, still bear witness to that old and ineradicable faith that everywhere there is a God to hear our prayers, if we will but call on Him, and to accept our offerings, whether they are offered as a ransom for sin, or as a token of a grateful heart.

Still farther east the double continent of America becomes visible, and in spite of the unchristian vandalism of its first discoverers and conquerors, there, too, we find materials for the study of an ancient, and, it would seem, independent faith. Unfortunately, the religious and mythological traditions collected by the first Europeans who came in contact with the natives of America, reach back but a short distance beyond the time when they were written down, and they seem in several cases to reflect the thoughts of the Spanish listeners as much as those of the native narrators. The quaint hieroglyphic manuscripts of Mexico and Guatemala have as yet told us very little, and the accounts written by natives in their native language have to be used with great caution. Still the ancient religion of the Aztecs of Mexico and of the Incas of Peru is full of interesting problems. As we advance towards the north and its red-skinned inhabitants, our information becomes more meagre still, and after what happened some years ago, no *Livre des Sauvages* is likely to come to our assistance again. Yet there are wild and home-grown specimens of religious faith to be studied even now among the receding and gradually perishing tribes of the Red Indians, and, in their languages as well as in their religions, traces may possibly still be found, before it is too late, of pre-historic migrations of men from the primitive Asiatic to the American continent, either across the stepping-stones of the Aleutic bridge in the north, or lower south by drifting with favourable winds from island to island, till the hardy canoe was landed or wrecked on the American coast, never to return again to the Asiatic home from which it had started.

And when in our religious survey we finally come back again to the Asiatic continent, we find here too, although nearly the whole of its area is now occupied by one or the other of the eight book-religions, by Mosaism, Christianity, and Mohammedanism, by Brahmanism, Buddhism, and Zoroastrianism, and in China by the religions of Confucius and Lao-tse, that nevertheless partly below the surface, and in some places still on the surface too, more primitive forms of worship have maintained themselves. I mean the Shamanism of the Mongolian race, and the beautiful half-Homeric mythology of the Finnish and Esthonian tribes.

And now that I have displayed this world-wide panorama before your eyes, you will share, I think, the feeling of dismay with which the student of the science of religion looks around, and asks himself where to begin and how to proceed. That there are materials in abundance, capable of scientific treatment, no one would venture to deny. But how are they to be held together? How are we to discover what all these religions share in common? How they differ? How they rise and how they decline? What they are and what they mean?

Let us take the old saying, *Divide et impera*, and translate it somewhat freely by 'Classify and understand,' and I believe we shall then lay hold of the old thread of Ariadne which has led the students of many a science through darker labyrinths even than the labyrinth of the religions of the world. All real science rests on classification, and only in case we cannot succeed in classifying the various dialects of faith, shall we have to confess that a science of religion is really an impossibility. If the ground before us has once been properly surveyed and carefully parcelled out, each scholar may then cultivate his own glebe, without wasting his energies, and without losing sight of the general purposes to which all special researches must be subservient.

How, then, is the vast domain of religion to be parcelled out? How are religions to be classified, or, we ought rather to ask first, how have they been classified before now? The simplest classification, and one which we find adopted in almost every country, is that into *true* and *false* religions. It is very much like the first classification of languages into one's own language and the languages of the rest of the world; as the Greeks would say, into the languages of the

Greeks and the Barbarians; or, as the Jews would say, into the languages of the Jews and the Gentiles; or, as the Hindus would say, into the languages of the Âryas and Mle*kkh*as; or, as the Chinese would say, into the languages of the Middle Empire and that of the Outer Barbarians. I need not say why that sort of classification is useless for scientific purposes.

There is another classification, apparently of a more scientific character, but if examined more closely, equally worthless to the student of religion. I mean the well-known division into *revealed* and *natural* religions.

I have first to say a few words on the meaning attached to natural religion. That word is constantly used in very different acceptations. It is applied by several writers to certain historical forms of religion, which are looked upon as not resting on the authority of revelation, in whatever sense that word may be hereafter interpreted. Thus Buddhism would be a natural religion in the eyes of the Brahmans, Brahmanism would be a natural religion in the eyes of the Mohammedans. With us, all religions except Christianity and, though in a lesser degree, Mosaism, would be classed as merely natural; and though natural does not imply false, yet it distinctly implies the absence of any sanction beyond the sense of truth, or the voice of conscience that is within us.

But Natural Religion is also used in a very different sense, particularly by the philosophers of the last century. When people began to subject the principal historical religions to a critical analysis, they found that after removing what was peculiar to each, there remained certain principles which they all shared in common.   These were supposed to be the principles of Natural Religion.

Again, when everything that seemed supernatural, miraculous, and irrational, had been removed from the pages of the New Testament, there still remained a kind of skeleton of religion, and this too was passed off under the name of Natural Religion.

During the last century, philosophers who were opposing the spread of scepticism and infidelity, thought that this kind of natural, or, as it was also called, rational religion, might serve as a breakwater against utter unbelief;—but their endeavours led to no result.   When Diderot said that all revealed religions were the heresies of Natural Religion, he meant by Natural Religion a body of truths implanted in human nature, to be discovered by the eye of reason alone, and independent of any such historical or local influences as give to each religion its peculiar character and individual aspect.   The existence of a deity, the nature of his attributes, such as Omnipotence, Omniscience, Omnipresence, Eternity, Self-existence, Spirituality, the Goodness also of the Deity, and, connected with it, the admission of an absolute distinction between Good and Evil, between Virtue and Vice, all this, and according to some writers, the Unity and Personality also of the Deity, were included in the domain of Natural Religion.   The scientific treatment of this so-called Natural Religion received the name of Natural Theology, a title rendered famous in the beginning of our century by the much praised and much abused work of Paley.

Natural Religion corresponds in the science of

religion to what in the science of language used to be called *Grammaire générale*, a collection of fundamental rules which were supposed to be self-evident, and indispensable in every grammar, but which, strange to say, never exist in their purity and completeness in any language that is or ever has been spoken by human beings. It is the same with religion. There never has been any real religion, consisting exclusively of the pure and simple tenets of Natural Religion, though there have been certain philosophers who brought themselves to believe that their religion was entirely rational, was, in fact, pure and simple Deism.

If we speak, therefore, of a classification of all historical religions into revealed and natural, what is meant by natural is simply the negation of revealed, and if we tried to carry out the classification practically, we should find the same result as before. We should have on one side Christianity alone, or, according to some theologians, Christianity and Judaism; on the other, all the remaining religions of the world.

This classification, therefore, whatever may be its practical value, is perfectly useless for scientific purposes. A more extended study shows us very soon that the claim of revelation is set up by the founders, or if not by them, at all events by the later preachers and advocates of most religions; and would therefore be declined by all but ourselves as a distinguishing feature of Christianity and Judaism. We shall see, in fact, that the claims to a revealed authority are urged far more strongly and elaborately by the believers in the Veda, than by the apologetical theolo-

gians among Jews and Christians. Even Buddha,
originally the most thoroughly human and self-de-
pendent among the founders of religion, is by a
strange kind of inconsistency represented, in later
controversial writings, as in possession of revealed
truth [1]. He himself could not, like Numa or Zoroaster, or Mohammed [2], claim communication with
higher spirits; still less could he, like the poets of
the Veda, speak of divine inspirations and god-given
utterances: for according to him there was none
among the spirits greater or wiser than himself, and
the gods of the Veda had become his servants and
worshippers. Buddha himself appeals only to what
we should call the inner light [3]. When he delivered
for the first time the four fundamental doctrines of
his system, he said, 'Mendicants, for the attainment
of these previously unknown doctrines, the eye, the
knowledge, the wisdom, the clear perception, the light
were developed within me.' He was called Sarva*gña*
or omniscient by his earliest pupils; but when in later
times, it was seen that on several points Buddha had
but spoken the language of his age, and had shared
the errors current among his contemporaries with
regard to the shape of the earth and the movement
of the heavenly bodies, an important concession was
made by Buddhist theologians. They limited the
meaning of the word 'omniscient,' as applied to
Buddha, to a knowledge of the principal doctrines
of his system, and concerning these, but these only,

[1] 'History of Ancient Sanskrit Literature,' by Max Müller, p. 83.
[2] Sprenger, 'Mohammad,' vol. ii. p. 426.
[3] Gogerly, 'The Evidences and Doctrines of Christian Religion.'
Colombo, 1862.   Part I.

they declared him to have been infallible. This may seem to be a late, and almost modern view, but whether modern or ancient, it certainly reflects great credit on the Buddhist theologians. In the Milinda Pra na, however, which is a canonical book, we see that the same idea was already rising in the mind of the great Nâgasena. Being asked by King Milinda whether Buddha is omniscient, he replies: 'Yes, Great King, the blessed Buddha is omniscient. But Buddha does not at all times exercise his omniscience. By meditation he knows all things; meditating he knows everything he desires to know.' In this reply a distinction is evidently intended between subjects that may be known by sense and reason, and subjects that can be known by meditation only. Within the domain of sense and reason, Nâgasena does not claim omniscience or infallibility for Buddha, but he claims for him both omniscience and infallibility in all that is to be perceived by meditation only, or, as we should say, in matters of faith.

I shall have to explain to you hereafter the extraordinary contrivances by which the Brahmans endeavoured to eliminate every human element from the hymns of the Veda, and to establish, not only the revealed, but the pre-historic or even ante-mundane character of their scriptures. No apologetic writers have ever carried the theory of revelation to greater extremes.

In the present stage of our inquiries, all that I wish to point out is this,—that when the founders or defenders of nearly all the religions of the world appeal to some kind of revelation in support of the truth of their doctrines, it could answer no useful purpose were we to attempt any classification on such disputed ground. Whether the claim of a natural or preternatural revelation, put forward by nearly all religions, is well founded or not, is not the question at present. It falls to the province of Theoretic Theology to explain the true meaning of revelation, for few words have been used so vaguely and in so many different senses. It falls to its province to explain, not only how the veil was withdrawn that intercepted for a time the rays of divine truth, but, what is a far more difficult problem, how there could ever have been a veil between truth and the seeker of truth, between the adoring heart and the object of the highest adoration, between the Father and his children.

In Comparative Theology our task is different: we have simply to deal with the facts such as we find them. If people regard their religion as revealed, it is to them a revealed religion, and has to be treated as such by every impartial historian.

But this principle of classification into revealed and natural religions appears still more faulty, when we look at it from another point of view. Even if we granted that all religions, except Christianity and Mosaism, derived their origin from those faculties of the mind only which, according to Paley, are sufficient by themselves for calling into life the fundamental tenets of what we explained before as natural religion, the classification of Christianity and Judaism on one side as *revealed*, and of the other religions as *natural*, would still be defective, for the simple reason that no religion, though founded on revelation, can ever be entirely separated from natural religion. The tenets of natural religion, though they never constituted by themselves a real historical religion, supply the only ground on which even revealed religions can stand, the only soil where they can strike root, and from which they can receive nourishment and life. If we took away that soil, or if we supposed that it, too, had to be supplied by revelation, we should not only run counter to the letter and spirit of the Old and the New Testament, but we should degrade revealed religion by changing it into a mere formula, to be accepted by a recipient incapable of questioning, weighing, and appreciating its truth; we should indeed have the germ, but we should have thrown away the congenial soil in which alone the germs of revealed truth can live and grow.

Christianity, addressing itself not only to the Jews, but also to the Gentiles, not only to the ignorant, but also to the learned, not only to the believer, but, in the first instance, to the unbeliever, presupposed in all of them the elements of natural religion, and with them the power of choosing between truth and untruth. Thus only could St. Paul say: 'Prove all things, hold fast that which is good.' (1 Thess. v. 21.)

The same is true with regard to the Old Testament. There, too, the belief in a Deity, and in some at least of its indefeasible attributes, is taken for granted, and the prophets who call the wayward Jews back to the worship of Jehovah, appeal to them as competent by the truth-testing power that is within them, to choose between Jehovah and the gods of the Gentiles, between truth and untruth. Thus Joshua gathered all the tribes of Israel to Shechem, and called for the elders of Israel, and for their heads, and for their judges, and for their officers; and they presented themselves before God.

'And Joshua said unto all the people: Thus saith the Lord God of Israel: Your fathers dwelt on the other side of the flood in old time, even Terah, the father of Abraham, and the father of Nachor: and they served other gods.'

And then, after reminding them of all that God has done for them, he concludes by saying:

'Now, therefore, fear the Lord, and serve him in sincerity and in truth; and put away the gods which your fathers served on the other side of the flood, and in Egypt, and serve ye the Lord.

'And if it seem evil unto you to serve the Lord, *choose you* this day whom ye will serve; whether the gods which your fathers served that were on the other side of the flood, or the gods of the Amorites in whose lands ye dwell: but as for me and my house, we will serve the Lord.'

In order to choose between different gods and different forms of faith, a man must possess the faculty of choosing, the instruments of testing truth and untruth, whether revealed or not: he must know that certain fundamental tenets cannot be absent in any true religion, and that there are doctrines against which his rational or moral conscience revolts as incompatible with truth. In short, there must be the foundation of religion, there must be the solid rock, before it is possible to erect an altar, a temple, or a church: and if we call that foundation natural religion, it is clear that no revealed religion can be thought of which does not rest more or less firmly on natural religion.

These difficulties have been felt distinctly by some

of our most learned divines, who have attempted various classifications of religions from their own point of view.   New definitions of natural religion have therefore been proposed in order to avoid the overlapping of the two definitions of natural and re-vealed religion[1].   Natural religion has, for instance, been explained as the religion of nature before revela-tion, such as may be supposed to have existed among the patriarchs, or to exist still among primitive people who have not yet been enlightened by Christianity or debased by idolatry.

According to this view we should have to distin-guish not two, but three classes of religion: the pri-mitive or natural, the debased or idolatrous, and the revealed. But, as pointed out before, the first, the so-called primitive or natural religion, exists in the minds of modern philosophers rather than of ancient poets and prophets. History never tells us of any race with whom the simple feeling of reverence for higher powers was not hidden under mythological disguises. Nor would it be possible even thus to separate the three classes of religion by sharp and definite lines of demarcation, because both the debased or idolatrous and the purified or revealed religions would of necessity include within themselves the elements of natural religion.

Nor do we diminish these difficulties in the classifi-catory stage of our science if, in the place of this simple natural religion, we admit with other theolo-gians and philosophers, a universal primeval revela-tion. This universal primeval revelation is only another name for natural religion, and it rests on

[1] See Professor Jowett's ' Essay on Natural Religion,' p. 458.

no authority but the speculations of philosophers.
The same class of philosophers, considering that language was too wonderful an achievement for the
human mind, insisted on the necessity of admitting a
universal primeval language, revealed directly by
God to men, or rather to mute beings; while the
more thoughtful and the more reverent among the
Fathers of the Church, and among the founders of
modern philosophy also pointed out that it was more
consonant with the general working of an all-wise
and all-powerful Creator, that he should have endowed human nature with the essential conditions of
speech, instead of presenting mute beings with grammars and dictionaries ready-made. Is an infant less
wonderful than a man? an acorn less wonderful than
an oak tree? a cell, including potentially within itself
all that it has to become hereafter, less wonderful than
all the moving creatures that have life? The same
applies to religion. A universal primeval religion revealed direct by God to man, or rather to a crowd of
atheists, may, to our human wisdom, seem the best
solution of all difficulties: but a higher wisdom
speaks to us from out the realities of history, and
teaches us, if we will but learn, that 'we have all to
seek the Lord, if haply we may feel after him, and
find him, though he be not far from every one of us.'

Of the hypothesis of a universal primeval revelation and all its self-created difficulties we shall have
to speak again: for the present it must suffice if we
have shown that the problem of a scientific classification of religions is not brought nearer to its solution
by the additional assumption of another purely hypothetical class of religions.

Another apparently more scientific classification is that into *national* and *individual* religions, the former comprehending religions the founders of which are unknown to us as they were to those who believed in them; the latter comprehending religious systems which bear the names of those by whom they were supposed to have been originally planned or established. To the former class, speaking only of the religions with which we are most familiar, would belong those of the ancient Brahmans, the Greeks, Romans, Teutons, Slaves, and Celts; to the latter those of Moses, Zoroaster, Buddha, Confucius, Lao-tse, Christ, and Mohammed.

This division, however, though easily applied in a general way, and useful for certain purposes, fails us as soon as we attempt to apply it in a more critical spirit. It is quite true that neither a Brahman, nor a Greek, nor a Roman would have known what to answer when asked, who was the founder of his religion, who first declared the existence of Indra, Zeus, or Jupiter; but the student of antiquity can still discover in the various forms which the ancient Aryan worship has assumed in India, Greece, and Italy, the influence of individual minds or schools. If, on the other hand, we ask the founders of so-called individual religions, whether their doctrine is a new one, whether they preach a new God, we almost always receive a negative answer. Confucius emphatically asserts that he was a transmitter, not a maker; Buddha delights in representing himself as a mere link in a long chain of enlightened teachers; Christ declares that he came to fulfil, not to destroy the Law or the Prophets; and even Mohammed insisted on tracing his faith back to Ibrâhym, i.e. Abraham, the friend of God, whom he called a Moslim, and not a Jew or Christian, (Koran iii. 60,) and who, he maintained, had founded the temple at Mekka[1]. To determine how much is peculiar to the supposed founder of a religion, how much he received from his predecessors, and how much was added by his disciples, is almost impossible; nay, it is perfectly true that no religion has ever struck root and lived, unless it found a congenial soil from which to draw its real strength and support. If they find such a soil, individual religions have a tendency to develope into *universal* religions, while national creeds remain more exclusive, and in many cases are even opposed to all missionary propaganda[2].

We have not finished yet. A very important and, for certain purposes, very useful classification has been that into *polytheistic, dualistic,* and *monotheistic* religions. If religion rests chiefly on a belief in a Higher Power, then the nature of that Higher Power would seem to supply the most characteristic feature by which to classify the religions of the world. Nor do I deny that for certain purposes such a classification has proved useful: all I maintain is that we should ·thus have to class together religions most heterogeneous in other respects, though agreeing in the number of their deities. Besides, it would certainly be necessary to add two other classes—the *henotheistic* and the *atheistic.* Henotheistic religions differ from polytheistic because, although they recog-

[1] Sprenger, 'Mohammad,' vol. iii. pp. 49, 489.
[2] See 'Hibbert Lectures,' by Professor Kuenen, 1882. 'National Religions and Universal Religions.'

nise the existence of various deities, or names of deities, they represent each deity as independent of all the rest, as the only deity present in the mind of the worshipper at the time of his worship and prayer. This character is most prominent in the religion of the Vedic poets. Although many gods are invoked in different hymns, sometimes also in the same hymn, yet there is no rule of precedence established among them; and, according to the varying aspects of nature, and the varying cravings of the human heart, it is sometimes Indra, the god of the blue sky, sometimes Agni, the god of fire, sometimes Varuna, the ancient god of the firmament, that are praised as supreme without any suspicion of rivalry, or any idea of subordination. This peculiar phase of religion, this worship of single gods, forms probably everywhere the first stage in the growth of polytheism, and deserves therefore a separate name [1].

As to atheistic religions, they might seem to be perfectly impossible; and yet the fact cannot be disputed away that the religion of Buddha was from the beginning purely atheistic. The idea of the Godhead, after it had been degraded by endless mythological absurdities which struck and repelled the heart of Buddha, was, for a time at least, entirely expelled from the sanctuary of the human mind: and the highest morality that was ever taught before the rise of Christianity was taught by men with whom the gods had become mere phantoms, without any altars, not even an altar to the Unknown God.

It will be the object of my next lecture to show

---

[1] 'History of Ancient Sanskrit Literature' by Max Müller, second edition, p. 532. 'Hibbert Lectures,' p. 236.

that the only scientific and truly genetic classification of religions is the same as the classification of languages, and that, particularly in the early history of the human intellect, there exists the most intimate relationship between language, religion, and nationality—a relationship quite independent of those physical elements, the blood, the skull, or the hair, on which ethnologists have attempted to found their classification of the human race.

THIRD LECTURE.

DELIVERED AT THE ROYAL INSTITUTION,
MARCH 5, 1870.

IF we approached the religions of mankind without any prejudices or predilections, in that frame of mind in which the lover of truth or the man of science ought to approach every subject, I believe we should not be long before recognising the natural lines of demarcation which divide the whole religious world into several great continents. I am speaking, of course, of ancient religions only, or of the earliest period in the history of religious thought. In that primitive period which might be called, if not prehistoric, at least purely ethnic, because what we know of it consists only in the general movements of nations, and not in the acts of individuals, of parties, or of states—in that primitive period, I say, nations have been called languages; and in our best works on the ancient history of mankind, a map of languages now takes the place of a map of nations. But during the same primitive period nations might with equal right be called religions; for there is at that time the same, nay, an even more intimate, relationship between religion and nationality than between language and nationality.

In order clearly to explain my meaning, I shall have to refer, as shortly as possible, to the specula-

G 2

tions of some German philosophers on the true relation between language, religion, and nationality—
speculations which have as yet received less attention
on the part of modern ethnologists than they seem to
me to deserve.

It was Schelling, one of the profoundest thinkers
of Germany, who first asked the question, What
makes an *ethnos*? What is the true origin of a
people? How did human beings become a people?
And the answer which he gave, though it sounded
startling to me when, in 1845, I listened, at Berlin, to
the lectures of the old philosopher, has been confirmed
more and more by subsequent researches into the
history of language and religion.

To say that man is a gregarious animal, and that,
like swarms of bees, or herds of wild elephants, men
keep together instinctively, and thus form themselves
into a people, is saying very little. It might explain
the agglomeration of one large flock of human beings,
but it would never explain the formation of peoples
possessing the consciousness of their national individuality.

Nor should we advance much towards a solution of
our problem, if we were told that men break up into
peoples as bees break up into swarms, by following
different queens, by owing allegiance to different governments. Allegiance to the same government, particularly in ancient times, is the result rather than
the cause of nationality; while in historical times,
such has been the confusion produced by extraneous
influences, by brute force, or dynastic ambition, that
the natural development of peoples has been entirely
arrested, and we frequently find one and the same

people divided by different governments, and different peoples united under the same ruler.

Our question, What makes a people? has to be considered in reference to the most ancient times. How did men form themselves into a people before there were kings or shepherds of men? Was it through community of blood? I doubt it. Community of blood produces families, clans, possibly races, but it does not produce that higher and purely moral feeling which binds men together and makes them a people.

It is language and religion that make a people, but religion is even a more powerful agent than language. The languages of many of the aboriginal inhabitants of Northern America are but dialectic varieties of one type, but those who spoke these dialects seem never to have coalesced into a people. They remained mere clans or wandering tribes, and even their antagonism to foreign invaders did not call out the sense of a national coherence and unity among them, because they were without that higher sense of unity which is called forth, or, at all events, strengthened, by worshipping the same god or gods. The Greeks[1], on the contrary, though speaking their strongly marked, and I doubt whether mutually intelligible dialects, the Æolic, the Doric, the Ionic, felt themselves at all times, even when ruled by different tyrants, or broken up into numerous republics, as one great Hellenic people. What was it, then, that

---

[1] Herodotus, viii. 144—Αὖτις δὲ τὸ Ἑλληνικὸν ἐὸν ὅμαιμόν τε καὶ ὁμόγλωσσον, καὶ θεῶν ἱδρύματά τε κοινὰ καὶ θυσίαι ἤθεά τε ὁμότροπα, τῶν προδότας γενέσθαι Ἀθηναίους οὐκ ἂν εὖ ἔχοι. See ' Edinb. Review,' 1874, p. 433.

preserved in their hearts, in spite of dialects, in spite
of dynasties, in spite even of the feuds of tribes and
the jealousies of states, the deep feeling of that ideal
unity which constitutes a people? It was their primitive religion; it was a dim recollection of the
common allegiance they owed from time immemorial
to the great father of gods and men; it was their
belief in the old Zeus of Dodona, the Panhellenic
Zeus.

Perhaps the most signal confirmation of this view
that it is religion even more than language which
supplies the foundation of nationality, is to be found
in the history of the Jews, the chosen people of God.
The language of the Jews differed from that of the
Phenicians, the Moabites, and other neighbouring
tribes much less than the Greek dialects differed
from each other. But the worship of Jehovah made
the Jews a peculiar people, the people of Jehovah,
separated by their God, though not by their language, from the people of Chemosh (the Moabites [1])
and from the worshippers of Baal and Ashtoreth.
It was their faith in Jehovah that changed the
wandering tribes of Israel into a nation.

'A people,' as Schelling says, 'exists only when it
has determined itself with regard to its mythology.
This mythology, therefore, cannot take its origin
after a national separation has taken place, after
a people has become a people: nor could it spring
up while a people was still contained as an invisible
part in the whole of humanity; but its origin must
be referred to that very period of transition before

[1] Numb. xxi. 29; Jeremiah xlviii. 7: 'And Chemosh shall go forth
into captivity, with his priests and his princes together.'

a people has assumed its definite existence, and when it is on the point of separating and constituting itself. The same applies to the language of a people; it becomes definite at the same time that a people becomes definite[1].'

Hegel, the great rival of Schelling, arrived at the same conclusion. In his Philosophy of History he says: 'The idea of God constitutes the general foundation of a people. Whatever is the form of a religion, the same is the form of a state and its constitution: it springs from religion, so much so that the Athenian and the Roman states were possible only with the peculiar heathendom of those peoples, and that even now a Roman Catholic state has a different genius and a different constitution from a Protestant state. The genius of a people is a definite, individual genius which becomes conscious of its individuality in different spheres: in the character of its moral life, its political constitution, its art, religion and science[2].'

But this is not an idea of philosophers only. Historians, and, more particularly, the students of the history of law, have arrived at very much the same conclusion. Though to many of them law seems naturally to be the foundation of society, and the

---

[1] 'Vorlesungen über Philosophie der Mythologie,' vol. i. p. 107 seq.

[2] Though these words of Hegel's were published long before Schelling's lectures, they seem to me to breathe the spirit of Schelling rather than of Hegel, and it is but fair therefore to state that Schelling's lectures, though not published, were printed and circulated among friends twenty years before they were delivered at Berlin. The question of priority may seem of little importance on matters such as these, but there is nevertheless much truth in Schelling's remark, that philosophy advances not so much by the answers given to difficult problems, as by the starting of new problems, and by asking questions which no one else would think of asking.

bond that binds a nation together, those who look below the surface have quickly perceived that law itself, at least ancient law, derives its authority, its force, its very life, from religion. Sir H. Maine is no doubt right when, in the case of the so-called Laws of Manu, he rejects the idea of the Deity dictating an entire code or body of law, as an idea of a decidedly modern origin. Yet the belief that the law-giver enjoyed some closer intimacy with the Deity than ordinary mortals, pervades the ancient traditions of many nations. Thus Diodorus Siculus (l. i. c. 94), tells us that the Egyptians believed their laws to have been communicated to Mnevis by Hermes; the Cretans held that Minos received his laws from Zeus, the Lacedæmonians that Lykurgos received his laws from Apollon. According to the Arians, their law-giver, Zathraustes, had received his laws from the Good Spirit; according to the Getæ, Zamolxis received his laws from the goddess Hestia; and, according to the Jews, Moses received his laws from the god Iao.

No one has pointed out more forcibly than Sir H. Maine that in ancient times religion as a divine influence was underlying and supporting every relation of life and every social institution. 'A supernatural presidency,' he writes, 'is supposed to consecrate and keep together all the cardinal institutions of those early times, the state, the race, and the family' (p. 6). 'The elementary group is the family; the aggregation of families forms the *gens* or the house. The aggregation of houses makes the tribe. The aggregation of tribes constitutes the commonwealth' (p. 128). Now the family is held together by the family *sacra* (p. 191), and so were the *gens*, the tribe, and the commonwealth; and strangers could only be admitted to these brotherhoods by being admitted to their *sacra* (p. 131)[1]. At a later time, law breaks away from religion (p. 193), but even then many traces remain to show that the hearth was the first altar, the father the first elder, his wife and children and slaves the first congregation gathered together round the sacred fire—the Hestia, the goddess of the house, and in the end the goddess of the people. To the present day, marriage, one of the most important of civil acts, the very foundation of civilised life, has retained something of the religious character which it had from the very beginning of history.

Let us see now what religion really is in those early ages of which we are here speaking: I do not mean religion as a silent power, working in the heart of man; I mean religion in its outward appearance, religion as something outspoken, tangible, and definite, that can be described and communicated to others. We shall find that in that sense religion lies within a very small compass. A few words, recognised as names of the deity; a few epithets that have been raised from their material meaning to a higher and more spiritual stage,—I mean words which expressed originally bodily strength, or brightness, or purity, and which gradually had come to mean greatness, goodness, and holiness; lastly, some

---

[1] A very different opinion is held by Varro. 'Varro propterea se prius de rebus humanis, de divinis autem postea scripsisse testatur, quod prius extiterint civitates, deinde ab eis hæc instituta sint . . . . sicut prior est, inquit, pictor quam tabula picta, prior faber quam ædificium: ita priores sunt civitates quam ea quæ a civitatibus instituta sunt.' (August. 'Civ. Dei,' 6. 4).

more or less technical terms expressive of such ideas
as *sacrifice, altar, prayer,* possibly *virtue* and *sin,*
body and *spirit*—this is what constitutes the outward
framework of the incipient religions of antiquity. If
we look at these simple manifestations of religion, we
see at once why religion, during those early ages of
which we are here speaking, may really and truly be
called a sacred dialect of human speech; how at all
events early religion and early language are most
intimately connected, religion depending entirely for
its outward expression on the more or less adequate
resources of language.

And if this dependence of early religion on language
is once clearly understood, it follows, as a matter of
course, that whatever classification has been found
most useful in the Science of Language ought to
prove equally useful in the Science of Religion. If
there is a truly genetic relationship of languages, the
same relationship ought to hold together the religions
of the world, at least the most ancient religions.

Before we proceed therefore to consider the proper
classification of religions, it will be necessary to say
a few words on the present state of our knowledge
with regard to the genetic relationship of languages.

If we confine ourselves to the Asiatic continent
with its important peninsula of Europe, we find that
in the vast desert of drifting human speech three, and
only three, oases have been formed in which, before
the beginning of all history, language became permanent and traditional, assumed in fact a new
character, a character totally different from the original character of the floating and constantly varying
speech of human beings. These three oases of lan-

guage are known by the name of *Turanian, Semitic,* and *Aryan.* In these three centres, more particularly in the *Aryan* and *Semitic,* language ceased to be natural; its growth was arrested, and it became permanent, solid, petrified, or, if you like, historical speech. I have always maintained that this centralisation and traditional conservation of language could only have been the result of religious and political influences, and I now intend to show that we really have clear evidence of three independent settlements of religion, the *Turanian,* the *Semitic,* and the *Aryan,* concomitantly with the three great settlements of language.

Taking Chinese for what it can hardly any longer be doubted that it is, viz. the earliest representative of Turanian speech, we find in China an ancient colourless and unpoetical religion, a religion we might almost venture to call monosyllabic, consisting of the worship of a host of single spirits, representing the sky, the sun, storms and lightning, mountains and rivers, one standing by the side of the other without any mutual attraction, without any higher principle to hold them together. In addition to this, we likewise meet in China with the worship of ancestral spirits, the spirits of the departed, who are supposed to retain some cognisance of human affairs, and to possess peculiar powers which they exercise for good or for evil. This double worship of human and of natural spirits constitutes the old popular religion of China, and it has lived on to the present day, at least in the lower ranks of society, though there towers above it a more elevated range of half religious and half philosophical faith, a belief in two higher Powers which, in the language of philosophy, may mean *Form* and *Matter*, in the language of Ethics, *Good* and *Evil*, but which in the original language of religion and mythology are represented as *Heaven* and *Earth*.

It is true that we know the ancient popular religion of China from the works of Confucius only, or from even more modern sources. But Confucius, though he is called the founder of a new religion, was really but the new preacher of an old religion. He was emphatically a transmitter, not a maker [1]. He says of himself, 'I only hand on; I cannot create new things. I believe in the ancients, and therefore I love them [2].'

We find, secondly, the ancient worship of the Semitic races, clearly marked by a number of names of the Deity, which appear in the polytheistic religions of the Babylonians, the Phenicians, and Carthaginians, as well as in the monotheistic creeds of Jews, Christians, and Mohammedans. It is almost impossible to characterise the religion of people so different from each other in language, in literature, and general civilisation, so different also from themselves at different periods of their history; but if I ventured to characterise the worship of all the Semitic nations by one word, I should say it was pre-eminently a worship of *God in History*, of God as affecting the destinies of individuals and races and nations rather than of God as wielding the powers of nature. The names of the Semitic deities are mostly words expressive of moral qualities; they mean the Strong, the Exalted, the Lord, the King; and they grow but seldom into divine personalities, definite in their outward appear-

[1] See Dr. Legge, 'Life of Confucius.' p. 96.
[2] Lün-yü (§ 1. a); Schott, 'Chinesische Literatur,' p. 7.

ance or easily to be recognised by strongly marked features of a real dramatic character. Hence many of the ancient Semitic gods have a tendency to run together, and a transition from the worship of single gods to the worship of one God required no great effort. In the monotonous desert, more particularly, the worship of single gods glided away almost imperceptibly into the worship of one God. If I were to add, as a distinguishing mark, that the Semitic religions excluded the feminine gender in their names of the Deity, or that all their female deities were only representatives of the active energies of older and sexless gods, this would be true of some only, not of all ; and it would require nearly as many limitations as the statement of M. Renan, that the Semitic religions were instinctively monotheistic [1].

We find lastly the ancient worship of the Aryan race carried to the most distant corners of the earth by its adventurous sons, and easily recognised, whether in the valleys of India or in the forests of Germany, by the common names of the Deity, all originally expressive of natural powers. Their worship is not, as has been so often said, a worship of nature. But if it had to be characterised by one word, I should venture to call it a worship of *God in Nature*, of God as appearing behind the gorgeous veil of Nature, rather than as hidden behind the veil of the sanctuary of the human heart. The gods of the Aryan pantheon assume an individuality so strongly marked and permanent, that with the Aryans, a transition to monotheism required a powerful struggle, and seldom took

---

[1] See my essay on ' Semitic Monotheism,' in ' Chips from a German Workshop,' vol. i. pp. 342 380.

effect without iconoclastic revolutions or philosophical despair.

These three classes of religion are not to be mistaken, as little as the three classes of language, the Turanian, the Semitic, and the Aryan. They mark three events in the most ancient history of the world, events which have determined the whole fate of the human race, and of which we ourselves still feel the consequences in our language, in our thoughts, and in our religion.

But the chaos which these three leaders in language, thought, and religion, the Turanian, the Semitic, and the Aryan, left behind, was not altogether a chaos. The stream of language from which these three channels had separated, rolled on; the sacred fire of religion from which these three altars had been lighted was not extinguished, though hidden in smoke and ashes. There was language and there was religion everywhere in the world, but it was natural and wild-growing language and religion; it had no history, it left no history, and it is therefore incapable of that peculiar scientific treatment which has been found applicable to a study of the languages and the religions of the Chinese, the Semitic, and the Aryan nations.

People wonder why the students of language have not succeeded in establishing more than three families of speech—or rather two, for the Turanian can hardly be called a family, in the strict sense of that word, until it has been fully proved that Chinese forms the centre of the two Turanian branches, the North Turanian on one side, and the South Turanian on the other, that Chinese[1] forms, in fact, the earliest settle-

---

[1] See my 'Lecture on the Stratification of Language,' p. 4.

ment of that unsettled mass of speech, which, at a later stage, became more fixed and traditional,—in the north, in *Tungusic*, *Mongolic*, *Tataric*, and *Finnic*, and in the south, in *Taic*, *Malaic*, *Bhotiya*, and *Tamulic*.

The reason why scholars have discovered no more than these two or three great families of speech is very simple. There were no more, and we cannot make more. Families of languages are very peculiar formations; they are, and they must be, the exception, not the rule, in the growth of language. There was always the possibility, but there never was, as far as I can judge, any necessity for human speech leaving its primitive stage of wild growth and wild decay. If it had not been for what I consider a purely spontaneous act on the part of the ancestors of the Semitic, Aryan, and Turanian races, all languages might for ever have remained ephemeral, answering the purposes of every generation that comes and goes, struggling on, now gaining, now losing, sometimes acquiring a certain permanence, but after a season breaking up again, and carried away like blocks of ice by the waters that rise underneath the surface. Our very idea of language would then have been something totally different from what it is now.

For what are we doing?

We first form our idea of what language ought to be from those exceptional languages which were arrested in their natural growth by social, religious, political, or at all events by extraneous influences, and we then turn round and wonder why all languages are not like these two or three exceptional channels of speech. We might as well wonder why all animals are not domesticated, or why, besides the garden anemone, there should be endless varieties of the same flower growing wild on the meadow and in the woods.

In the Turanian class, in which the original concentration was never so powerful as in the Aryan and Semitic families, we can still catch a glimpse of the natural growth of language, though confined within certain limits. The different settlements of this great floating mass of homogeneous speech do not show such definite marks of relationship as Hebrew and Arabic, Greek and Sanskrit, but only such sporadic coincidences and general structural similarities as can be explained by the admission of a primitive concentration, followed by a new period of independent growth. It would be wilful blindness not to recognise the definite and characteristic features which pervade the North Turanian languages: it would be impossible to explain the coincidences between Hungarian, Lapponian, Esthonian, and Finnish, except on the supposition that there was a very early concentration of speech from which these dialects branched off. We see this less clearly in the South Turanian group, though I confess my surprise even here has always been, not that there should be so few, but that there should be even these few relics, attesting a former community of these divergent streams of language. The point in which the South Turanian and North Turanian languages meet goes back as far as Chinese; for that Chinese is at the root of Mandshu and Mongolian as well as of Siamese and Tibetan becomes daily more apparent through the researches of Mr. Edkins and other Chinese scholars.

I readily admit that there is no hurry for pronouncing definitely on these problems, and I am well aware of what may be said against these wide generalisations affecting the 'origin of species' in language. My chief object in publishing, more than twenty years ago, my Letter to Bunsen 'On the Turanian Languages,' in which these views were first put forward, was to counteract the dangerous dogmatic scepticism which at that time threatened to stop all freedom of research, and all progress in the Science of Language. No method was then considered legitimate for a comparative analysis of languages except that which was, no doubt, the only legitimate method in treating, for instance, the Romance languages, but was not therefore the only possible method for a scientific treatment of all other languages. No proofs of relationship were then admitted even for languages outside the pale of the Aryan and Semitic families, except those which had been found applicable for establishing the relationship between the various members of these two great families of speech. My object was to show that, during an earlier phase in the development of language, no such proofs ought ever to be demanded, because, from the nature of the case, they could not exist, while yet their absence would in no way justify us in denying the possibility of a more distant relationship. At present a complete change has taken place in the Science of Language, as in other branches of natural science. Owing chiefly to the influence of the ideas which Darwin has brought again into the foreground of all natural philosophy, students are now directing their attention everywhere to the general rather than to the special. Every kind of change, under the name

H

of development, seems now conceivable and admissible, and when all races of men have been traced back to one common source, and even beyond the level of humanity, no difficulty is felt any longer as to the possibility of a relationship between any of the so-called Turanian languages, nay, of a common beginning for all varieties of human speech. This phase of thought in its extreme form will no doubt pass away like the former, but these oscillations should teach us at least this one lesson that no dictatorial authority should ever stop the progress of science, and that nothing is so dangerous as a belief in our own infallibility.

If we turn away from the Asiatic continent, the original home of the Aryan, the Semitic, and the Turanian languages, we find that in Africa, too, a comparative study of dialects has clearly proved a concentration of African speech, the results of which may be seen in the uniform *Bântu* dialects, (Kafir, Setchuâna, Damara, Otyiherero, Angola, Kongo, Kisuahéli, etc.), spoken from the equator to the Keiskamma[1]. North of this body of Bântu or Kafir speech, we have an independent settlement of Semitic speech in the Berber and the Galla dialects; south of it we have only the Hottentot and Bushman tongues, which are now declared by Dr. Th. Hahn to be closely allied to each other. Whether there is any real linguistic relationship between these languages in the South of Africa and the Nubian, and even the ancient Egyptian, and whether these languages were separated

[1] Bleek, 'Comparative Grammar of the South African Languages,' p. 2. See also Dr. Bleek's 'Report concerning his Researches into the Bushman Language,' published in 1873.

from each other by the intrusion of the Kafir tribes
is a problem the solution of which must be left to
the future. So much only is certain that the ancient
Egyptian represents to us an independent primeval
concentration of intellectual work in the country
of the Nile, independent, so far as we know at
present, of the ancient Aryan and Semitic concentration of language and religion.

But while the spoken languages of the African
continent enable us to perceive in a general way the
original articulation of the primitive population of
Africa—for there is a continuity in language which
nothing can destroy—we know, and can know, but
little of the growth and decay of African religion.
In many places Mohammedanism and Christianity
have swept away every recollection of the ancient
gods; and even when attempts have been made by
missionaries or travellers to describe the religious
status of Zulus or Hottentots, they could only see the
most recent forms of African faith, and these were
but too often depicted in their ridiculous rather than
in their serious character. It is here where the theory
of a primitive fetishism has done most mischief in
blinding the eyes even of accurate observers as to
anything that might lie beyond the growth of fetish
worship.

The only African religion of which we possess
ancient literary records is the religion of Egypt,
which has long been a riddle to us, as it was to the
Greeks and Romans. At last, however, the light is
beginning to dawn on the darkest chambers of the
ancient temples of Egypt, and on the deepest recesses
of the human heart, from which sprang both the belief

and the worship of the ancient gods.   At first sight
nothing seems more confused, perplexing, and un-
promising than the religion of Egypt, exhibiting at
one time a grovelling worship of animals, at another
the highest flights of a mysterious wisdom.   It can
hardly be said that even now, after the decipherment
of the ancient language of Egypt, this strange contrast
has been entirely accounted for.   Still no one can
rise from the perusal of M. Le Page Renouf's excellent
'Hibbert Lectures' without feeling convinced that there
is reason in the religion of Egypt also, nay, that the
growth of religious ideas there is wonderfully alike
the growth of religious ideas among the Aryan nations.

The religion of the Egyptians was not from the first
a mere worship of brutes.   Egyptian zoolatry belonged
to a period of decay, and was based upon symbols derived from mythology.   Egyptian, like Aryan, mythology dealt originally with those phenomena of nature
which are conspicuously the result of law, such as the
rising and setting of the sun, the moon, and the
stars: and a recognition of law and order as existing
throughout the universe, underlies the whole system
of Egyptian religion.   Like the Sanskrit *Rita*, the
Egyptian Maât, derived from merely sensuous impressions, became in the end the name for moral order
and righteousness.

But besides the several powers recognised in their
mythology, most of which have now been traced back
to a solar origin, the Egyptians from the very first
spoke of the One Power also, by whom the whole
physical and moral government of the universe is
directed, upon whom each individual depends, and to
whom it is responsible.   And lastly they paid honour

to the departed, because death was considered as the beginning of a new life, a life that will never end.

With all this, mythology, as an inevitable disease of language, was terribly aggravated in Egypt by the early development of art and the forms which it assumed. The Power which the Egyptians recognised without any mythological adjunct, to whom no temple was ever raised (as little as there was in India a sanctuary dedicated to Para-Brahman, the Highest Brahman), 'who was not graven on stone,' 'whose shrine was never found with painted figures,' 'who had neither ministrants nor offerings,' and 'whose abode was unknown,' must practically have been forgotten by the worshippers of the magnificent temples of Memphis, Heliopolis, Abydos, Thebes, or Dendera, where quite other deities received the homage of prayer, and praise, and sacrifice. Efforts, however, are visible, in Egypt as in India, to cling to the notion of the unity of God. The 'self-existent, or self-becoming One, the One, the One of One, the One without a second' (as in Sanskrit, svayambhû, Ekam advitîyam), ' the Beginner of becoming, from the first, who made all things, but was not made,' are expressions constantly met with in the religious texts, and applied to this or that god (henotheistically), each in his turn being considered as the supreme God of gods, the Maker and Creator of all things. Thus Râ, originally the sun, proceeding from Nu, 'the father of the gods,' and himself the father of Shu (air) and Tefnut (dew), was worshipped as the supreme celestial deity. Osiris, the eldest of the five children of Seb (earth) and Nut (heaven), 'greater than his father, more powerful than his mother,' the husband of Isis, the father of Horus, was another representation of the sun, conceived chiefly in his character of conqueror of darkness (Set).   Râ, we read, 'is the soul of Osiris, and Osiris the soul of Râ.'   Horus again is a name of the sun, originally of the morning sun, 'whose eyes are restored at the dawn of day.'   Thoth represents the moon, 'the measurer of the earth,' 'the distributor of time,' and, at last, the inventor of letters and arts. Truly does M. Le Page Renouf remark: 'Sanskrit scholars who do not know a word of Egyptian, and Egyptologists who do not know a word of Sanskrit, will give different names to these personages.   But the comparative mythologist will hardly hesitate about assigning his real name to each of them, whether Aryan or Egyptian.'

We may sum up in the words of Mariette: 'On the summit of the Egyptian pantheon hovers a sole God, immortal, uncreate, invisible, and hidden in the inaccessible depths of his own essence.   He is the creator of heaven and earth; he made all that exists, and nothing was made without him.   This is the God, the knowledge of whom was reserved for the initiated, in the sanctuaries.   But the Egyptian mind could not, or would not, remain at this sublime altitude.   It considered the world, its formation, the principles which govern it, man and his earthly destiny, as an immense drama in which the one Being is the only actor.   All proceeds from him, and all returns to him. But he has agents who are his own personified attributes, who become deities in visible forms, limited in their activity, yet partaking of his own powers and qualities [1].'

---

[1] In this account of the Egyptian religion I have chiefly followed M.

If we turn from Africa to America, we find there in the North numerous languages as witnesses of ancient migrations, but of ancient religion we have hardly anything. In the South we know of two linguistic and political centres; and there, in Mexico and Peru, we meet with curious, though not always trustworthy, traditions of an ancient and well-established system of religious faith and worship.

Lastly, as it is possible to reconstruct an original Polynesian language from what is common to the dialects of the islands reaching from America to Africa (Madagascar), fragments of an original Polynesian religion also are gradually brought to light, which would amply repay the labours of a new Humboldt.

The Science of Religion has this advantage over the Science of Language, if advantage it may be called, that in several cases where the latter has materials sufficient to raise problems of the highest importance, but not sufficient for their satisfactory solution, the former has no materials at all that would justify even a mere hypothesis. In many parts of the world where dialects, however degenerate, still allow us a dark glimpse of a distant past, the old temples have completely vanished, and the very names of the ancient deities are clean forgotten. We know nothing, we must be satisfied with knowing nothing, and the true scholar leaves the field which proves all the more attractive to the dabblers in *a priori* theories.

But even if it were otherwise, the students of religion would, I think, do well to follow the example of

Le Page Renouf's 'Hibbert Lectures' of 1879, 'Lectures on the Origin and Growth of Religion, as illustrated by the Religion of Ancient Egypt;' also De Rougé, 'Sur la Religion des anciens Égyptiens,' in 'Annales de Philosophie Chrétienne,' Nov. 1869.

the students of language, and to serve their first apprenticeship in a comparative study of the Aryan and Semitic religions. If it can be proved that the religions of the Aryan nations are united by the same bonds of a real relationship which have enabled us to treat their languages as so many varieties of the same type, and if the same fact can be established with reference to the Semitic world, the field thus opened is vast enough, and its careful clearing and cultivation will occupy several generations of scholars. And this original relationship, I believe, can be proved. Names of the principal deities, words also expressive of the most essential elements of religion, such as *prayer, sacrifice, altar, spirit, law,* and *faith,* have been preserved among the Aryan and among the Semitic nations, and these relics admit of one explanation only. After that, a comparative study of the Turanian religions may be approached with better hope of success; for that there was not only a primitive Aryan and a primitive Semitic religion, but likewise a primitive Turanian religion, before each of these primeval races was broken up and became separated in language, worship, and national sentiment, admits, I believe, of little doubt at present.

Let us begin with our own ancestors, the Aryans. In a lecture which I delivered in this place some years ago, I drew a sketch of what the life of the Aryans must have been before their first separation, that is, before the time when Sanskrit was spoken in India, or Greek in Asia Minor and Europe. The outline of that sketch and the colours with which it was filled were simply taken from language. We argued that it would be possible, if we took all the words which

LECTURE III. **105**

exist in the same form in French, Italian, and Spanish, to show what words, and therefore what things,
must have been known to the people who did not as
yet speak French, Italian, and Spanish, but who spoke
that language which preceded these Romance dialects.
We happen to know that language: it was Latin;
but if we did not know a word of Latin or a single
chapter of Roman history, we should still be able, by
using the evidence of the words which are common to
all the Romance languages, to draw some kind of picture of what the principal thoughts and occupations
of those people must have been who lived in Italy a
thousand years at least before the time of Charle-
magne. We could easily prove that those people
must have had *kings* and *laws*, *temples* and *palaces*,
ships and *carriages*, *high roads* and *bridges*, and nearly
all the ingredients of a highly civilised life. We could
prove this, as I said, by simply taking the names of
all these things as they occur in French, Spanish, and
Italian, and by showing that as Spanish did not borrow them from French, or Italian from Spanish, they
must have existed in that previous stratum of language from which these three modern Romance dialects took their origin.

Exactly the same kind of argument enabled us to
put together a kind of mosaic picture of the earliest
civilisation of the Aryan people before the time of
their separation. As we find in Greek, Latin, and
Sanskrit, also in Slavonic, Celtic, and Teutonic, the
same word for *house*, we are fully justified in conclud-
ing that before any of these languages had assumed a
separate existence, a thousand years at least before
Agamemnon and before Manu, the ancestors of the

Aryan races were no longer dwellers in tents, but builders of permanent houses[1]. As we find the name for town the same in Sanskrit and Greek[2], we can conclude with equal certainty that, if not towns, in our sense of the word, at all events strongholds or camps were known to the Aryans before Greek and before Sanskrit was spoken. As we find the name for king the same in Sanskrit, Latin, Teutonic, and Celtic[3], we know again that some kind of kingly government was established and recognised by the Aryans during the same pre-historic period.

I must not allow myself to be tempted to draw the whole of that picture of primeval civilisation over again[4]. I only wish to call back to your recollection the fact that in exploring together the ancient archives of language, we found that the highest God had received the same name in the ancient mythology of India, Greece, Italy, and Germany, and had retained that name, whether worshipped on the Himalayan mountains, or among the oaks of Dodona, on the Capitol, or in the forests of Germany. I pointed out that his name was *Dyaus* in Sanskrit, *Zeus* in Greek, *Jovi-s* in Latin, *Tiu* in German; but I hardly dwelt with sufficient strength on the startling nature of this discovery. These names are not mere names: they are historical facts, ay, facts more immediate, more trustworthy, than many facts of medieval history. These words are not mere words, but they bring before us, with all the vividness of an event which

---

[1] Sk. dama, δόμος, domus, Goth. timrjan, 'to build,' Sl. dom; Sk. vesa, οἶκος, vicus, Goth. veih-s.

[2] Sk. pur, purî, or puri, Gk. πόλις; Sk. vâstu, 'house,' Gk. ἄστυ.

[3] Sk. Râg, râgan, rex, Goth. reiks, Ir. riogh.

[4] See 'Selected Essays,' vol. i. p. 317 *seq.*

we witnessed ourselves but yesterday, the ancestors
of the whole Aryan race, thousands of years it may
be before Homer and the Veda, worshipping an unseen
Being, under the selfsame name, the best, the most
exalted name which they could find in their vocabu-
lary—under the name of Light and Sky.

And let us not turn away, and say that this was,
after all, but nature-worship and idolatry. No, it was
not meant for that, though it may have been degraded
into that in later times. *Dyaus* did not mean the blue
sky, nor was it simply the sky personified: it was
meant for something else. We have in the Veda the
invocations *Dyaūs pítar*, the Greek Ζεῦ πάτερ, the
Latin *Jupiter;* and that means in all the three languages what it meant before these three languages were
torn asunder—it means Heaven-Father! These two
words are not mere words; they are to my mind the
oldest poem, the oldest prayer of mankind, or at least
of that pure branch of it to which we belong—and I
am as firmly convinced that this prayer was uttered,
that this name was given to the unknown God before
Sanskrit was Sanskrit and Greek was Greek, as, when
I see the Lord's Prayer in the languages of Polynesia
and Melanesia, I feel certain that it was first uttered
in the language of Jerusalem. We little thought when
we heard for the first time the name of Jupiter, degraded it may be by Homer or Ovid into a scolding
husband or a faithless lover, what sacred records lay
enshrined in that unholy name. We shall have to
learn the same lesson again and again in the Science
of Religion, viz. that the place whereon we stand is
holy ground. Thousands of years have passed since
the Aryan nations separated to travel to the North

and the South, the West and the East.   They have
each formed their languages, they have each founded
empires and philosophies, they have each built temples
and razed them to the ground; they have all grown
older, and it may be wiser and better; but when they
search for a name for what is most exalted and yet
most near and dear to every one of us, when they
wish to express both awe and love, the infinite and
the finite, they can but do what their old fathers did
when gazing up to the eternal sky, and feeling the
presence of a Being as far as far and as near as near
can be, they can but combine the selfsame words, and
utter once more the primeval Aryan prayer, Heaven-
Father, in that form which will endure for ever, 'Our
Father, which art in heaven.'

Let us now turn to the early religion of the
Semitic nations.   The Semitic languages, it is well
known, are even more closely connected together
than the Aryan languages, so much so that a comparative grammar of the Semitic languages seems to
have but few of the attractions possessed by a
comparative study of Sanskrit, Greek, and Latin.
Semitic scholars complain that there is no work
worth doing in comparing the grammars of Hebrew,
Syriac, Arabic, and Ethiopic, for they have only to be
placed side by side[1] in order to show their close
relationship.   I do not think this is quite true, and
I still hope that M. Renan will carry out his original
design, and, by including not only the literary
branches of the Semitic family, but also the ancient
dialects of Phœnicia, Arabia, Babylon, and Nineveh,
produce a comparative grammar of the Semitic lan-

[1] See Bunsen's 'Christianity and Mankind,' vol. iii. p. 246 *seq.*

guages that may hold its place by the side of Bopp's great work on the Comparative Grammar of the Aryan Languages.

But what is still more surprising to me is that no Semitic scholar should have followed the example of the Aryan scholars, and collected from the different Semitic dialects those common words which must have existed before Hebrew was Hebrew, before Syriac was Syriac, and before Arabic was Arabic, and from which some kind of idea might be formed as to what were the principal thoughts and occupations of the Semitic race in its earliest undivided state. The materials seem much larger and much more easily accessible[1]. And though there may be some difficulty arising from the close contact which continued to exist between several branches of the Semitic family, it would surely be possible, by means of phonetic rules, to distinguish between common Semitic words, and words borrowed, it may be, by the Arabs from Aramæan sources. The principal degrees of relationship, for instance, have common names among the Semitic as among the Aryan nations, and if it was important to show that the Aryans had named and recognised not only the natural members of a family, such as father and mother, son and daughter, brother and sister, but also the more distant members, the father and mother-in-law, the son and daughter-in-law, the brother and sister-in-law, would it not be of equal interest to show that the Semitic nations had reached the same degree of civilisation long before the time of the laws of Moses?

---

[1] See Bunsen's 'Christianity and Mankind,' vol. iii. p. 246, iv. p. 345.

Confining ourselves to the more immediate object of our researches, we see without difficulty, that the Semitic, like the Aryan languages, possess a number of names of the Deity in common, which must have existed before the *Southern* or *Arabic*, the *Northern* or *Aramaic*, the *Middle* or *Hebraic* branches became permanently separated, and which, therefore, allow us an insight into the religious conceptions of the once united Semitic race long before Jehovah was worshipped by Abraham, or Baal was invoked in Phœnicia, or El in Babylon.

It is true, as I pointed out before, that the meaning of many of these names is more general than the original meaning of the names of the Aryan gods. Many of them signify *Powerful, Venerable, Exalted, King, Lord,* and they might seem, therefore, like honorific titles, to have been given independently by the different branches of the Semitic family to the gods whom they worshipped each in their own sanctuaries. But if we consider how many words there were in the Semitic languages to express greatness, strength, or lordship, the fact that the same appellatives occur as the proper names of the deity in Syria, in Carthage, in Babylon, and in Palestine, admits of one historical explanation only. There must have been a time for the Semitic as well as for the Aryan races, when they fixed the names of their deities, and that time must have preceded the formation of their separate languages and separate religions.

One of the oldest names of the deity among the ancestors of the Semitic nations was *Él.* It meant Strong. It occurs in the Babylonian inscriptions as

Ilu, God [1], and in the very name of Bab-il, the gate or temple of Il. In Hebrew it occurs both in its general sense of strong or hero, and as a name of God. We have it in *Beth-el*, the house of God, and in many other names. If used with the article as *ha-El*, the Strong One, or the God, it always is meant in the Old Testament for Jehovah, the true God. El, however, always retained its appellative power, and we find it applied therefore, in parts of the Old Testament, to the gods of the gentiles also.

The same El was worshipped at Byblus by the Phœnicians, and he was called there the son of Heaven and Earth [2]. His father was the son of *Eliun*, the most high God, who had been killed by wild animals. The son of Eliun, who succeeded him, was dethroned, and at last slain by his own son *El*, whom Philo identifies with the Greek Kronos, and represents as the presiding deity of the planet Saturn [3]. In the Himyaritic inscriptions, too, the name of El has been discovered [4], and more lately in many Arab proper names [5], but as a deity El was forgotten among the Arabs from the very earliest times.

[1] Schrader, in the 'Zeitschrift der Deutschen Morgenländischen Gesellschaft,' vol. xxiii. p. 350; xxvi. p. 180.

[2] Bunsen, 'Egypt,' iv. 187. 'Fragmenta Hist. Græc.' vol. iii. p. 567.

[3] 'Fragmenta Hist. Græc.' vol. iii. pp. 567-571. That El is the presiding deity of the planet Saturn according to the Chaldæans is also confirmed by Diodorus Siculus, ii. pp. 30-33. See also Eusebius, 'Præp. evang.' I. c. x. p. 90, ed. Gaisford, Κρόνος τοίνυν, ὃν οἱ Φοίνικες Ἦλον προσαγορεύουσι, and Bernays' notes, 'Zu Sanchuniathon,' in Rhein. Mus. 1864, p. 632, who corrects Ἦλον into Ἦλ.

[4] Osiander, 'Zeitschrift der Deutschen Morgenländischen Gesellschaft,' vol. x. p. 61.

[5] Nöldeke, 'Monatsberichte der Berl. Akademie,' 1880, p. 768.

With the name of *El*, Philo connected the name of *Elohím*, the plural of *Eloah*. In the battle between *El* and his father, the allies of *El*, he says, were called *Eloeim*, as those who were with *Kronos* were called *Kronioi*[1]. This is, no doubt, a very tempting etymology of *Eloah;* but as the best Semitic scholars, and particularly Professor Fleischer, have declared against it, we shall have, however reluctantly, to surrender it.

Eloah is the same word as the Arabic, *Ilâh*, God. In the singular, *Eloah* is used in the Bible synonymously with *El;* in the plural it may mean gods in general, or false gods, but it becomes in the Old Testament the recognised name of the true God, plural in form, but singular in meaning. In Arabic, *Ilâh*, without the article, means a God in general: with the article Al-Ilâh, or Allâh[2], becomes the name of the God of Mohammed, as it was the name of the God of Abraham and of Moses.

The origin of *Eloah* or *Ilâh* has been frequently discussed by European as well as by native scholars. The Kâmûs says that there were twenty, Mohammad El Fâsî that there were thirty, opinions about it. Professor Fleischer[3], whose judgment in such matters

---

[1] 'Fragmenta Hist. Græc.' vol. iii. p. 568, 18 : οἱ δὲ σύμμαχοι "Ηλου τοῦ Κρόνου 'Ελοείμ ἐπεκλήθησαν, ὡς ἂν Κρόνιοι οὗτοι ἦσαν οἱ λεγόμενοι ἐπὶ Κρόνου. The plural of El, i.e. Elîm, gods, occurs in Phœnician; Nöldeke, l. c. p. 775.

[2] اِلَا, اَللَّا, اِلَّاَ, اِلَا. On the original meaning of this Allâh see Sprenger, 'Mohammad,' i. p. 286.

[3] See a note by Professor Fleischer in Delitzsch, 'Commentar über die Genesis,' 3rd ed., 1860, p. 64; also 'Zeitschrift der Deutschen Morgenländischen Gesellschaft,' vol. x. p. 60; and 'Sitzungsberichte der königl. Sächsischen Gesellschaft der Wissenschaften, Philosoph. Hist. Classe,' vol. xviii (1866), pp. 290–292. Dr. W. Wright adopts

we may trust implicitly, traces *El*, the strong one, back to a root *ûl* (with middle vav, aval), to be thick and dense, to be fleshy and strong[1]. But he takes *Eloah* or *Ilâh* for an abstract noun, in the sense of fear[2], derived from a totally different root, viz. *alah*, to be agitated, confounded, perplexed. From meaning fear, *Eloah* came to mean the object of fear or reverence, and thus rose to be a name of God. In the same way we find *pachad*, which means fear, used in the sense of God; Gen. xxxi. 42—'Except the God of my father, the God of Abraham, and the fear of Isaac had been with me.' And again, v. 54—'And Jacob sware by the fear of his father Isaac.' In Aramaic, *dachlâ*, fear, is the recognised name for God or for an idol, while in Sanskrit also, Brahman is called 'a great fear[3].'

The same ancient name appears also in its feminine form as *Allât*[4]. Her famous temple at *Tâif*, in Arabia, was second only in importance to the sanctuary at Mekkah, and was destroyed at the command of Mohammed. The worship of *Allât*, however, was not confined to this one place; and there can be no doubt that the Arabian goddess *Alilat*, mentioned by Herodotus[5], is the same as the *Allât* of the Korân.

Professor Fleischer's derivation; likewise Professor Kuenen in his work, 'De Godsdienst van Israel,' p. 45.

[1] Professor Nöldeke, l. c. p. 774, assigns to this root the meaning of being in front, leading.

[2] Kuenen, 'Religion of Israel,' i. p. 41, Eloah is only used by poets, and its primitive meaning is 'fear,' hence, 'that which is feared.'

[3] Ka*th*a-upanishad, vi. 2, mohad bhaya*m* va*g*ram udyata*m* ya*h*.

[4] Osiander, 'Zeitschrift der Deutschen Morgenländischen Gesellschaft,' vii. 479-482, اللات Allât, goddess, is contracted from الإلٰهة Al-Ilâhat.

[5] Herod. iii. 8: Ὀνομάζουσι (οἱ Ἀράβιοι) τὸν μὲν Διόνυσον Ὀροτάλ,

Another famous name of the deity, traces of which can be found among most of the Semitic nations, is *Baal*, or *Bel*. The Assyrians and Babylonians[1], the Phœnicians and Carthaginians, the Moabites and Philistines, and, we must add, the Jews also, all knew of *Bel* or *Baal* as a great, or even as the supreme God. Baal can hardly be considered as a strange and foreign god in the eyes of the Jewish people, who, in spite of the protests of the Hebrew prophets, worshipped him so constantly in the groves of Jerusalem[2]. He was felt by them almost as a home deity, or at all events, as a Semitic deity, and among the gods whom the fathers served on the other side of the flood, Baal or Bel held most likely a very prominent place. Though originally *one*[3], Baal became divided into many divine personalities through the influence of local worship. We hear of a Baal-tsur, Baal-tsidon, Baal-tars, originally the Baal of Tyre, of Sidon, and Tarsus. On two candelabra found in the island of Malta we read the Phœnician dedication to ' Melkarth, the Baal of Tyre.'

τὴν δὲ Οὐρανίην 'Αλιλάτ. In Herod. i. 131, 138, this name is corrupted to 'Αλιττα. See Osiander, ' Zeitschrift der Deutschen Morgenländischen Gesellschaft,' vol. ii. pp. 482, 483. Sprenger, 'Mohammad,' i. p. 292, says, ' I hesitate to identify the Alilat of Herodotus with the al-Lât of Tàyif, for even if it could be proved that this goddess had been worshipped in his time, he (Herodotus) would not have heard of her. Arabia and its worship extended at that time far to the North, and one should compare the importance of Palmyra with that of Tàyif. Secondly, the form Lât is purer Arabic and older than Ilât, always supposing that the root is lâh, and not alh.' See also his ' Remarks on Arabian idols,' l. c. p. 361. Orotal has been explained as 'light' or 'fire' of El. Kuenen, ' Religion of Israel,' vol. i. p. 228.

[1] ' Fragmenta Hist. Græc.' vol. ii. p. 498, 2.
[2] Ibid. vol. iii. p. 568, 21.
[3] M. de Vogüé, ' Journal Asiatique,' 1867, p. 135.

At Shechem Baal was worshipped as *Baal-berith*[1], supposed to mean the god of treaties; at Ekron the Philistines worshipped him as *Baal-zebub*[2], the lord of flies, while the Moabites, and the Jews too, knew him also by the name of *Baal-peor*[3]. On Phœnician coins Baal is called Bâal-Shâmayîm, on Palmyrenian inscriptions (de Vogüé, No. 73), Baal-shamên, the Baal of heaven, which is the *Beelsamén* of Philo, identified by him with the sun[4]. 'When the heat became oppressive, the ancient races of Phœnicia,' he says, 'lifted their hand heavenward to the sun. For him they considered the only God, the lord of heaven, calling him Beel-samên[5], which with the Phœnicians is lord of heaven, and with the Greeks Zeus.' We likewise hear of *Baalîm*, or many Baals or gods. And in the same way as by the side of the male *Ilâh* or *Allâh* we found a female *Allât*, we also find by the side of the male Baal, a female deity *Baalt*, the Biltu of the Assyrians[6], the Baaltis of the Phœnicians. It may be that the original conception of female deities differs among Semitic and Aryan nations, and that these feminine forms of *Allâh* and *Baal* were at first intended only to express the energy or activity, or the

---

[1] Judges viii. 33 ; ix. 4.   [2] 2 Kings i. 2, 3, 16.
[3] Numbers xxv. 3.
[4] 'Fragmenta Hist. Græc.' vol. iii. p. 565, 5. It is impossible to change ἥλιον to ἧλον, because El or Kronos is mentioned afterwards.
[5] Is this the same as Barsamus, mentioned by Moses of Chorene (His. Arm. vol. i. p. 13) as a deified hero worshipped by the Syrians? Or is Barsamus the Son of Heaven? See Rawlinson, 'Ancient Monarchies,' vol. i. p. 116.
[6] See Schrader, 'Zeitschrift der Deutschen Morgenl. Gesellschaft,' xxvi. p. 193. Professor Nöldeke is inclined to treat 'Abraham and Sarah,' 'the High Father and the Princess,' as a similar originally divine pair.

collective powers of the deity, not a separate being, least of all a wife. This opinion[1] is certainly confirmed when we see that in many Carthaginian inscriptions the goddess *Tanit* is called *the face of Baal*[2], and that in the inscription of Eshmunazar, the Sidonian Astarte is called the *name of Baal*[3]. In course of time, however, this abstract idea was supplanted by that of a female power, and even a wife, and as such we find *Baaltis* worshipped by Phœnicians[4], Babylonians, and Assyrians[5], for the name of Mylitta in Herodotus[6] is, according to Dr. Oppert, a mere corruption of Baaltis.

Another female goddess is *Ashtoreth* or *Ashtaroth* (plural), a name which presupposes a masculine deity, *Ashtar*. Traces of this god or goddess have been discovered in the *Ishtar* of the Babylonian inscriptions, where Ishtar is always feminine, the Queen of heaven and earth[7]. A Palmyrene inscription also, according to some authorities, and the Moabite stone speak of the same deity. In her case, however, the female character became preponderant, and as such she was worshipped, not only by Carthaginians, Phœnicians, and Philistines, but likewise by the Jews[8] when they forsook the Lord, and served Baal and Ashtaroth[9]. The Syrians called her 'Atharathah, the Atargatis of Strabo[10]. The Phœnicians called her Astarte, and by

---

[1] De Vogüé, 'Journal Asiatique,' 1867, p. 138.

[2] פן־בעל cf. פְּנִיאֵל.   [3] שם־בעל, cf. שם יהוח.

[4] 'Fragmenta Hist. Græc.' vol. iii. p. 569, 25.

[5] Ibid. vol. iv. p. 283, 9.   [6] Herod. i. 131, 199.

[7] See Schrader, Z. d. D. M. G. xxvi. p. 169.

[8] 1 Kings xi. 5 ; also Genesis xiv. 5.   [9] Judges ii. 13.

[10] See Nöldeke, 'Z. d. D. M. G.' xxiv. 92, 109; Strabo, p. 667, 42; 636, 48.

that ominous name she became known to Greeks and
Romans. She may have been a moon-goddess, as
Kuenen supposes ('Religion of Israel,' vol. i. p. 90), and
she was originally a *numen virginale* before her service
degenerated into wild excesses. When Jeremiah speaks
of the Queen of Heaven[1], this is probably meant for
Astarte, or Baaltis. Even in Southern Arabia there
are traces of the worship of this ancient goddess.
For in Sanâ, the ancient capital of the Himyaritic
kingdom, there was a magnificent palace and temple
dedicated to Venus (Bait Ghumdân), and the name of
Athtar has been read in the Himyaritic inscriptions:
nay, it is preceded in one place by the verb in the
masculine gender[2].

Another word meaning originally king, which
must have been fixed upon as a name of the Deity
in pre-historic times, is the Hebrew *Melech*. We find
it in *Moloch*, who was worshipped, not only in
Carthage, in the Islands of Crete and Rhodes, but
likewise in the valley of Hinnom. We find the same
word in *Milcom*, the god of the Ammonites, who had
a sanctuary in Mount Olivet[3]; and the gods *Adram-
melech* and *Anammelech*, to whom the Sepharvites
burnt their children in the fire[4], seem again but local
varieties of the same ancient Semitic idol.

---

[1] Jer. vii. 18, מְלֶכֶת הַשָּׁמַיִם.

[2] Osiander, 'Zeitschrift der Deutschen Morgenländischen Gesellschaft.' vii. p. 472; Gildemeister, 'Zeitsch. der D. M. G.' vol. xxiv.
pp. 180, 181; Lenormant, 'Comptes-rendus des séances de l'Acad.
des Inscriptions et Belles-lettres de l'année 1867;' Levy, 'Zeitschrift
der D. M. G.' vol. xxiv. p. 189.

[3] 2 Kings xxiii. 13.

[4] 2 Kings xvii. 31. There was also an Assyrian god *Adar*, see
Schrader, Z. d. D. M. G. xxvi. pp. 140, 149, and another god Anu, see
Schrader, l. c. p. 141.

Adonâi, which in Hebrew means my lord, and in the Old Testament is used exclusively of Jehovah, appears in Phœnicia as the name of the Supreme Deity, and after undergoing manifold mythological transformations, the same name has become familiar to us through the Greek tales about the beautiful young Adonis, loved by Aphrodite, and killed by the wild boar of Ares.

Elyôn, which in Hebrew means the Highest, is used in the Old Testament as a predicate of God. It occurs also by itself as a name of Jehovah. Melchizedek is called emphatically the priest of *El Elyôn*, the priest of the most high God.

But this name again is not restricted to Hebrew. It occurs in the Phœnician cosmogony as *Eliun*, the highest God, the Father of Heaven, who was the father of *El*. Dr. Oppert has identified this Eliun with the *Ilinus* mentioned by Damascius.

Another word used in the Bible, sometimes in combination with El, and more frequently alone, as a name of the supreme deity, is *Shaddai*[1], the violent or powerful. It has been derived from a kindred root to that which has yielded the substantive *Shéd*, meaning demon in Syriac and in the language of the Talmud, and the plural *Shedîm*, a name for false gods or idols in the Old Testament. M. de Vogüé[2] supposed that it was the same name as *Set* or *Sed* of the hieroglyphic inscriptions. It occurs there as the name of a god introduced by the Shepherds, and having Baal as one of his epithets. Lepsius[3], however, is op-

[1] שׁדי‎ or אֵל שַׁדַּי‎   [2] 'Journal Asiatique,' 1867, p. 160.
[3] Lepsius, 'Der erste Aeg. Götterkreis,' p. 48. See also Nöldeke,

posed to this identification. The same deity *Shaddai*, the Powerful, has, by a clever conjecture, been discovered as one of the deities worshipped by the ancient Phœnicians[1].

While these names of the Deity and some more are shared in common by all, or by the most important branches of the Semitic family, and must therefore have existed previous to the first Semitic separation, there are others which are generally supposed to be peculiar to one or the other branch. They either started into existence after the first Semitic Separation, or at all events they became in after times the peculiar gods of their own peculiar people, such as Chemosh of the Moabites, Milcom of the Ammonites, Ashtaroth of the Sidonians[2].

Thus the name of Jehovah, or *Jahveh*[3], as it seems originally to have been pronounced[4], has generally been supposed to be a divine name peculiar to the Jews. It is true that in a well-known passage of Lydus, IAO[5] is said to have been the name of God among the Chaldæans. But granting that IAO was the same word as Jahveh or Jehovah or Jah (as in

'Zur Kritik des A. T.' p. 160, note; and Cheyne, in the *Academy*, 1875, p. 653.

[1] Bunsen, 'Egypt,' iv. 221; De Vogüé, 'Mélanges d'Archéologie,' p. 77. See also Nöldeke, l. c. p. 775.

[2] 1 Kings xi. 5, 7; 2 Kings xxii. 13; Judges xi. 23, 24.

[3] Theodoret. 'Quæst. xv. ad Exodum' (420 A. D.): καλοῦσι δὲ αὐτὸ Σαμαρεῖται ΙΑΒΕ, Ἰουδαῖοι δὲ ΙΑΩ. Diod. Sic. i. 94 (59 B. C.): παρὰ δὲ τοῖς Ἰουδαίοις Μωυσῆν τὸν Ἰαὼ ἐπικαλούμενον θεόν, κ. τ. λ.

[4] See Kuenen, 'Hibbert Lectures,' p. 308.

[5] Lydus, 'De Mensibus,' iv. 38, 14: Οἱ Χαλδαῖοι τὸν θεὸν ΙΑΩ λέγουσι, ἀντὶ τοῦ φῶς νοητόν· τῇ Φοινίκων γλώσσῃ καὶ ΣΑΒΑΩΘ δὲ πολλαχοῦ λέγεται, οἷον ὁ ὑπὲρ τοὺς ἑπτὰ πόλους, τουτέστιν ὁ δημιουργός: Bunsen, 'Egypt,' iv. 193; Renan, 'Sanchoniathon,' p. 44, note. And see Diodorus Siculus, i. 94, 2.

Hallelu-jah), may not Lydus by the Chaldæans have simply meant the Jews? We should be driven to a different conclusion, if *Jahu* did really occur as a divine name in the Assyrian inscriptions. Sir Henry Rawlinson, however, to whom I applied for information, declares himself to be doubtful, as yet, whether the Jahu who is mentioned in the Assyrian inscriptions is really an Assyrian name. He thinks it may be a Syrian word that found an entrance into Assyrian, like several other foreign words. Other scholars, on the contrary, such as Professor Schrader, express themselves less doubtfully on this point, and claim Jahu as one of the old Assyrian gods. Nay, they now go even a step further, and trace his first beginning back to Accadian. Thus Professor Delitzsch maintains that the simple sound I signified in Accadian 'god' and 'the supreme god,' just as ili, ila (Hebrew él) did; that the Assyrians pronounced this I with the nominative termination ia-u; that accordingly the character for I was called by the Assyrians ia-u; and that it can only be regarded as an accident that hitherto Ya-u, as the name of the deity, has not been met with in any Assyrian inscription [1].

It is difficult either to accept or to reject statements of facts put forward with so much authority, and it seems to me the most respectful attitude which we can assume with regard to the new evidence placed before us by Assyrian and Accadian scholars, if for the present we keep at a certain distance, and wait before finally recasting our received notions of Semitic religion. That the Babylonian and Assyrian docu-

---

[1] See Kuenen, 'Hibbert Lectures,' p. 311.

ments are being deciphered in a truly scientific spirit
has never been a matter of doubt to me, since the
first publication of the Babylonian version of the
Behistûn inscriptions. Nor have I been in the least
surprised at the frequent changes in the reading of
certain names, and in the rendering of certain sentences. Though unable to follow the bold investigators
of these Semitic documents, it was not difficult for any
one acquainted with the history of the decipherment
of the Persian Cuneiform inscriptions, to understand
why there should be at first so much uncertainty in
reading an alphabet like that of the Semitic Cuneiform texts. With regard to the Sumerian decipher-
ments, I have no right to say even so much as this,
but here too I feel we ought to learn to wait, and
not discourage those laborious explorers who try to
translate a language of which as yet no more is
really known than that it is neither Semitic nor
Aryan. All I can say is, that if their endeavours are
ever crowned with complete success, their achievement
will be more wonderful than the decipherment of all
other inscriptions.

Taking this view of the matter, I have, whenever I
had to treat of the religion of the Semitic races, simply
abstained from touching on Babylonian or Assyrian,
still more on Accadian and Sumerian ground. I preferred leaving a gap to filling it with materials which,
from the nature of the case, were as yet so pliant and
so brittle. I greatly admire the courage of other
students of ancient religion, and particularly of Professor Tiele, who in his 'Comparative History of Ancient Religions' has made such excellent use of the
same materials. But I cannot disregard the warning

voices of other scholars, such as, for instance, M. Guyard, who remarks that the gods of the Sumerian and Accadian religions called 'Moulge, Silik-moulon-chi' are in reality the names of Bel and Mardak, wrongly deciphered[1].   It might be said that M. Guyard is not a quite impartial authority in such questions.   But he quotes Mr. Pinches, whose authority will hardly be questioned, and who remarks that such names of Accadian kings as Hammurabi and Burnaburias, should really be read Kimtu rapastu and Kidin-bel-matâti.

I say again that even such portents are not enough to shake my faith in that method of Babylonian and even of Accadian decipherment which has been followed for years by so many eminent scholars, but I think the historian of ancient religions is justified in waiting before he either accepts or definitely rejects the new light that the ancient Cuneiform Inscriptions are meant to shed over the most remote periods of Semitic thought. That some of our best Semitic scholars should be less patient, and point out what seems to them utter impossibilities in the conclusions to which Babylonian and Accadian researches seem to lead, is perfectly natural. Such criticism should be welcomed, not resented. Thus Professor Kuenen, the great historian of the 'Religion of Israel,' objects to the Accadian derivation of Jehovah or Jahveh, because he sees difficulties which must be removed before such a derivation could be accepted. He remarks that as early as the inscription of Mesha, about 900 B.C., the name of Jahveh occurs in its quadriliteral forms, Y(a)hw(e)h, and such a form could never have grown out of Iau; while Iau, as he shows,

---

[1] See 'Athenæum,' 17 June, 1882.

might well be understood as a secondary development
of Y(a)hw(e)h. 'In the eighth century,' as the same
scholar adds[1], 'the name of Jahveh was regarded by
many, rightly or wrongly, as a derivative of the verb
to be. It was explained as *he is*, and in it was seen
the expression of the unchangeableness and faithful-
ness of the God to whose essence the name corres-
ponded.' Professor Kuenen holds, in fact, that Moses
was the first to call the god of the sons of Israel
Jahveh[2], instead of his old name El-Shaddai, and I
only wonder that he did not mention that the name
of Jahveh occurs for the first time in the name of the
mother of Moses, *Jochebed*, 'she whose glory is Jehovah.' He leaves it open to explain Jahveh, either as
He who is, or as He who alone is, while the other gods
are not; but he inclines himself to take the root in
a causal sense, and to take the name of Jahveh as
meaning he who gives life, who causes everything to
exist, the creator. This would make Jahveh almost
a reproduction of the old Vedic A s u r a, the life-giver,
from a s, to breathe, to be, a s u, breath, a s u r a, the
living and enlivening god, the *Ahura* of the Avesta,
showing again how the same thoughts and the same
names may crop up on Aryan and Semitic ground
without necessitating in the least the admission of an
actual contact during pre-historic periods of Aryans
and Semites in Iran[3].

But whether for the present we include or exclude
the name of Jehovah from the stock of divine names

---

[1] Kuenen, 'Hibbert Lectures,' p. 311; Kuenen, 'Religion of Israel,'
vol. i. p. 42.

[2] Kuenen, 'Religion of Israel,' vol. i. p. 278.

[3] Ibid. p. 254.

shared in common by the whole Semitic race, we
have, I think, sufficient witnesses to establish the fact
that there was a period during which the ancestors of
the Semitic family had not yet been divided either
in language or religion.   That period transcends the
recollection of every one of the Semitic races in the
same way as neither Hindus, Greeks, nor Romans
have any recollection of the time when they spoke
a common language, and worshipped their Father in
heaven by a name that was as yet neither Sanskrit,
nor Greek, nor Latin.   I do not hesitate to call this
pre-historic period historical in the best sense of the
word.   It was a real period, because, unless it was
real, all the realities of the Semitic languages and the
Semitic religions, such as we find them after their
separation, would be unintelligible.   Hebrew, Syriac,
and Arabic point to a common source as much as
Sanskrit, Greek, and Latin; and unless we can bring
ourselves to doubt that the Hindus, the Greeks, the
Romans, and the Teutons derived the worship of their
principal deity from their common Aryan sanctuary,
we shall not be able to deny that there was likewise
a primitive religion of the whole Semitic race, and
that *El*, the Strong One in heaven, was invoked by
the ancestors of all the Semitic races, before there
were Babylonians in Babylon, Phœnicians in Sidon
and Tyrus, before there were Jews in Mesopotamia
or Jerusalem.   The evidence of the Semitic is the
same as that of the Aryan languages: the conclusion
cannot be different.

   We now come to the third nucleus of language,
and, as I hope to show, of religion also—that which
forms the foundation of the Turanian world.   The

subject is extremely difficult, and I confess I doubt
whether I shall succeed in engaging your sympathy
in favour of the religious opinions of people so strange,
so far removed from us, as the Chinese, the Mongolians, the Samoyedes, the Finns, and Lapps. We
naturally take an interest in the ancient history of
the Aryan and Semitic nations, for, after all, we are
ourselves Aryan in language, and Semitic, at least to
a certain extent, in religion. But what have we in
common with the Turanians, with Chinese and Samoyedes? Very little, it may seem, and yet it is not
the yellow skin and the high cheekbones that make
the man. Nay, if we look but steadily into those
black Chinese eyes, we shall find that there, too, there
is a soul that responds to a soul, and that the God
whom they *mean* is the same God whom we *mean*,
however helpless their utterance, however imperfect
their worship.

That the languages of the Finns Lapps, Samoyedes,
Turks Mongol and Tungusians presuppose an early,
though, it may be, not a very firm settlement, is now
admitted by all competent authorities. That the
Tamulic, Lohitic, Gangetic, Malaic and Taic languages
presuppose a similar concentration, is as yet an hypothesis only, while the convergence of these two
branches, the North Turanian and South Turanian,
towards the most ancient Chinese as their common
centre, though it may be called plausible, has certainly
not yet been established by sufficient scientific evidence. If therefore we endeavour to discover among
the religions of these people fragments and, more particularly, linguistic fragments which betray the same
origin, and must have descended from one and the same

source, we must never forget that, as yet, we are building
hypothesis on hypothesis only, and that our pleading for
the existence of common Turanian concepts of the Divine
cannot count on the same willing acceptance which
is readily accorded to arguments in favour of common
Aryan and Semitic concepts of the Deity. On the
other hand it should be borne in mind that, if we
succeeded in establishing the existence of names of
the Deity shared in common by some at least of the
Turanian peoples, this would supply a new and very
important support of the theory that the Turanian
languages possess indeed a common prehistoric beginning, and a common historic continuity.

If we take the religion of China as the earliest
representative of Turanian worship, the question is,
whether we can find any names of the Deity in
Chinese which appear again in the religions and mythologies of other Turanian tribes, such as the Mandshus, the Mongolians, the Tatars, or Finns. I confess
that, considering the changing and shifting character
of the Turanian languages, considering also the long
interval of time that must have passed between the
first linguistic and religious settlement in China, and
the later gradual and imperfect consolidation of the
other Turanian races, I was not very sanguine in my
expectation that any such names as *Dyaus pitar*
among the Aryans, or *El* and *Baal* among the Shemites, could have survived in the religious traditions
of the vast Turanian world. Such preconceived
opinions, however, ought not to keep us from further
researches, and if what we find is but little, we must
never forget that we have hardly a right to expect
even this little. There are in researches of this kind

different degrees of certainty, and I am the very last person to slur them over, and to represent all our results as equally certain. But if we want to arrive at *terra firma*, we must not mind a plunge now and then; and if we wish to mount a ladder, we must not be afraid of taking the first step. The coincidences between the religious phraseology of Chinese and other Turanian languages are certainly not like the coincidences between Greek and Sanskrit, or between Hebrew and Phœnician; but they are such that they ought not to be passed over by the pioneers of a new science.

You remember that the popular worship of ancient China was a worship of single spirits, of powers, or, we might almost say, of names, the names of the most prominent powers of nature which are supposed to exercise an influence for good or evil on the life of man. We find a belief in spirits of the sky, the sun, the moon, the stars, the earth, the mountains, the rivers; to say nothing as yet of the spirits of the departed.

In China, where there always has been a strong tendency towards order and regularity, some kind of system has been superinduced by the recognition of two powers, one active, the other passive, one male, the other female, which comprehend everything, and which, in the mind of the more enlightened, tower high above the great crowd of minor spirits. These two powers are within and beneath and behind everything that is double in nature, and they have frequently been identified with heaven and earth.

We can clearly see, however, that the spirit of heaven occupied from the beginning a much higher position than the spirit of the earth.   It is in the historical books only, in the Shu-king[1], that we are told that heaven and earth together are the father and mother of all things.   In the most ancient poetry Heaven alone is both father and mother[2].   This spirit of heaven is known in Chinese by the name of *Tien*, and wherever in other religions we should expect the name of the supreme deity, whether Jupiter or Allah, we find in Chinese the name of *Tien* or sky.   This *Tien*, according to the Imperial Dictionary of Kanghee, means the Great One, he that dwells on high and regulates all below.   We see in fact that *Tien*, originally the name of sky, has passed in Chinese through nearly all the phases, from the lowest to the highest, through which the Aryan name for sky, *dyaus*, passed in the poetry, the religion, the mythology, and philosophy of India and Greece.   The sign of *tien* in Chinese is 天, and this is compounded of two signs: 大 *ta*, which means *great*, and — *yih*, which means *one*.   The sky, therefore, was conceived as the One, the Peerless, and as the Great, the High, the Exalted.   I remember reading in a Chinese book, 'As there is but one sky, how can there be many gods?'   In fact, their belief in *Tien*, the spirit of heaven, moulded the whole of the religious phraseology of the Chinese.   'The glorious heaven,' we read, 'is called bright, it accompanies you wherever you

[1] In the 'Shu-king' (3, 11) Tien is called Shang-tien, or High Heaven, which is synonymous with Shang-te, High Spirit, another very common name of the supreme deity.   The Confucians never made any image of Shang-te, but the Tao-sse represented their (Yah-hwang) Shang-te under the human form.—Medhurst, 'Inquiry,' p. 46.

[2] Chalmers, 'Origin of the Chinese,' p. 14; Medhurst, l. c. p. 124, contrast between Shin and Shangti.

go; the glorious heaven is called luminous, it goes wherever you roam.' *Tien* is called the ancestor of all things; the highest that is above. He is called the great framer, who makes things as a potter frames an earthen vessel. The Chinese also speak of the decrees and the will of Heaven, of the steps of Heaven or Providence. The sages who teach the people are sent by heaven, and Confucius himself is said to have been used by heaven as the 'alarum' of the world. The same Confucius, when on the brink of despondency, because no one would believe in him, knows of one comfort only: that comfort is: 'Heaven knows me.' It is clear from many passages that with Confucius *Tien* or the Spirit of Heaven was the supreme deity, and that he looked upon the other gods of the people, the spirits of the air, the mountains and the rivers, the spirits also of the departed, very much with the same feelings with which Sokrates regarded the mythological deities of Greece. Thus when asked on one occasion how the spirits should be served, he replied: 'If we are not able to serve men, how can we serve the spirits?' And at another time he said, in his short and significant manner: 'Respect the Gods, and keep them at a distance[1].'

We have now to see whether we can find any traces of this belief in a supreme spirit of heaven among the other branches of the Turanian class, the Mandshus, Mongolians, Tatars, Finns, or Lapps. As there are many names for sky in the Turanian dialects, it would not be absolutely necessary that we should find the same name which we found in Chinese: yet, if traces of that name could be found among Mongolians and

[1] Medhurst, 'Reply to Dr. Boone,' p. 32.

Tatars, our argument would, no doubt, gain far greater strength.   It is the same in all researches of comparative mythology.   If we find the same conceptions, the same myths and legends, in India, Greece, Italy, and Germany, there is, no doubt, some presumption in favour of their common origin, but no more.   But if we meet with gods and heroes, having the same names in the mythology of the Veda, and in the mythology of Greece and Rome and Germany, we stand on firmer ground.   We have then to deal with real facts that cannot be disputed, and all that remains is to explain them.

In Turanian mythology, however, such facts are not easily brought together.   With the exception of China, we know very little of the ancient history of the Turanian races, and what we know of their present state comes frequently from prejudiced observers.   Besides, their old heathendom is fast disappearing before the advance of Buddhism, Mohammedanism, and Christianity.   Yet if we take the accounts of the most trustworthy travellers in Central and Northern Asia, and more particularly the careful observations of Castrén, we cannot but recognise some most striking coincidences in the scattered notices of the religion of the Tungusic, Mongolic, Tataric, and Finnic tribes.   Everywhere we find a worship of the spirits of nature, of the spirits of the departed, though behind and above it there rises the belief in some higher power, known by different names, sometimes called the Father, the Old One, who is the Maker and Protector of the world, and who always resides in heaven [1].

Chinese historians are the only writers who give us

[1] Castrén, ' Vorlesungen über Finnische Mythologie,' p. 2.

an account of the earlier history of some of these
Turanian tribes, particularly of the Huns, whom they
call *Hiongnu*, and of the Turks, whom they call *Tukiu*.
They relate that the Huns worshipped the sun, the
moon, the spirits of the sky and the earth, and the
spirits of the departed, and that their priests, the
Shamans, possessed a power over the clouds, being
able to bring down snow, hail, rain, and wind[1].

Menander, a Byzantine historian, relates of the Turks
that in his time they worshipped the fire, the water,
and the earth, but that at the same time they believed
in a God, the maker of the world, and offered to him
sacrifices of camels, oxen, and sheep.

Still later we get some information from medieval
travellers, such as Plano Carpini[2] and Marco Polo[3],

---

[1] Castrén, 'Vorlesungen über Finnische Mythologie,' p. 36.

[2] 'They believe in one God, the Maker of all things, visible and
invisible, and the Distributor of good and evil in this world, but they
worship him not with prayers or praises or any kind of service.
Natheless they have certain idols of felt, imitating the human face,
and having underneath the face something resembling teats; these
they place on either side the door. These they believe to be the
guardians of the flocks, from whom they have the boons of milk and
increase. Others they fabricate of bits of silk, and these are highly
honoured .... and whenever they begin to eat and drink, they first
offer these idols a portion of their food or drink.' See 'Marco Polo,' ed.
Yule, vol. i. p. 249.

[3] 'This is the fashion of their religion. They say there is a Most
High God of Heaven, whom they worship daily with thurible and
incense, but they pray to Him only for health of mind and body. But
they have also certain other gods of theirs called Natigay, and they say
he is the god of the Earth, who watches over their children, cattle, and
crops. They show him great worship and honour, and every man hath
a figure of him in his house, made of felt and cloth; and they also make
in the same manner images of his wife and children. The wife they put
on the left hand, and the children in front. And when they eat, they
take the fat of the meat and grease the god's mouth withal, as well as
the mouths of his wife and children. Then they take off the broth and

who say that the Mongol tribes paid great reverence to the sun, the fire, and the water, but that they believed also in a great and powerful God, whom they called *Natagai* (Natigay) or *Itoga.*

In modern times we have chiefly to depend on Castrén, who had eyes to see and ears to hear what few other travellers would have seen or heard, or understood. Speaking of the Tungusic tribes, he says, ' they worship the sun, the moon, the stars, the earth, fire, the spirits of forests, rivers, and certain sacred localities ; they worship even images and fetishes, but with all this they retain a faith in a supreme being which they call *Buga*[1].' 'The Samoyedes,' he says, ' worship idols and various natural objects; but they always profess a belief in a higher divine power which they call *Num.*'

This deity which is called *Num* is also called *Juma* by the Samoyedes[2], and is in fact the same deity which in the grand mythology of Finland is known under the name of *Jumala.* The mythology of Finland has been more carefully preserved than the mythologies of all the other Altaic races, and in their ancient epic poems which have been kept up by oral tradition for centuries, and have been written down

---

sprinkle it before the door of the house ; and that done, they deem that their god, and his family have had their share of the dinner.' 'Marco Polo,' ed. Yule, vol. i. p. 248.   Colonel Yule traces these Nagatay back to the Ongot of the Tunguses, and the Nogat of the Buriates. Marco Polo himself ascribes the same worship of the Nagatay to the Cathayans, i. e. Chinese (vol. i. p. 437), but Colonel Yule thinks that this may be due to a confusion of Chinese with Tartars. See also vol. ii. p. 478.

[1] Is this the Russian 'bog,' god?

[2] Castrén, 'Vorlesungen über Finnische Mythologie,' p. 13.

but very lately, we have magnificent descriptions of *Jumala*, the deity of the sky.

Jumala meant originally the sky. It is derived, as Castrén has shown (p. 24), from *Juma*, thunder, and *la*, the place, meaning therefore the place of thunder, or the sky. It is used first of all for sky, secondly for the god of the sky, and thirdly for gods in general. The very same word, only modified according to the phonetic rules of each language, occurs among the Lapps (p. 11), the Esthonians, the Syrjanes, the Tcheremissians, and the Votyakes (p. 24). We can watch the growth and the changes of this heavenly deity as we catch a glimpse here and there of the religious thoughts of the Altaic tribes. An old Samoyede woman who was asked by Castrén (p. 16) whether she ever said her prayers, replied: 'Every morning I step out of my tent and bow before the sun, and say: "When thou risest, I, too, rise from my bed." And every evening I say: "When thou sinkest down, I, too, sink down to rest."' That was her prayer, perhaps the whole of her religious service;— a poor prayer it may seem to us, but not to her: for it made that old woman look twice at least every day away from earth and up to heaven; it implied that her life was bound up with a larger and higher life; it encircled the daily routine of her earthly existence with something of a divine light. She herself was evidently proud of it, for she added, with a touch of self-righteousness : 'There *are* wild people who never say their morning and evening prayers.'

While in this case the deity of the sky is represented, as it were, by the sun, we see Jumala, under different circumstances, conceived as the deity of the sea.

When walking one evening with a Samoyede sailor along the coast of the Polar Sea, Castrén asked him: 'Tell me, where is Num?' (i.e. Jumala.)   Without a moment's hesitation the old sailor pointed to the dark, distant sea, and said: '*He is there.*'

Again, in the epic poem Kalevála, when the hostess of Pohjola is in labour, she calls on Jumala, and says: 'Come now into the bath, Jumala, into the warmth, O Lord of the air!' (p. 19).

At another time Jumala is the god of the air, and is invoked in the following lines (p. 21):

> Harness now thyself, Jumala,
> Ruler of the air, thy horses!
> Bring them forth, thy rapid racers,
> Drive the sledge with glittering colours,
> Passing through our bones, our ankles,
> Through our flesh that shakes and trembles,
> Through our veins which seem all broken.
> Knit the flesh and bones together,
> Fasten vein to vein more firmly.
> Let our joints be filled with silver,
> Let our veins with gold be running!

In all these cases the deity invoked is the same, it is the deity of the sky, Jumala; but so indefinite is his character, that we can hardly say whether he is the god of the sky, or the sun, or the sea, or the air, or whether he is a supreme deity reflected in all these aspects of nature.

However, you will naturally ask, where is there any similarity between the name of that deity and the Chinese deity of the sky, *Tien?* The common worship of *Jumala* may prove some kind of religious concentration among the different Altaic nations in the North of Asia, but it does not prove any pre-historic community of worship between those nations and the ancient inhabitants of China. It is true that the Chinese *Tien*, with its three meanings of sky, god of the sky, and god in general, is the exact counterpart of the North Turanian Jumala; but still we want more; we want, if possible, traces of the same name of the deity in China, in Mongolia, and Tatary, just as we found the name of Jupiter in India and Italy, and the name of El in Babylon and Palestine.

Well, let us remember that Chinese is a monosyllabic language, and that the later Turanian dialects have entered into the agglutinative stage, that is to say, that they use derivative suffixes, and we shall then without much difficulty discover traces of the Chinese word *Tien*, with all its meanings, among some at least of the most important of the Turanian races. In the Mongolian language we find *Teng-ri*[1], and this means, first, sky; then, god of the sky; then, god in general; and, lastly, spirit or demon, whether good or bad.

Thus we have gained the first firm ground, and we may now advance another step. It is a fortunate accident that this very word *tengri* is one of the few that can be traced back historically from its modern

---

[1] Turkish 'tangry' (طانكری or تكری, tengri), the Yakute 'tangara.' The Buriates place Dsaiagachi or 'Chief Creator of Fortune' in the middle of their hut, the place of honour. At the door is the Emelgelji, the tutelary of the herds and young cattle, made of sheepskins. Outside the hut is the Chandaghatu, a name implying that the idol was formed of a white hareskin, the tutelary of the chase, and perhaps of war. All these have been expelled by Buddhism except Dsaiagachi, who is called *Tengri*, and introduced among the Buddhist divinities. See 'Marco Polo,' ed. Yule, vol. i. p. 250. 'The Supreme Good Spirit appears to have been called by the Mongols *Tengri* (heaven) and Khormuzda, and is identified by Schmidt with the Persian Hormuzd. In Buddhist times he became identified with Indra, l. c. vol. i. p. 249.

to its more ancient forms.   Chinese writers, when
speaking of the ancient history of the Huns, tell us
that the title which the Huns gave to their leaders
was *tangli-kutu* (or *tchen-jü*)[1].   This title is said to
have had in their language the meaning of 'Son of
Heaven,' which reminds us of the still current title of
the Emperor of China, viz. 'Son of Heaven[2],' *tien-tze*,
conveying the meaning, not, as is commonly supposed, of 'Son of God,' but 'Son of Heaven,' or, as
we should say, 'Emperor by the grace of God.'
Taking therefore *tien-tze* as corresponding to *tangli-
kutu*, we arrive at the following equation:

Hunnish	Mongolian	Chinese
tang-li	*teng-ri*	*tien.*

Again, in the historical accounts which the Chinese
give of the *Tukiu*, the ancestors of the Turks, it is
said that they worshipped the Spirits of the Earth,
and that they called these spirits *pu-teng-i-li*.   Here
the first syllable must be intended for earth, while in
teng-i-li we have again the same word as the Mongolian *tengri*, only used, even at that early time, no
longer in the sense of heaven, or god of heaven, but
as a name of gods and spirits in general.   We find
a similar transition of meaning in the modern Yakute
word *tangara*.   It means the sky, and it means God;
but among the Christian converts in Siberia, *tangara*
is also used to signify 'the Saints.'   The wild reindeer
is called in Yakute 'God's reindeer,' because it lives in
the open air, or because God alone takes care of it.
   Here, then, we have the same kind of evidence
which enabled us to establish a primitive Aryan and

[1] See Schott, 'Ueber das Altaische Sprachgeschlecht,' p. 9.
[2] See Schott, 'Chinesische Literatur,' p. 63.

a primitive Semitic religion: we have a common
name, and this name given to the highest deity,
preserved in the monosyllabic language of China,
and in the cognate, though agglutinative, dialects of
some of the principal North Turanian tribes.   We
find in these words, not merely a vague similarity
of sound and meaning, but, by watching their growth
in Chinese, Mongolian, and Turkish, we are able to
discover in them traces of organic identity.   Everywhere they begin with the meaning of sky, they rise
to the meaning of God, and they sink down again to
the meaning of gods and spirits.   The changes in the
meaning of these words run parallel with the changes
that took place in the religions of these nations
which comprehended the first intimation of the
Divine under the name of the sky, and thus formed
for themselves a god of the sky.   By his various
manifestations that god of the sky became more and
more mythologically individualised, was broken up
into many gods, and these many gods led again in
the end to the concept of a God in general.   Thus
only can we explain historically, i. e. phonetically and
etymologically, the connection between the French
divinité and the Vedic *Dyaus*, sky; and the same
applies to the Yakute *tangara*, Saint, in its historical
relation to the Chinese *tien*, sky.

Did we allow ourselves to be guided by mere similarity of sound and meaning, it would be easy to take
another step and to attempt a comparison between
divine names occurring in the Northern and the
Southern branches of the Turanian class.   We saw,
for instance, that the name of the supreme deity
among the Samoyedes was *Num*, and we are told

that among the Tibetans *Nam* means godhead. In mere sound *Nam* is no doubt much nearer to *Num* than *Num* is to the Finnish *Jumula*. Nevertheless the real affinity of the Samoyede *Num* and the Finnish *Jumala* admits of no doubt, while it would be mere guesswork to connect Samoyede *Num* and Tibetan *Nam*[1], unless the phonetic rules had first been established which would justify the change of a into u, and a common source had been discovered from which both words could have sprung.

If we now turn for a moment to the minor spirits believed in by the large masses in China, we shall easily see that they, too, in their character are strikingly like the spirits worshipped by the North Turanian tribes. These spirits in Chinese are called *Shin*[2], which is really the name given to every invisible power or influence which can be perceived in operation in the universe. Some *Shin* or spirits receive real worship, which is graduated according to their dignity; others are looked upon with fear. The spirits of pestilence are driven out and dispersed by exorcism; many are only talked about. There are so many spirits that it seems impossible to fix their exact number. The principal classes[3] are the celestial spirits (*tien shin*), the terrestrial spirits (*ti ki*), and the ancestral spirits (*jin kwei*), and this is the

[1] This is probably intended for the word which Jaeschke in his 'Tibetan-English Dictionary,' p. 309, writes ꙙnam. This means heaven, sky. He adds that ꙙnam-t'el-dkár-po is said to be a deity of the Horpa or Mongols. Nám-mk'a is 'the space above us where the birds are flying, and the saints are soaring, where it lightens and thunders,' etc.

[2] Medhurst, 'Reply,' p. 11.

[3] Ibid. p. 21.

order[1] in which they are ranked according to their dignity. Among celestial spirits (*tien shin*) we find the spirits of the sun and the moon and the stars, the clouds, wind, thunder, and rain; among terrestrial spirits, those of the mountains, the fields, the grain, the rivers, the trees, the year. Among the departed spirits are those of the emperors, the sages, and other public benefactors, which are to be revered by the whole nation, while each family has its own *manes* which are treated with special reverence and honoured by many superstitious rites[2].

The same state of religious feeling is exhibited among the North Turanian tribes, only without those minute distinctions and regulations in which the Chinese mind delights. The Samoyedes, as we saw, believed in a supreme god of heaven, called *Num*; but Castrén, who lived so long among them, says: 'The chief deities invoked by their priests or sorcerers, the Shamans, are the so-called *Tadebcjos*[3], invisible spirits dwelling in the air, the earth, the water, and everywhere in nature. I have heard many a Samoyede say that they were merely the spirits of the departed, but others look upon them as a class of inferior deities.'

The same scholar tells us (p. 105) that 'the mytho-

---

[1] Medhurst, 'Reply,' p. 22. 'The spirits of heaven are called *shin*; the spirits of earth are called *ki*; when men die, their wandering and transformed souls and spirits are called *kwei*.'

[2] Ibid. p. 43. 'The great sacrifices are offered only to *Te* or *Shang-te*, the same as *Tien*. The five *T's* which used to be joined with *Shang-te* at the great border sacrifice were only the five powers or qualities of *Shang-te* personified. Since the year A.D. 1369 the worship of these five *Te* has been abolished.'

[3] Castrén, 'Finnische Mythologie,' p. 122.

logy of the Finns is flooded with names of deities.
Every object in nature has a genius, called *haltia*,
which is supposed to be its creator and protector.
These spirits were not tied to these outward objects,
but were free to roam about, and had a body and
soul, and their own well-marked personality. Nor
did their existence depend on the existence of a
single object; for though there was no object in
nature without a genius, the genius was not confined to any single object, but comprehended the
whole class or genus. This mountain-ash, this
stone, this house has its own genius, but the same
genius cares for all other mountain-ashes, stones, and
houses.'

We have only to translate this into the language
of logic, and we shall understand at once what has
happened here as elsewhere in the growth of religious
ideas and mythological names. What we call a general concept, or what used to be called ' *essentia generalis*,' ' the tree-hood,' ' the stone-hood,' ' the house-
hood,' in fact, the genus tree, stone, and house, is what
the Finns and Samoyedes call the genius, the *haltia*,
the *tadebcjo*, and what the Chinese call *Shin*. We
speak very glibly of an *essentia generalis*, but to the
unschooled mind this was too great an effort. Something substantial and individual had to be retained
when trees had to be spoken of as a forest, or days
as a year; and in this transition period from individual to general conceptions, from the intuitional to
the conceptual, from the real to the abstract, the
shadow, the ghost, the power or the spirit of the
forest, of the year, of the clouds, and the lightning,
took possession of the human mind, and a class of

beings was called into existence which stands before
us as so-called deities in the religion and mythology
of the ancient world.

The worship of ancestral spirits is likewise shared
in common by the North Turanian races and the
Chinese. I do not lay much stress on that fact,
because the worship of the spirits of the departed is
perhaps the most widely spread form of natural superstition all over the world. It is nevertheless of some
interest that we should meet this superstition so fully
developed in China and in the whole North of Asia.
Most of the Finnish and Altaic tribes, says Castrén
(p. 119), cherish a belief that death, which they look
upon with terrible fear, does not entirely destroy
individual existence. And even those who do not
profess belief in a future life, observe certain ceremonies which show that they think of the departed
as still existing. They take food, dresses, oxen,
knives, tinder-boxes, kettles, and sledges, and place
them on the graves; nay, if pressed, they would confess that this is done to enable the departed to hunt,
to fish, and to fight, as they used to do when alive.
Lapps and Finns admit that the body decays, but
they imagine that a new body is given to the dead
in the lower world. Others speak of the departed as
ghosts or spirits, who either stay in the grave or in
the realm of the dead, or who roam about on earth,
particularly in the dead of night, and during storm
and rain. They give signs of themselves in the howl-
ing of the wind, the rustling of leaves, the crackling
of the fire, and in a thousand other ways. They are
invisible to ordinary mortals, but the sorcerers or
Shamans can see them, and can even divine their

thoughts. It is curious that in general these spirits are supposed to be mischievous; and the most mischievous of all are the spirits of the departed priests (p. 123). They interrupt the sleep, they send illness and misfortunes, and they trouble the conscience of their relatives. Everything is done to keep them away. When the corpse has been carried out of the house, a redhot stone is thrown after the departed, as a charm to prevent his return. The offerings of food and other articles deposited on the grave are accounted for by some as depriving the dead of any excuse for coming to the house, and fetching these things himself. Among the Tchuvashes a son uses the following invocation when offering sacrifice to the spirit of his father: 'We honour thee with a feast; look, here is bread for thee, and different kinds of meat; thou hast all thou canst want: but do not trouble us, do not come near us' (p. 122).

It is certainly a general belief that if they receive no such offerings, the dead revenge themselves by sending diseases and other misfortunes. The ancient Hiongnu or Huns killed the prisoners of war on the tombs of their leaders; for the Shamans assured them that the anger of the spirits could not be appeased otherwise. The same Huns had regular sacrifices in honour of their ancestral spirits. One tribe, the Topas, which had migrated from Siberia to Central Asia, sent ambassadors with offerings to the tombs of their ancestors. Their tombs were protected with high palings, to prevent the living from clambering in, and the dead from clambering out. Some of these tombs were magnificently adorned[1], and at last grew

---

[1] Castrén, 'Finnische Mythologie,' p. 122.

almost, and in China[1] altogether, into temples where the spirits of the departed were actually worshipped. All this takes place by slow degrees; it begins with placing a flower on the tomb; it ends with worshipping the spirits of departed emperors[2] as equals of the Supreme Spirit, the *Shang-te* or *Tien*, and as enjoying a divine rank far above other spirits or *Shin*.

The difference, at first sight, between the minute ceremonial of China and the homely worship of Finns and Lapps may seem enormous; but if we trace both back as far as we can, we see that the early stages of their religious belief are curiously alike. First, a worship of heaven, as the emblem of the most exalted conception which the untutored mind of man can entertain, expanding with the expanding thoughts of its worshippers, and eventually leading and lifting the soul from horizon to horizon to a belief in that which is beyond all horizons, a belief in that which is infinite. Secondly, a belief in deathless spirits or powers of nature; which supplies the more immediate and every-day wants of the religious instinct of man, satisfies the imagination, and furnishes the earliest poetry with elevated themes. Lastly, a belief in the existence of ancestral spirits: which implies, consciously or unconsciously, in a spiritual or in a material form, that which is one of the life-springs of all religion, a belief in immortality.

Allow me in conclusion to recapitulate shortly the results of this Lecture.

[1] When an emperor died, and men erected an ancestral temple, and set up a parental tablet (as a resting-place for the 'shin' or spirit of the departed), they called him Te.—Medhurst, 'Inquiry,' p. 7; from the *Le-ke*, vol. i. p. 49.

[2] Medhurst, 'Inquiry,' p. 45.

We found, first of all, that there is a natural connexion between language and religion, and that therefore the classification of languages is applicable also to the ancient religions of the world.

We found, secondly, that there was a common Aryan religion before the separation of the Aryan race; a common Semitic religion before the separation of the Semitic race; and a common Turanic religion before the separation of the Chinese and the other tribes belonging to the Turanian class.   We found, in fact, three ancient centres of religion as we had before three ancient centres of language, and we have thus gained, I believe, a truly historical basis for a scientific treatment of the principal religions of the world.

FOURTH LECTURE.

DELIVERED AT THE ROYAL INSTITUTION,
MARCH 12, 1870.

WHEN I came to deliver the first of this short course of lectures, I confess I felt sorry for having undertaken so difficult a task; and if I could have withdrawn from it with honour, I should gladly have done so. Now that I have only this one lecture left, I feel equally sorry, and I wish I could continue my course in order to say something more of what I wished to say, and what in four lectures I could say but very imperfectly. From the announcement of my lectures you must have seen that in what I called 'An Introduction to the Science of Religion' I did not intend to treat of more than some preliminary questions. I chiefly wanted to show in what sense a truly scientific study of religion was possible, what materials there are to enable us to gain a trustworthy knowledge of the principal religions of the world, and according to what principles these religions may be classified. It would perhaps have been more interesting to some of my hearers if we had rushed at once into the ancient temples to look at the broken idols of the past, and to discover, if possible, some of the fundamental ideas that found expression in the ancient systems of faith and worship. But in order

L

to explore with real advantage any ruins, whether
of stone or of thought, it is necessary that we should
know where to look and how to look.   In most
works on the history of ancient religions we are
driven about like forlorn tourists in a vast museum
where ancient and modern statues, gems of Oriental
and European workmanship, original works of art
and mere copies are piled up together, and at the
end of our journey we only feel bewildered and disheartened.   We have seen much, no doubt, but we
carry away very little.   It is better, before we enter
into these labyrinths, that we should spend a few
hours in making up our minds as to what we really
want to see and what we may pass by; and if in
these introductory lectures we have only arrived at
a clear view on these points, you will find hereafter
that our time has not been altogether spent in vain.

You will have observed that I have carefully abstained from entering on the domain of what I call
Theoretic, as distinguished from *Comparative Theology*.
Theoretic theology, or, as it is sometimes called, the
philosophy of religion, has, as far as I can judge, its
right place at the end, not at the beginning of Comparative Theology.   I have made no secret of my own
conviction that a study of Comparative Theology will
produce with regard to Theoretic Theology the same
revolution which a study of Comparative Philology
has produced in what used to be called the Philosophy
of language.   You know how all speculations on the
nature of language, on its origin, its development, its
natural growth and inevitable decay have had to be
taken up afresh from the very beginning, after the
new light thrown on the history of language by the

comparative method. I look forward to the same results with respect to philosophical inquiries into the nature of religion, its origin, and its development. I do not mean to say that all former speculations on these subjects will become useless. Plato's *Cratylus*, even the *Hermes* of Harris, and Horne Tooke's *Diversions of Purley* have not become useless after the work done by Grimm and Bopp, by Humboldt and Bunsen. But I believe that philosophers who speculate on the origin of religion and on the psychological conditions of faith, will in future write more circumspectly, and with less of that dogmatic assurance which has hitherto distinguished so many speculations on the philosophy of religion, not excepting those of Schelling and Hegel. Before the rise of geology it was easy to speculate on the origin of the earth; before the rise of glossology, any theories on the revealed, the mimetic, the interjectional, or the conventional origin of language might easily be held and defended. Not so now, when facts have filled the place that was formerly open to theories, and when those who have worked most carefully among the *débris* of the earth or the strata of languages are most reluctant to approach the great problem of the first beginnings.

So much in order to explain why in this introductory course I have confined myself within narrower limits than some of my hearers seem to have expected. And now, as I have but one hour left, I shall try to make the best use of it I can, by devoting it entirely to a point on which I have not yet touched, viz. on the right spirit in which ancient religions ought to be studied and interpreted.

No judge, if he had before him the worst of criminals, would treat him as most historians and theologians have treated the religions of the world. Every act in the lives of their founders which shows that they were but men, is eagerly seized and judged without mercy; every doctrine that is not carefully guarded is interpreted in the worst sense that it will bear; every act of worship that differs from our own way of serving God is held up to ridicule and contempt. And this is not done by accident, but with a set purpose, nay, with something of that artificial sense of duty which stimulates the counsel for the defence to see nothing but an angel in his own client, and anything but an angel in the plaintiff on the other side. The result has been—as it could not be otherwise—a complete miscarriage of justice, an utter misapprehension of the real character and purpose of the ancient religions of mankind; and, as a necessary consequence, a failure in discovering the peculiar features which really distinguish Christianity from all the religions of the world, and secure to its founder his own peculiar place in the history of the world, far away from Vasishtha, Zoroaster, and Buddha, from Moses and Mohammed, from Confucius and Lao-tse. By unduly depreciating all other religions, we have placed our own in a position which its founder never intended for it; we have torn it away from the sacred context of the history of the world; we have ignored, or wilfully narrowed, the sundry times and divers manners in which, in times past, God spake unto the fathers by the prophets; and instead of recognising Christianity as coming in the fulness of time, and as the fulfilment of the hopes and desires of the whole world, we have brought ourselves to look upon its advent as the only broken link in that unbroken chain which is rightly called the Divine government of the world.

Nay, worse than this: there are people who, from mere ignorance of the ancient religions of mankind, have adopted a doctrine more unchristian than any that could be found in the pages of the religious books of antiquity, viz. that all the nations of the earth, before the rise of Christianity, were mere outcasts, forsaken and forgotten of their Father in heaven, without a knowledge of God, without a hope of salvation. If a comparative study of the religions of the world produced but this one result, that it drove this godless heresy out of every Christian heart, and made us see again in the whole history of the world the eternal wisdom and love of God towards all His creatures, it would have done a good work.

And it is high time that this good work should be done. We have learnt to do justice to the ancient poetry, the political institutions, the legal enactments, the systems of philosophy, and the works of art of nations differing from ourselves in many respects; we have brought ourselves to value even the crude and imperfect beginnings in all these spheres of mental activity; and I believe we have thus learnt lessons from ancient history which we could not have learnt anywhere else. We can admire the temples of the ancient world, whether in Egypt, Babylon, or Greece; we can stand in raptures before the statues of Phidias; and only when we approach the religious conceptions which find their expression in the temples of Athene and in the statues of Zeus, we turn away with pity or scorn, we call these gods mere idols and images, and class their worshippers—Perikles, Phidias, Sokrates, and Plato—with the worshippers of stocks and stones.   I do not deny that the religions of the Babylonians, Egyptians, Greeks, and Romans were imperfect and full of errors, particularly in their later stages, but I maintain that the fact of these ancient people having any religion at all, however imperfect, raises them higher, and brings them nearer to us, than all their works of art, all their poetry, all their philosophy.   Neither their art nor their poetry nor their philosophy would have been possible without religion ; and if we will but look without prejudice, if we will but judge as we ought always to judge, with unwearying love and charity, we shall be surprised at that new world of beauty and truth which, like the azure of a vernal sky, rises before us from behind the clouds of the ancient mythologies.

We can speak freely and fearlessly ; *we* can afford to be charitable.   There was a time when it was otherwise.   There was a time when people imagined that truth, particularly the highest truth, the truth of religion, could only conquer by blind zeal, by fire and sword.   At that time all idols were to be overthrown, their altars to be destroyed, and their worshippers to be cut to pieces.   But there came a time when the sword was to be put up into its place. . . . And if even after that time there was a work to work and a fight to fight, which required the fiery zeal of apostles and martyrs, that time also is now past ; the conquest is gained, and we have time to reflect calmly on what is past and what is still to come.

Surely we need not be afraid of Baal or Jupiter.

Our dangers and our difficulties are now of a very different kind. Those who believe that there is a God, and that He created heaven and earth, and that He ruleth the world by His unceasing providence, cannot believe that millions of human beings, all created like ourselves in the image of God, were, in their time of ignorance, so utterly abandoned that their whole religion was falsehood, their whole worship a farce, their whole life a mockery. An honest and independent study of the religions of the world will teach us that it was not so—will teach us the same lesson which it taught St. Augustine, that there is no religion which does not contain some grains of truth. Nay, it will teach us more; it will enable us to see in the history of the ancient religions, more clearly than anywhere else, the *Divine education of the human race.*

I know this is a view which has been much objected to, but I hold it as strongly as ever. If we must not read in the history of the whole human race the daily lessons of a Divine teacher and guide, if there is no purpose, no increasing purpose in the succession of the religions of the world, then we might as well shut up the godless book of history altogether, and look upon men as no better than the grass which is to-day in the field and to-morrow is cast into the oven. Man would then be indeed of less value than the sparrows, for none of them is forgotten before God.

But those who imagine that, in order to make sure of their own salvation, they must have a great gulf fixed between themselves and all the other nations of the world—between their own religion and the re-

ligions of Zoroaster, Buddha, or Confucius—can hardly
be aware how strongly the interpretation of the history of the religions of the world, as an education of
the human race, can be supported by authorities
before which they themselves would probably bow in
silence. We need not appeal to an English bishop to
prove the soundness, or to a German philosopher to
prove the truth, of this view. If we wanted authorities we could appeal to Popes, to the Fathers of the
Church, to the Apostles themselves, for they have all
upheld the same view with no wavering or uncertain
voice.

I pointed out before that the simultaneous study
of the Old and the New Testament, with an occasional reference to the religion and philosophy of
Greece and Rome, had supplied Christian divines
with some of the most useful lessons for a wider
comparison of all the religions of the world. In
studying the Old Testament, and observing in it the
absence of some of the most essential truths of Christianity, they, too, had asked with surprise why the
interval between the fall of man and his redemption
had been so long, why men were allowed so long to
walk in darkness, and whether the heathens had
really no place in the counsels of God. Here is the
answer of a Pope, of Leo the Great[1] (440–461):

'Let those who with impious murmurings find fault
with the Divine dispensations, and who complain
about the lateness of Our Lord's nativity, cease from
their grievances, as if what was carried out in this
last age of the world, had not been impending in time
past. . . . What the apostles preached, the prophets

---

[1] Hardwick, 'Christ and other Masters,' vol. i. p. 85.

had announced before, and what has always been believed, cannot be said to have been fulfilled too late. By this delay of His work of salvation the wisdom and love of God have only made us more fitted for His call; so that, what had been announced before by many signs and words and mysteries during so many centuries, should not be doubtful or uncertain in the days of the Gospel. . . . God has not provided for the interests of men by a new counsel or by a late compassion; but He had instituted from the beginning for all men one and the same path of salvation.'

This is the language of a Pope—of Leo the Great.

Now let us hear what Irenæus says, and how he explains to himself the necessary imperfection of the early religions of mankind. 'A mother,' he says, 'may indeed offer to her infant a complete repast, but her infant cannot yet receive the food which is meant for full-grown men. In the same manner God might indeed from the beginning have offered to man the truth in its completeness, but man was unable to receive it, for he was still a child.'

If this, too, is considered a presumptuous reading of the counsels of God, we have, as a last appeal, the words of St. Paul, that 'the law was the schoolmaster to the Jews,' joined with the words of St. Peter, 'Of a truth I perceive that God is no respecter of persons, but in every nation he that feareth him and worketh righteousness is accepted with him.'

But, as I said before, we need not appeal to any authorities, if we will but read the records of the ancient religions of the world with an open heart and in a charitable spirit—in a spirit that thinketh

no evil, but rejoices in the truth wherever it can be
found.

I suppose that most of us, sooner or later in life,
have felt how the whole world—this wicked world,
as we call it—is changed as if by magic, if once we
can make up our mind to give men credit for good
motives, never to be suspicious, never to think evil,
never to think ourselves better than our neighbours.
Trust a man to be true and good, and, even if he is
not, your trust will tend to make him true and good.
It is the same with the religions of the world.   Let
us but once make up our mind to look in them for
what is true and good, and we shall hardly know our
old religions again.   If they are the work of the devil,
as many of us have been brought up to believe,
then never was there a kingdom so divided against
itself from the very beginning.   There is no religion—
or if there is, I do not know it—which does not say,
'Do good, avoid evil.'   There is none which does not
contain what Rabbi Hillel called the quintessence of
all religions, the simple warning, 'Be good, my boy.'
'Be good, my boy,' may seem a very short catechism;
but let us add to it, 'Be good, my boy, for God's sake,'
and we have in it very nearly the whole of the Law
and the Prophets.

I wish I could read you the extracts I have collected
from the sacred books of the ancient world, grains of
truth more precious to me than grains of gold; prayers
so simple and so true that we could all join in them if
we once accustomed ourselves to the strange sounds of
Sanskrit or Chinese.   I can to-day give you a few
specimens only.

Here is a prayer of Vasish*tha*, a Vedic prophet,

addressed to Varu*n*a, the Greek Οὐρανός, an ancient name of the sky and of the god who resides in the sky.

I shall read you one verse at least in the original—it is the 86th hymn of the seventh book of the Rig-veda—so that you may hear the very sounds which more than three thousand years ago were uttered for the first time in a village on the borders of the Sut-ledge, then called the *S*atadru, by a man who felt as we feel, who spoke as we speak, who believed in many points as we believe—a dark-complexioned Hindu, shepherd, poet, priest, patriarch, and certainly a man who, in the noble army of prophets, deserves a place by the side of David. And does it not show the indestructibility of the spirit, if we see how the waves which, by a poetic impulse, he started on the vast ocean of thought have been heaving and spreading and widening, till after centuries and centuries they strike to-day against our shores and tell us, in accents that cannot be mistaken, what passed through the mind of that ancient Aryan poet when he felt the presence of an almighty God, the maker of heaven and earth, and felt at the same time the burden of his sin, and prayed to his God that He might take that burden from him, that He might forgive him his sin? When you listen to the strange sounds of this Vedic hymn, you are listening, even in this Royal Institution, to spirit-rapping—to real spirit-rapping. Vasish*tha* is really among us again, and if you will accept me as his interpreter, you will find that we can all understand what the old poet wished to say[1]:

[1] M. M., 'History of Ancient Sanskrit Literature,' p. 540.

'Dhîrâ tv asya mahinâ *g*anûmshi,
  vi yas tastambha rodasî *k*id urvî,
  pra nâkam *ri*shvam nunude br*i*hanta*m*,
  dvitâ nakshatram papratha*k ka* bhûma.

'Wise and mighty are the works of him who stem-
med asunder the wide firmaments (heaven and earth).
He lifted on high the-bright and glorious heaven; he
stretched out apart the starry sky and the earth.

'Do I say this to my own self? How can I get near
unto Varu*n*a? Will he accept my offering without
displeasure? When shall I, with a quiet mind, see
him propitiated?

'I ask, O Varu*n*a, wishing to know this my sin;
I go to ask the wise.   The sages all tell me the same:
"Varu*n*a it is who is angry with thee."

'Was it for an old sin, O Varu*n*a, that thou wishest
to destroy thy friend, who always praises thee? Tell
me, thou unconquerable Lord! and I will quickly
turn to thee with praise, freed from sin.

'Absolve us from the sins of our fathers, and from
those which we committed with our own bodies.
Release Vasish*th*a, O King, like a thief who has
feasted on stolen cattle; release him like a calf from
the rope.

'It was not our own doing, O Varu*n*a, it was a
slip; an intoxicating draught, passion, dice. thoughtlessness.   The old is there to mislead the young;
even sleep is not free from mischief.

'Let me, freed from sin, do service to the angry
god, like a slave to his lord [1].   The lord god enlight-
eneth the foolish; he, the wisest, leads his worshipper
to wealth.

[1] See Benfey, 'Göttinger Gelehrte Nachrichten,' 1874, p. 370.

'O lord Varu*n*a, may this song go well to thy heart! May we prosper in acquiring and keeping! Protect us, O gods, always with your blessings.'

I am not blind to the blemishes of this ancient prayer, but I am not blind to its beauty either, and I think you will admit that the discovery of even one such poem among the hymns of the *R*ig-veda, and the certainty that such a poem was composed in India at least three thousand years ago, without any inspiration but that which all can find who seek for it if haply they may find it, is well worth the labour of a life. It shows that man was never forsaken of God, and that conviction is worth more to the student of history than all the dynasties of Babylon and Egypt, worth more than all lacustrian villages, worth more than the skulls and jaw-bones of Neanderthal or Abbeville.

I add a few more translations of Vedic hymns, some of which have been published elsewhere, while one is given here for the first time [1].

Prayer for Forgiveness (*R*ig-veda VII. 89).

1. Let me not yet, O Varu*n*a, enter into the house of earth; have mercy, almighty, have mercy!

2. If I move along trembling, like a cloud driven by the wind; have mercy, almighty, have mercy!

3. Through want of strength, thou strong and bright god, have I gone astray; have mercy, almighty, have mercy!

4. Thirst came upon the worshipper, though he

stood in the midst of the waters; have mercy, almighty, have mercy!

5. Whenever we men, O Varuna, commit an offence before the heavenly host, whenever we break the law through thoughtlessness; punish us not, O god, for that offence.

SONG OF PRAISE ADDRESSED TO VARUNA
(RIG-VEDA I. 25).

1. However we break thy laws from day to day, men as we are, O god, Varuna,

2. Do not deliver us unto death, nor to the blow of the furious; nor to the wrath of the spiteful!

3. To propitiate thee, O Varuna, we unbend thy mind with songs, as the charioteer (unties) a weary steed.

4. Away from me they flee dispirited, intent only on gaining wealth; as birds to their nests.

5. When shall we bring hither the man, who is victory to the warriors; when shall we bring Varuna, the wide-seeing, to be propitiated?

[6. They (Mitra and Varuna) take this in common; gracious, they never fail the faithful giver.]

7. He who knows the place of the birds that fly through the sky, who on the waters knows the ships;—

8. He, the upholder of order, who knows the twelve months with the offspring of each, and knows the month that is engendered afterwards;—

9. He who knows the track of the wind, of the wide, the bright, the mighty; and knows those who reside on high;—

10. He, the upholder of order, Varuna, sits down among his people; he, the wise, sits there to govern.

11. From thence perceiving all wondrous things, he sees what has been and what will be done.

12. May he, the wise Âditya, make our paths straight all our days; may he prolong our lives!

13. Varuna, wearing golden mail, has put on his shining cloak; the spies sat down around him.

14. The god whom the scoffers do not provoke, nor the tormentors of men, nor the plotters of mischief;

15. He, who gives to men glory, and not half glory, who gives it even to our own selves;—

16. Yearning for him, the far-seeing, my thoughts move onwards, as kine move to their pastures.

17. Let us speak together again, because my honey has been brought: that thou mayest eat what thou likest, like a friend[1].

18. Did I see the god who is to be seen by all, did I see the chariot above the earth? He must have accepted my prayers.

19. O hear this my calling, Varuna, be gracious now! longing for help, I have called upon thee.

20. Thou, O wise god, art lord of all, of heaven and earth: listen on thy way!

21. That I may live, take from me the upper rope, loose the middle, and remove the lowest!

In most of the hymns of the Rig-veda, however, the gods assume a far more mythological character than in these songs addressed to Varuna, though the spiri-

---

[1] See Bollensen, in *Orient und Occident*, ii. p. 147. One might read hotrâ-iva, 'because honey has been brought by me, as by a priest, sweet to taste.'

tual and ethical character of the deity is but seldom
entirely lost. If we take for instance a short hymn addressed to Agni or Fire, we easily see that Agni (ignis)
is conceived as the representative of fire, yet we also
perceive even here a more distant background, or a
true divine element, only enveloped in a mythological
shell.

HYMN TO AGNI (RIG-VEDA II. 6).

1. Agni, accept this log which I offer to thee, accept
this my service; listen well to these my songs.

2. With this log, O Agni, may we worship thee,
thou son of strength, conqueror of horses! and with
this hymn, thou high-born!

3. May we, thy servants, serve thee with songs, O
granter of riches, thou who lovest songs and delightest
in riches!

4. Thou lord of wealth and giver of wealth, be thou
wise and powerful; drive away from us the enemies!

5. He gives us rain from heaven, he gives us in-
violable strength, he gives us food a thousandfold.

6. Youngest of the gods, their messenger, their in-
voker, most deserving of worship, come, at our praise,
to him who worships thee and longs for thy help.

7. For thou, O sage, goest wisely between these
two creations (heaven and earth, gods and men), like
a friendly messenger between two hamlets!

8. Thou art wise, and thou hast been pleased:
perform thou, intelligent Agni, the sacrifice without
interruption, sit down on this sacred grass!

Here we may clearly observe that peculiar blending
of ethical and physical elements in the character of
one and the same deity, a blending which seems

strange to us, but must have been perfectly natural
in an earlier stage of religious thought, for we meet
with the same ideas everywhere, whenever we are able
to trace back the growth of religious concepts to their
first beginnings, not only among the Aryan nations,
but in Africa, in America, and even in Australia,
though nowhere with the same clearness and fulness
as in the hymns of the Vedic Aryans.

I have often expressed my opinion that we ought
to be careful in ascribing the same high antiquity to
everything occurring in the Rig-veda. Not that I re-
tract what I tried to prove in my 'History of Ancient
Sanskrit Literature,' that the whole collection of the
hymns must have been finished to the last letter
before the beginning of the Brâhmana period. Nor
am I aware that a single weak joint has been discovered by any of my numerous critics in the chain
of arguments on which I relied. But scientific honesty obliges me nevertheless to confess openly that
I cannot even now feel quite convinced in my own
mind that all the hymns, all the verses, all the words
and syllables in our text of the Rig-veda are really
of the same high antiquity. No doubt, we should
approach all such questions without any preconceived
opinions, but we cannot on the other hand forget all
we have been taught by a study of post-Vedic literature, or by a study of other ancient literatures. We
must wait for further evidence, and be careful not to
force these researches into a false direction by premature dicta. In order to give a specimen of what
I mean, I shall give a translation of the well-known
hymn to Visvakarman from the last Mandala, a Mandala which has generally been considered, though, as

yet, without very definite reasons, as a repository of more modern poems.

The very name of the deity, addressed in this hymn, Viśvakarman, indicates that the poet did not belong to the earliest period of Vedic religion. It occurs as a proper name in the tenth Maṇḍala only. Originally Viśvakarman, the maker of all things, is an epithet of several old gods. Indra is called Viśvakarman[1], likewise Sûrya, the sun[2], and Viśvakrit, he who makes everything, occurs in the Atharva-veda[3] as an epithet of Agni, the fire, who in the Brâhmaṇas[4] also is identified with Viśvakarman. Viśvakarman, as an independent, but very abstract deity appears, like Praǵâpati and similar divine individuals, as the creator, or, more correctly, as the fashioner and architect of the universe. In the hymns dedicated to him some rays break through here and there from the dark mythological background through which and from which the concept of Viśvakarman arose. Sometimes we are still able to recognise the traces of Agni, sometimes of Sûrya, although the poets themselves think of him chiefly as the Creator. Thus we read in one verse:

'The seer and a priest, who offering all the worlds as a sacrifice, came down as our father, he, appearing first, entered among mortals, desiring wealth with blessing.'

This, at first sight, is not very clear, nor do I pretend to say that this verse has as yet been rendered quite intelligible, in spite of the efforts of various translators and commentators. Still we may see a little light, if we remember that Viśvakarman, the

---

[1] Rig-Veda, viii. 98, 2. [2] Ibid. x. 170, 4.
[3] Atharva-veda, vi. 47, 1. [4] Satapatha-brâhmaṇa, ix. 2, 2.

maker of all things, was originally Agni, the god of
fire, and more particularly, the god of the fire and the
light of the morning.   Agni, as the god of the
morning (aushasya), is often conceived as a priest,
who, with his splendour, pours out the whole world
and offers it as a morning sacrifice.   Such a sacrifice
is represented as taking place either at the beginning
of every day, or at the beginning of a new year, or,
by another step, at the beginning of the world.   The
light of the morning sun was perceived by the poet as
illuminating the world, like the actual fires lighted in
the morning on every hearth.   Or the poet might see
in the light of the rising sun a power that brings
forth the whole world, brings it into sight and being,
in fact makes or creates the world.   This is a poetical,
perhaps a fantastic idea; nevertheless it is conceivable; and in interpreting the words of the Veda,
we must never rest till we arrive at something that
is at least conceivable.

The poet again seems to think of Agni, the fire,
when he says of Visvakarman that he settled down
as a father among men.   The germ of this conception
lies in the light of the morning appearing first as
something distant and divine, but then, unlike other
divine powers, remaining with men on earth, on the
very hearth of every dwelling.   This thought that
Agni is the first to take up his abode with men, that
his presence is the condition of all human activity,
workmanship, and art, and that through his blessing
alone men obtain health and wealth, is expressed in
many Vedic songs in ever varying ways.

If we transfer these thoughts to the Visvakarman,
the maker or shaper of all things, some of the dark

words of the first verse become more intelligible, while some of the translations hitherto published leave the impression as if some of the Vedic poets had really connected no thought whatever with their metrical effusions.

1. [1]'What was the place, what was the support, and where was it, from whence the all-seeing Visvakarman (the maker of all things), when producing the earth, displayed the heaven by his might?

2. 'He, the *one* God, whose eyes are everywhere, whose mouth, whose arms, whose feet are everywhere; he, when producing heaven and earth, forges them together with his arms and with the wings.

3. [2]'What was the forest, what was the tree[3], from which they cut out heaven and earth? Ye wise, seek in your mind that place on which he stood when supporting the worlds.

4. 'O Visvakarman, rejoicing in the sacrifice, teach thy friends what are thy highest abodes, and what are thy lowest, and what are these thy middle abodes! Sacrifice for thyself, increasing thy body[4].

[1] Dr. Muir translates this verse: 'Our father, who, a rishi and a priest, celebrated a sacrifice offering up all these creatures, he, earnestly desiring substance, he, the archetype, entered into later man.' Langlois: 'Que le richi (divin), notre pontife et notre père, qui par son sacrifice a formé tous ces mondes, vienne s'asseoir (à notre foyer). Qu'il désire et bénisse nos offrandes. Habitant des régions supérieures, il descend aussi vers nous.'
[2] Cf. Svetâsvatara Upan. iii. 3.
[3] We say ὕλη or *materies*, matter; Rig-Veda, x. 31, 7.
[4] This expression also 'Sacrifice for thyself, increasing thy body,' refers primarily to Agni. It was a familiar idea with the Brahmans to look upon the fire both as the subject and the object of a sacrifice. The fire embraced the offering, and was thus a kind of priest; it carried it to the gods, and was thus a kind of mediator between gods and men.

5. 'Maker of all things, growing by the oblations, sacrifice for thyself, for earth and for heaven! Let other men walk around in darkness, but among us let the wise man be powerful!

6. 'Let us invoke to-day, for our protection in battle, the lord of speech, Visvakarman, the maker of all things, who inspires our mind. May he accept all our offerings, he who is a blessing to everybody, and who performs good deeds for our safety!'

My next extract will be from the Zendavesta, the sacred book of the Zoroastrians, older in its language than the cuneiform inscriptions of Cyrus, Darius, Xerxes, those ancient kings of Persia who knew that they were kings by the grace of *Auramazda*, the Zend *Ahurô mazdâo*[1], and who placed his sacred image high on the mountain-records of Behistun. That ancient book, or its fragments at least, have survived many dynasties and kingdoms, and are still believed in by a small remnant of the Persian race, now settled at Bombay, and known all over the world by the name of Parsis.

The first extract is taken from the Yaçna, forming its thirtieth chapter. It has been translated or, I

But the fire represented also something divine, a god to whom honour was due, and thus it became both the object and the subject of the sacrifice. Hence the idea that Agni sacrifices himself, that he offers a sacrifice to himself, and likewise that he offers himself as a sacrifice. This led to many later legends, see Roth, 'Nirukta,' p. 142. Agni was also conceived as representing the rising sun and the morning, and from that point of view sunrise was conceived as the great sacrifice in nature, the light serving, like a sacrificial flame, for the glory of heaven and earth, and, at the same time, for his own glory. Hence lastly those cosmogonic ideas by which the daily sacrifice is conceived as the sacrifice of creation and as the glory of the creator.

[1] 'Lectures on the Science of Language,' vol. i. p. 239.

should rather say, a decipherment of it has been attempted by several scholars, more particularly by Professor Spiegel and Professor Haug[1]. It has also been referred to by Bunsen in his 'God in History' (vol. i. p. 277, of Miss Winkworth's translation), and I may quote from him what will serve as a living, though imaginary, background for this striking hymn.

'Let us picture to ourselves,' he writes, 'one of the holy hills dedicated to the worship of fire, in the neighbourhood of the primeval city of marvels in Central Asia,—Bactra "the glorious," now called Balkh, "the mother of cities." From this height we look down in imagination over the elevated plateau, which lies nearly 2000 feet above the level of the sea, sloping downwards toward the North and ending in a sandy desert, which does not even allow the stream Bactrus to reach the neighbouring Oxus. On the southern horizon, the last spurs of the Hindukush, or, as the historian of Alexander terms it, the Indian Caucasus, rear their lofty peaks 5000 feet high. Out of those hills,—the Paropamisus or Hindukush,—springs the chief river of the country, the Bactrus or Dehas, which near the city divides into hundreds of canals, making the face of the country one blooming garden of richest fruits. To this point converge the caravans, which travel across the mountains to the land of marvels, or bring treasures from thence..... Thither, on occasion of the peaceful sacrifice by fire, from whose ascending flame auguries were to be drawn, Zarathustra had convened the nobles of the land, that he might per-

---

[2] ' Essays on the Sacred Language of the Parsees,' 1862, p. 141.

form a great public religious act. Arrived there, at the head of his disciples, the seers and preachers, he summons the princes to draw nigh, and to choose between faith and superstition.'

I give the translation of the hymn, partly after Haug (1858), partly after Spiegel (1859), and I have likewise availed myself of some important emendations proposed by Dr. Hübschmann[1]. Yet, I must confess that, in numerous passages, my translation is purely tentative, and all I can answer for is the general tenour of the hymn.

1. 'Now I shall proclaim to all who have come to listen, the praises of thee, the all-wise Lord, and the hymns of Vohumano (the good spirit). Wise Asha! I ask that (thy) grace may appear in the lights of heaven.

2. 'Hear with your ears what is best, perceive with your mind what is pure, so that every man may for himself choose his tenets. Before the great doom, may the wise be on our side!

3. 'Those old Spirits who are twins, each with his own work, made known[2] what is good and what is evil in thoughts, words, and deeds. Those who are good, distinguished between the two, not those who are evil-doers.

4. 'When these two Spirits came together, they made first life and death, so that there should be at last the most wretched life for the bad, but for the good blessedness.

---

[1] 'Ein Zoroastrisches Lied, mit Rücksicht auf die Tradition übersetzt und erklärt' von Dr. H. Hübschmann: München, 1872.

[2] Haug does not admit the causative meaning of asrvâtem, but takes it in the sense of *audiverunt* or *auditi sunt*, i.e. they were known, they existed.

5. 'Of these two Spirits the evil one chose the worst deeds; the kind Spirit, he whose garment is the immovable sky, chose what is right; and they also who faithfully please Ahuramazda by good works.

6. 'Those who worshipped the Devas and were deceived, did not rightly distinguish between the two; those who had chosen the worst Spirit came to hold counsel together, and ran to Aeshma in order to afflict the life of man.

7. 'And to him (the good) came might, and with wisdom virtue; and the everlasting Armaiti herself made his body vigorous. It fell to thee to be rich by her gifts.

8. 'But when the punishment of their crimes will come, and, oh Mazda, thy power will be known as the reward of piety for those who delivered (Druj) falsehood into the hand of truth (Asha),

9. 'Let us then be of those who further this world; oh Ahuramazda, oh bliss-conferring Asha! Let our mind be there where wisdom abides.

10. 'Then indeed there will be the fall of the pernicious Druj, but in the beautiful abode of Vohumano, of Mazda and of Asha, will be gathered for ever those who dwell in good report.

11. 'Oh men, if you cling to these commandments which Mazda has given, . . . which are a torment to the wicked, and a blessing to the righteous, then there will be victory through them.'

The next three verses are taken from the forty-third chapter of the Yaçna[1].

---

[1] 'Yasna,' xliv. 3, ed. Brockhaus, p. 130; Spiegel, 'Yasna,' p. 146; Haug, 'Essays,' p. 150.

'I ask thee, tell me the truth, O Ahura! Who was from the beginning the father of the pure world? Who has made a path for the sun and for the stars? Who (but thou) makes the moon to increase and to decrease? That, O Mazda, and other things, I wish to know.

'I ask thee, tell me the truth, O Ahura! Who holds the earth and the clouds that they do not fall? Who holds the sea and the trees? Who has given swiftness to the wind and the clouds? Who is the creator of the good spirit?

'I ask thee, tell me the truth, O Ahura! Who has made the kindly light and the darkness, who has made the kindly sleep and the awaking? Who has made the mornings, the noons, and the nights, they who remind the wise of his duty?'

Whatever the difficulties may be, and they are no doubt most formidable, that prevent us from deciphering aright the words of the Zendavesta, so much is clear, that in the Bible of Zoroaster every man is called upon to take his part in the great battle between Good and Evil which is always going on, and is assured that in the end good will prevail.

What shall I quote from Buddha? for we have so much left of his sayings and his parables that it is indeed difficult to choose. In a collection of his sayings, written in Pâli—of which I have lately published a translation[1]—we read:

1. 'All that we are is the result of what we have thought: it is founded on our thoughts, it is made up

---

[1] The Dhammapada, a Collection of Verses, being one of the canonical books of the Buddhists, translated from Pâli by F. Max Müller, in 'Sacred Books of the East,' vol. x. 1881.

of our thoughts.   If a man speaks or acts with an
evil thought, pain follows him as the wheel follows
the foot of the ox that draws the cart.

49. 'As the bee collects honey and departs without
injuring the flower, or its colour, or scent, so let a sage
dwell on earth.

62. '"These sons belong to me, and this wealth
belongs to me," with such thoughts a fool is tor-
mented.   He himself does not belong to himself, how
much less sons and wealth!

121, 122. 'Let no man think lightly of evil, saying
in his heart, It will not come nigh unto me.   Let no
man think lightly of good, saying in his heart, It will
not benefit me.   Even by the falling of water-drops
a water-pot is filled.

173. 'He whose evil deeds are covered by good
deeds, brightens up this world like the moon when
she rises from behind the clouds.

223. 'Let a man overcome anger by love, evil by
good, the greedy by liberality, the liar by truth[1].

252. 'The fault of others is easily perceived, but
that of oneself is difficult to perceive; a man winnows
his neighbour's faults like chaff, but his own fault he
hides, as a cheat hides the bad die from the player[2].

264. 'Not by tonsure does an undisciplined man
who speaks falsehood become a saint: can a man be
a saint who is still held captive by desires and
greediness?

394. 'What is the use of platted hair, O fool?

---

[1] See Rom. xii. 21.   'Be not overcome of evil, but overcome evil with
good.'
[2] See Matt. vii. 3.   'And why beholdest thou the mote that is in thy
brother's eye, but considerest not the beam that is in thine own eye?'

what of the raiment of goat-skins? Within thee there is ravening, but the outside thou makest clean[1].'

In no religion are we so constantly reminded of our own as in Buddhism, and yet in no religion has man been drawn away so far from truth as in the religion of Buddha. Buddhism and Christianity are indeed the two opposite poles with regard to the most essential points of religion: Buddhism ignoring all feeling of dependence on a higher power, and therefore denying the very existence of a supreme Deity; Christianity resting entirely on a belief in God as the Father, in the Son of Man as the Son of God, and making all men children of God by faith in His Son. Yet between the language of Buddha and his disciples and the language of Christ and His apostles there are strange coincidences. Even some of the Buddhist legends and parables sound as if taken from the New Testament, though we know that many of them existed before the beginning of the Christian era.

Thus we read of Ânanda, the disciple of Buddha, who, after a long walk in the country, meets with Mâtangî, a woman of the low caste of the Kândâlas, near a well, and asks her for some water. She tells him what she is, and that she must not come near him. But he replies, ' My sister, I ask not for thy caste or thy family, I ask only for a draught of water.' She afterwards becomes herself a disciple of Buddha[2].

---

[1] See Luke xi. 39. ' Now do ye Pharisees make clean the outside of the cup and the platter; but your inward part is full of ravening and wickedness.'

[2] Burnouf, ' Introduction à l'Histoire du Buddhisme,' p. 205.

Sometimes the same doctrine which in the New Testament occurs in the simple form of a commandment, is inculcated by the Buddhists in the form of a parable.

A Buddhist priest, we read[1], was preaching to the multitudes that had gathered round him. In the crowd there was a king whose heart was full of sorrow, because he had no son to perpetuate his race. While he was listening, the preacher said:

'To give away our riches is considered the most difficult virtue in the world; he who gives away his riches is like a man who gives away his life: for our very life seems to cling to our riches. But Buddha, when his mind was moved by pity, gave his life, like grass, for the sake of others; why should we think of miserable riches! By this exalted virtue, Buddha, when he was freed from all desires, and had obtained divine knowledge, attained unto Buddhahood. Therefore let a wise man, after he has turned away his desires from all pleasures, do good to all beings, even unto sacrificing his own life, that thus he may attain to true knowledge.

'Listen to me: There was formerly a prince, free from all worldly desires. Though he was young and handsome, yet he left his palace, and embraced the life of a travelling ascetic. This ascetic coming one day to the house of a merchant, was seen by his young wife, and she, touched by the loveliness of his eyes, exclaimed: "How was this hard mode of life embraced by such a one as thou art? Blessed, indeed, is that woman on whom thou lookest with thy lovely eyes!"

[1] 'Somadeva,' vi. 28, 1 seq.

'When he heard this, the ascetic plucked out one eye, placed it into his hand, and said: " Mother, look at this! Take this hideous ball of flesh, if you like it. The other eye is like unto this; tell me, what is there lovely in them?"'

The preacher continued in the same strain, quoting other parables to the same purpose, and finished by inculcating the lesson that the true sage should neither care for riches, nor for his life, and that he should not cling to his wife and children, for they are like the grass that is cast away.

It is impossible to read such parables without being reminded of verses of the Bible, such as (Matt. v. 29): 'And if thy right eye offend thee, pluck it out, and cast it from thee[1];' and again (Matt. xix. 29): 'Every one that hath forsaken houses, or brethren, or sisters, or father, or mother, or wife, or children;' and again (Luke xii. 28): 'The grass which is to-day in the field, and to-morrow is cast into the oven.'

In the same collection, the Ocean of the rivers of stories, by Somadeva (vi. 27), we read of a merchant who had embraced the religion of Sugata, and showed great respect to the Buddhist monks. His young son, however, despised his father, and called him a sinner.

'Why do you abuse me?' said the father.

The son replied: 'You have abandoned the law of the Vedas, and followed a new law which is no law. You have forsaken the Brâhmans, and worship the Sramanas. What is the use of the Saugata religion,

---

[1] In the *Dialogi Creaturarum*, p. D 4b, it is told of Democritus that he pulled out his eyes, (1) because they prevented him from meditation, (2) because he saw the wicked flourish, (3) because he could not look on women without concupiscence.

which is followed only by men of low birth, who want
to find a refuge in the monasteries, who are happy
when they have thrown away their loin cloth, and
shaved off every hair on their head; who eat whatever they please, and perform neither ablutions nor
penances ?'

The father replied: 'There are different forms of
religion: one looks to another world, the other is intended for the masses. But surely true Brahmanism
also consists in avoiding of passion, in truthfulness,
kindness towards all beings, and in not recklessly
breaking the rules of caste. Therefore you should not
always abuse my religion which grants protection to
all beings. For surely there is no doubt that to be
kind cannot be unlawful, and I know no other kindness but to give protection to all living beings. Therefore if I am too much attached to my religion whose
object is love, and whose end is deliverance, what sin
is there in me, O child?'

However, as the son did not desist from his abuse,
his father took him before the king, and the king
ordered him to be executed. He granted him two
months to prepare for death. At the end of the two
months the son was brought before the king again,
and when the king saw that he had grown thin and
pale, he asked for the reason. The culprit replied that
seeing death approach nearer and nearer every day, he
could not think of eating. Then the king told him,
that he threatened to have him executed in order that
he might know the anguish that every creature feels
at the approach of death, and that he might learn to
respect a religion which enforces compassion for all
beings. Having known the fear of death, he ought

now to strive after spiritual freedom, and never again abuse his father's religion[1].

The son was moved, and asked the king how he could obtain spiritual freedom. The king hearing that there was a fair in the town, ordered the young man to take a vessel brimful of oil, and to carry it through the streets of the town without spilling a drop. Two executioners with drawn swords were to walk behind him, and at the first drop being spilled, they were to cut off his head. When the young man, after having walked through all the streets of the city, returned to the king without having spilled one drop, the king said: 'Did you to-day, while walking through the streets, see anybody?'

The young man replied: 'My thoughts were fixed on the vessel, and I saw and heard nothing else.'

Then the king said: 'Let thy thoughts be fixed in the same way on the Highest! He who is collected, and has ceased to care for outward life, will see the truth, and having seen the truth, will not be caught again by the net of works. Thus I have taught you in few words the way that leads to spiritual freedom.'

According to Buddha, the motive of all our actions should be *pity*, or what we should call *love* for our neighbour, and the same sentiment is inculcated again and again in the sacred poetry of the Brahmans. Thus we read in the Mahâbhârata, Udyoga-parva, cap. 38, 'Thou shalt not do to others what thou likest not thyself. This is the law in short, everything else proceeds from passion.'

Mahâbhârata, Anusâsana-parva, cap. 145:
'Not to hurt anybody by word, thought, or deed,

[1] Cf. 'Mahâvamsa,' p. 33.

and to be benevolent and charitable. This is the eternal law of the good.'

Mahâbhârata, Sânti-parva, cap. 160:

'Forgiveness and patience, kindness and equableness, truthfulness and uprightness, restraint of the senses and energy, gentleness and modesty and gravity, generosity and calmness, contentment, kindliness of speech, and absence of hatred and malice—these together make up self-control.'

Mahâbhârata, Sânti-parva, cap. 110:

'Those who are dreaded by none and who themselves dread no one, who regard all mankind like themselves, such men surmount all difficulties.'

Mahâbhârata, Anusâsana-parva, cap. 144:

'Those who always treat friends and foes with an equal heart, being friends to all, such men shall go to heaven[1].'

And as in Buddhism and Brahmanism, so again in the writings of Confucius, we find what we value most in our own religion. I shall quote but one saying of the Chinese sage[2]:

'What you do not like when done to yourself, do not do that to others.'

One passage only from the founder of the second religion in China, from Lao-tse (cap. 25)[3]:

'There is an infinite Being[4], which existed before heaven and earth.

[1] See Muir, 'Metrical Translations,' *passim*; 'the Pandit,' December, 1867.

[2] Dr. Legge's 'Life and Teachings of Confucius,' p. 47.

[3] 'Le Livre de la Voie et de la Vertu, composé dans le VI⁰ siècle avant l'ère chrétienne, par Lao-tseu,' traduit par Stanislas Julien. Paris, 1842, p. 91.

[4] Stan. Julien translates, 'Il est un être confus,' and he explains

'How calm it is! how free!

'It lives alone, it changes not.

'It moves everywhere, but it never suffers.

'We may look on it as the Mother of the Universe.

'I, I know not its name.

'In order to give it a title, I call it *Tao* (the Way).

'When I try to give it a name, I call it *Great*.

'After calling it *Great*, I call it *Fugitive*.

'After calling it *Fugitive*, I call it *Distant*.

'After calling it *Distant*, I say it comes back to me.'

Need I say that Greek and Roman writers abound in the most exalted sentiments on religion and morality, in spite of their mythology and in spite of their idolatry? When Plato says that men ought to strive after likeness with God, do you think that he thought of Jupiter, or Mars, or Mercury? When another poet exclaimed that the conscience is a god for all men, was he so very far from ·a knowledge of the true God?

On African ground the hieroglyphic and hieratic texts of the ancient Egyptians show the same strange mixture of sublime and childish, nay worse than childish, thoughts to which all students of primitive religion have become accustomed, nay from which they must learn to draw some of their most important lessons. It is easy to appreciate what is simple, and true, and beautiful in the Sacred Books of the East, but those who are satisfied with such gems, are like botanists who should care for roses

confus according to the Chinese commentaries by ' ce qu'il est impossible de distinguer clairement. Si par hazard on m'interroge sur cet être (le Tao), je répondrai : Il n'a ni commencement, ni fin,' etc. See, however, Dr. J. Legge, ' The Religions of China,' 1880, p. 213.

N

and lilies only, and in whose eyes the thorns and briers are mere weeds and rubbish. This is not the true spirit in which the natural development either of the flowers of the earth or of the products of the mind can be studied, and it is surprising to see how long it takes before the students of anthropology will learn that one simple lesson.

In a papyrus at Turin[1], the following words are put into the mouth of 'the almighty God, the self-existent, who made heaven and earth, the waters, the breaths of life, fire, the gods, men, animals, cattle, reptiles, birds, fishes, kings, men and gods.' . . . 'I am the maker of heaven and of the earth, I raise its mountains and the creatures which are upon it; I make the waters, and the Mehura comes into being. . . . I am the maker of heaven, and of the mysteries of the twofold horizon. It is I who have given to all the gods the soul which is within them. When I open my eyes, there is light; when I close them, there is darkness. . . . I make the hours, and the hours come into existence. I am Chepera in the morning, Râ at noon, Tmu in the evening.'

And again: 'Hail to thee, O Ptah-tanu, great god who concealeth his form, . . . thou art watching when at rest; the father of all fathers and of all gods. . . . Watcher, who traversest the endless ages of eternity. The heaven was yet uncreated, uncreated was the earth, the water flowed not; thou hast put together the earth, thou hast united thy limbs, thou hast reckoned thy members; what thou hast found apart, thou hast put into its place; O God, architect of the world, thou art without a father, begotten by thine own

---

[1] Le Page Renouf, 'Hibbert Lectures,' p. 221.

blessing; thou art without a mother, being born through repetition of thyself. Thou drivest away the darkness by the beams of thine eyes. Thou ascendest into the zenith of heaven, and thou comest down even as thou hast risen. When thou art a dweller in the infernal world, thy knees are above the earth, and thine head is in the upper sky. Thou sustainest the substances which thou hast made. It is by thine own strength that thou movest; thou art raised up by the might of thine own arms. . . . The roaring of thy voice is in the cloud; thy breath is on the mountain-tops; the waters of the inundation cover the lofty trees of every region. . . . Heaven and earth obey the commands which thou hast given; they travel by the road which thou hast laid down for them, they transgress not the path which thou hast prescribed to them, and which thou hast opened to them. . . . Thou restest, and it is night; when thine eyes shine forth, we are illuminated. . . . O let us give glory to the God who hath raised the sky, and who causeth his disk to float over the bosom of Nut, who hath made the gods and men and all their generations, who hath made all land and countries and the great sea, in his name of " Let-the-earth-be." . . . The babe which is brought forth daily, the ancient one who traverses every path, the height which cannot be attained.'

The following are extracts from a hymn addressed to Amon, the great divinity of Thebes, preserved in the Museum at Bulak:

'Hail to thee, Amon Râ, Lord of the thrones of the earth—the ancient of heaven, the oldest of the earth, Lord of all existences, the support of things, the support of all things. The One in his works, single

among the gods; the beautiful bull of the cycle of the
gods, chief of all the gods; Lord of truth, father of
the gods; maker of men, creator of beasts, maker of
herbs, feeder of cattle, good power begotten of Ptah
. . . to whom the gods give honour . . . Most glorious
one, Lord of terror, chief maker of the earth after his
image, how great are his thoughts above every god!
Hail to thee, Râ, Lord of law, whose shrine is hidden,
Lord of the gods; Chepra in his boat, at whose command the gods were made.   Atmu, maker of men,
. . . giving them life, . . . listening to the poor who
is in distress, gentle of heart when one cries to him
. . . Lord of wisdom, whose precepts are wise, at
whose pleasure the Nile overflows: Lord of mercy,
most loving, at whose coming men live: opener of
every eye, proceeding from the firmament, causer of
pleasure and light; at whose goodness the gods rejoice; their hearts revived when they see him.   O Râ,
adored in Thebes, high crowned in the house of the
obelisk (Heliopolis), sovereign of life, health, and
strength, sovereign Lord of all the gods; who art
visible in the midst of the horizon, ruler of the past
generations and the nether world; whose name is
hidden from his creatures . . . Hail to thee the one,
alone with many hands, lying awake while all men
sleep, to seek out the good of his creatures, Amon,
sustainer of all things.   Tmu and Horus of the
horizon pay homage to thee in all their words.   Sa-
lutation to thee, because thou abidest in us, adoration
to thee because thou hast created us.'

Are there many prayers uttered by kings like this
of King Rameses II?

Who then art thou, O my father Amon?   Doth a

father forget his son? Surely a wretched lot awaiteth
him who opposeth thy will; but blessed is he who
knoweth thee, for thy deeds proceed from a heart full
of love. I call upon thee, O my father Amon! behold
me in the midst of many peoples, unknown to me; all
nations are united against me, and I am alone; no
other is with me. My many soldiers have abandoned
me, none of my horsemen hath looked towards me;
and when I called them, none hath listened to my
voice. But I believe that Amon is worth more to me
than a million of soldiers, than a hundred thousand
horsemen, and ten thousands of brothers and sons,
even were they all gathered together. The work of
many men is nought; Amon will prevail over them.'

The following are a few passages translated from
the book of Ptahhotep, which has been called 'the
most ancient book of the world,' and would indeed
have a right to that title if, as we are told, the Paris
MS. containing it was written centuries before Moses
was born, while the author lived during the reign of
King Assa Tatkarâ of the fifth dynasty[1]:

'If thou art a wise man, bring up thy son in the
love of God.'

'God loveth the obedient and hateth the dis-
obedient.'

'A good son is spoken of as the gift of God.'

In the Maxims of Ani we read:

'The sanctuary of God abhors' (noisy manifestations?). Pray humbly with a loving heart all the
words of which are uttered in secret. He will protect thee in thine affairs; He will listen to thy words.
He will accept thine offerings.'

[1] Le Page Renouf, 'Hibbert Lectures,' p. 76.

'The God of the world is in the light above the firmament. His emblems are upon earth; it is to them that worship is rendered daily.'

In conclusion, I add a few sayings from funeral monuments, put into the mouth of the departed [1]:

'Not a little child did I injure. Not a widow did I oppress. Not a herdsman did I ill-treat. There was no beggar in my days; no one starved in my time. And when the years of famine came, I ploughed all the lands of the province to its northern and southern boundaries, feeding its inhabitants and providing their food. There was no starving person in it, and I made the widow as though she possessed a husband.'

In another inscription the departed says:

'Doing that which is right, and hating that which is wrong, I was bread to the hungry, water to the thirsty, clothing to the naked, a refuge to him that was in want; that which I did to him, the great God hath done to me!'

It is difficult to stop quoting. With every year new treasures are brought to light from the ancient literature of Egypt, and I doubt not that in time, particularly if the hieroglyphic documents continue to be deciphered in a truly scholarlike spirit, Egypt will become one of the richest mines to the student of religion.

But we must look now at some at least of the black inhabitants of Africa, I mean those whose language and religion have been carefully studied and described to us by trustworthy men, such as Bishop Colenso, Bishop Callaway, Dr. Bleek, Dr. Theophilus Hahn; and more particularly the Bântu tribes, occupying the

---

[1] Le Page Renouf, 'Hibbert Lectures,' p. 72.

Eastern coast from beyond the Equator to the Cape.
What darkness there is at present among these races
we have learnt from the history of the last wars, but
we should not forget how highly some of these races,
particularly the Zulus, are spoken of by English
missionaries.   If the number of converts among them
is as yet small, perhaps it is well that it should be so.
Bishop Callaway tells us that one lad, the first he
baptized in Natal, told him that his mother, who witnessed the battle between the English troops under
Cathcart and the Basutos, and observed the terrible
effect of our artillery, was so much struck with the
power displayed, that she concluded that they who
could shake the very earth, could not be mistaken in
anything, and advised her son to accept their religion.
It is only the old story, that truth is on the side of
the big battalions.   But the same Bishop is evidently
gaining influence by better means, and chiefly by
schools which, as he truly says, 'must be the seed-bed
of the Church, because Christianity flourishes with
more vigour in the cultivated than in the uncultivated
mind.'   One of the Zulus, whose confidence Dr. Callaway had gained, said to him [1]:

'We did not hear first from the white men about
the King who is above.   In summer-time, when it
thunders, we say, "The King is playing."   And if
there is one who is afraid, the elder people say to him,
"It is nothing but fear.   What thing belonging to the
King have you eaten?"'

Another very old man stated (p. 50): 'When we
were children, it was said : "The King is in heaven."
We used constantly to hear this when we were children;

[1] Dr. Callaway, 'Unkulunkulu,' p. 19.

they used to point to the King on high; we did not hear his name; we heard only that the King is on high. We heard it said that the creator of the world (Umdabuko) is the King which is above"' (p. 60).

A very old woman when examined by one of her own countrymen, said (p. 53): 'When we speak of the origin of corn, asking, "Whence came this?" the old people said, "It came from the creator who created all things; but we do not know him." When we asked continually, "Where is the creator? for our chiefs we see," the old men denied, saying, "And those chiefs, too, whom we see, they were created by the creator." And when we asked, "Where is he? for he is not visible at all; where is he then?" we heard our fathers pointing towards heaven, and saying, 'The Creator of all things is in heaven. And there is a nation of people there, too . . . ." It used to be said constantly, " He is the King of kings." Also when we heard it said that the heaven had eaten the cattle at such a village (i.e. when the lightning had struck them), we said, "The King has taken the cattle from such a village." And when it thundered the people took courage by saying, "The King is playing."'

Again, another very old man, belonging to the Amantanja tribe, who showed four wounds, and whose people had been scattered by the armies of Utshaka, said (p. 56): 'The old faith of our forefathers was this; they said, "There is Unkulunkulu, who is a man, who is of the earth." And they used to say, "There is a king in heaven." When it hailed, and thundered, they said, "The king is arming; he will cause it to hail; put things in order." . . As to the source of being I know that only which is in heaven (p. 59). The ancient men said, "The source of being (Umdabuko) is above, which gives life to men" . . . . It was said at first, the rain came from the King, and that the sun came from him, and the moon which gives a white light during the night, that men may go and not be injured.

'If lightning struck cattle, the people were not distressed. It used to be said (p. 60): "The King has slaughtered for himself among his own food. Is it yours? Is it not the King's? He is hungry; he kills for himself." If a village is struck by lightning, and a cow is killed, it is said, "This village will be prosperous." If a man is struck and dies, it is said, "The King has found fault with him."'

Another name of the Creator is Itongo, the Spirit, and this is the account given by a native (p. 94): 'When he says Itongo, he is not speaking of a man who has died and risen again; he is speaking of the Up-bearer of the earth, which supports men and cattle. The Up-bearer is the earth by which we live; and there is the Up-bearer of the earth by which we live, and without which we could not be, and by which we are.'

Thus we find among a people who were said to be without any religious life, without any idea of a Divine power, that some of the most essential elements of religion are fully developed,—a belief in an invisible God, the Creator of all things, residing in heaven, sending rain and hail and thunder, punishing the wicked, and claiming his sacrifice from among the cattle on a thousand hills. This shows how careful we should be before we accept purely negative evidence on the religion or the absence of all religion

among savage tribes. Suppose an educated native of
India or China were to appear suddenly in the Black
country, and address some questions in scarcely intelligible English[1] to a dust-begrimed coal-heaver, and
ask him what his ancestors had told him about the
source of being — what account could he give to his
countrymen of the state of religious faith in England,
if all his information had been gathered from the
answers which he would be likely to receive from
such witnesses! Perhaps he would never hear the
name of God except in a 'God bless you!' which people
uttered in England as well as in Germany and many
other countries, when any one present sneezed. It was
in such an exclamation that Dr. Callaway first discovered one of the names of the deity among the Zulus.
Asking an old man who lived at the mission station,
whether the word Utikxo had come into use after the
arrival of the missionaries, he received the answer
(p. 64): 'No; the word Utikxo is not a word we learnt
from the English; it is an old word of our own. It
used to be always said when a man sneezes, "May
Utikxo ever regard me with favour."' This Utikxo
was supposed to have been concealed by Unkulunkulu
(p. 67), and to be seen by no one. Men saw Unkulunkulu, and said that he was the creator of all things
(Umveliqangi) ; they said this, because they did not
see Him who made Unkulunkulu ; they therefore said
that Unkulunkulu was God.

After these crude fragments picked up among the

---

[1] P. 67. 'On the arrival of the English in this land of ours, the
first who came was a missionary named Uyegana. On his arrival he
taught the people, but they did not understand what he said . . . . and
although he did not understand the people's language, he jabbered
constantly to the people, and they could not understand what he said.'

uncultured races of Africa, who have *not yet* arrived at
any positive form of faith, let us now, in conclusion,
look at a few specimens of religious thought, emanat-
ing from those who *no longer* hold to any positive
form of faith. I take as their representative Faizi, the
brother of Abulfazl, one of that small company at the
Court of the Emperor Akbar, who, after a comparative
study of the religions of the world, had renounced the
religion of Mohammad, and for whom, as we shall see[1],
the orthodox Badáoní could not invent invective strong
enough to express his horror. Faizi was one of those
men whom their contemporaries call heretics and blas-
phemers, but whom posterity often calls saints and
martyrs, the salt of the earth, the light of the world; a
man of real devotion, real love for his fellow-creatures,
real faith in God, the Unknown God, whom we ignorantly worship, whom no human thought and no human
language can declare, and whose altar,—the same that
St. Paul saw at Athens—will remain standing for ever
in the hearts of all true believers.

'Take Faizi's Díwán to bear witness to the wonderful speeches of a free-thinker who belongs to a thousand
sects.

'I have become dust, but from the odour of my
grave, people shall know that man rises from such
dust.

'They may know Faizi's[2] end from the beginning:
without an equal he goes from the world, and without
an equal he rises.

'In the assembly of the day of resurrection, when
past things shall be forgiven, the sins of the Ka'bah

---

[1] See p. 218.   [2] Faizi means also the heart.

will be forgiven for the sake of the dust of Christian churches[1].

'O Thou who existest from eternity and abidest for ever, sight cannot bear Thy light, praise cannot express Thy perfection;

'Thy light melts the understanding, and Thy glory baffles wisdom; to think of Thee destroys reason, Thy essence confounds thought.

'Thy holiness pronounces that the blood-drops of human meditation are shed in vain in search of Thy knowledge: human understanding is but an atom of dust.

'Thy jealousy, the guard of Thy door, stuns human thought by a blow in the face, and gives human ignorance a slap on the nape of the neck.

'Science is like blinding sand of the desert on the road to Thy perfection. The town of literature is a mere hamlet compared with the world of Thy knowledge.

'My foot has no power to travel on this path which misleads sages; I have no power to bear the odour of the wine, it confounds my mind.

'Man's so-called foresight and guiding reason wander about bewildered in the city of Thy glory.

'Human knowledge and thought combined can only spell the first letter of the alphabet of Thy love.

'Mere beginners and such as are far advanced in knowledge are both eager for union with Thee; but

---

[1] The sins of Islam are as worthless as the dust of Christianity. On the day of resurrection, both Muhammadans and Christians will see the vanity of their religious doctrines. Men fight about religion on earth; in heaven they shall find out that there is only one true religion, the worship of God's spirit.

the beginners are tattlers, and those that are advanced are triflers.

'Each brain is full of thought of grasping Thee; the brow of Plato even burned with the fever-heat of this hopeless thought.

'How shall a thoughtless man like me succeed, when Thy jealousy strikes a dagger into the liver of saints?

'O that Thy grace would cleanse my brain; for if not, my restlessness will end in madness.

'To bow down the head upon the dust of Thy threshold and then to look up, is neither right in faith, nor permitted by truth.'

'O man, thou coin bearing the double stamp of body and spirit, I do not know what thy nature is; for thou art higher than heaven and lower than earth.

'Thy frame contains the image of the heavenly and the lower regions; be either heavenly or earthly, thou art at liberty to choose.

'Do not act against thy reason, for it is a trustworthy counsellor; put not thy heart on illusions, for the heart is a lying fool.

'If thou wishest to understand the secret meaning of the words, "to prefer the welfare of others to thy own," treat thyself with poison, and others with sugar.

'Accept misfortune with a joyful look, if thou art in the service of Him whom people serve.

'Plunged into the wisdom of Greece, my mind rose again from the deep in the land of Ind; be thou as if

thou hadst fallen into this deep abyss (of my knowledge, i. e. learn of me).

'If people would withdraw the veil from the face
of my knowledge, they would find that what those
who are far advanced in knowledge call certainty, is
with me the faintest dawn of thought.

'If people would take the screen from the eye of
my knowledge, they would find that what is revelation (ecstatic knowledge) for the wise, is but drunken
madness for me.

'If I were to bring forth what is in my mind, I
wonder whether the spirit of the age could bear it.

'My vessel does not require the wine of the friend-
ship of time; my own blood is the basis of the wine
of my enthusiasm.'

I wish we could explore together in this spirit the
ancient religions of mankind, for I feel convinced that
the more we know of them, the more we shall see
that there is not one which is entirely false; nay,
that in one sense every religion was a true religion,
being the only religion which was possible at the time,
which was compatible with the language, the thoughts,
and the sentiments of each generation, which was
appropriate to the age of the world. I know full
well the objections that will be made to this. Was
the worship of Moloch, it will be said, a true religion
when they burnt their sons and their daughters in
the fire to their gods? Was the worship of Mylitta,
or is the worship of Kâlî a true religion, when within
the sanctuary of their temples they committed abo-
minations that must be nameless? Was the teaching
of Buddha a true religion, when men were asked to

believe that the highest reward of virtue and meditation consisted in a complete annihilation of the
soul?

Such arguments may tell in party warfare, though
even there they have provoked fearful retaliation.
Can that be a true religion, it has been answered,
which consigned men of holy innocence to the flames,
because they held that the Son was like unto the
Father, but not the same as the Father, or because
they would not worship the Virgin and the Saints?
Can that be a true religion which screened the same
nameless crimes behind the sacred walls of monasteries? Can that be a true religion which taught the
eternity of punishment without any hope of pardon
or salvation for the sinner, not penitent in proper
time?

People who judge of religions in that spirit will
never understand their real purport, will never reach
their sacred springs. These are the excrescences, the
inevitable excrescences of all religions. We might as
well judge of the health of a people from its hospitals,
or of its morality from its prisons. If we want to
judge of a religion, we must try to study it as much
as possible in the mind of its founder; and when that
is impossible, as it is but too often, try to find it in
the lonely chamber and the sick-room, rather than in
the colleges of augurs and the councils of priests.

If we do this, and if we bear in mind that religion
must accommodate itself to the intellectual capacities
of those whom it is to influence, we shall be surprised
to find much of true religion where we only expected degrading superstition or an absurd worship
of idols.

The intention of religion, wherever we meet it, is always holy. However imperfect, however childish a religion may be, it always places the human soul in the presence of God; and however imperfect and however childish the conception of God may be, it always represents the highest ideal of perfection which the human soul, for the time being, can reach and grasp. Religion therefore places the human soul in the presence of its highest ideal, it lifts it above the level of ordinary goodness, and produces at least a yearning after a higher and better life—a life in the light of God.

The expression that is given to these early manifestations of religious sentiment is no doubt frequently childish: it may be irreverent or even repulsive. But has not every father to learn the lesson of a charitable interpretation in watching the first stammerings of religion in his children? Why, then, should people find it so difficult to learn the same lesson in the ancient history of the world, and to judge in the same spirit the religious utterances of the childhood of the human race? Who does not recollect the startling and seemingly irreverent questionings of children about God, and who does not know how perfectly guiltless the child's mind is of real irreverence? Such outbursts of infantine religion hardly bear repeating. I shall only mention one instance. I well recollect the dismay which was created by a child exclaiming, 'Oh! I wish there was at least *one* room in the house where I could play alone, and where God could not see me!' People who heard it were shocked; but to my mind, I confess, this childish exclamation sounded more truthful and wonderful than even the Psalm of David,

'Whither shall I go from Thy Spirit? or whither shall I flee from Thy presence?'

It is the same with the childish language of ancient religion. We say very calmly that God is omniscient and omnipresent. Hesiod speaks of the sun, as the eye of Zeus, that sees and perceives everything. Aratus wrote, 'Full of Zeus are all the streets, all the markets of men; full of Him is the sea and the harbours .... and we are also His offspring.'

A Vedic poet, though of more modern date than the one I quoted before, speaking of the same Varuna whom Vasishtha invoked, says: 'The great lord of these worlds sees as if he were near. If a man thinks he is walking by stealth, the gods know it all. If a man stands or walks or rides, if he goes to lie down or to get up, what two people sitting together whisper, King Varuna knows it, he is there as a third. This earth, too, belongs to Varuna, the king, and this wide sky with its ends far apart. The two seas (the sky and the ocean) are Varuna's loins; he is also contained in this small drop of water. He who should flee far beyond the sky, even he would not be rid of Varuna, the king. His spies proceed from heaven towards this world; with thousand eyes they overlook this earth. King Varuna sees all this, what is between heaven and earth, and what is beyond. He has counted the twinklings of our eyes. As a player throws down the dice, he settles all things [1].'

I do not deny that there is in this hymn much that is childish, that it contains expressions unworthy of the majesty of the Deity; but if I look at the language and the thoughts of the people who composed

[1] 'Chips from a German Workshop,' i. 41. 'Atharva-veda,' iv. 16.

these hymns more than three thousand years ago, I wonder rather at the happy and pure expression which they have given to these deep thoughts than at the occasional harshnesses which jar upon our ears.

These are the words of a Hindu convert, when he went back to India to preach the Gospel: 'Now I am not going to India to injure the feelings of the people by saying, "Your Scripture is all nonsense, anything outside the Old and New Testament is good for nothing." No, I tell you, I will appeal to the Hindu philosophers and moralists and poets, at the same time bringing to them my light, and reasoning with them in the spirit of Christ. That will be my work. We have sayings to this effect: "He who would be greatest shall be least." You cannot call this nonsense, for it is the saying of our Saviour, "Whosoever would be chief among you, let him be your servant." The missionaries, kind, earnest, devoted as they are, do not know these things, and at once exclude everything bearing the name of Hindu. Go to Egypt, and you will find some pieces of stone, beautifully carved and ornamented, that seem to have been part of some large building, and by examining these, you can imagine how magnificent this structure must have been. Go to India, and examine the common sayings of the people, and you will be surprised to see what a splendid religion the Hindu religion must have been[1].'

Much the same might be said of the religion of the Indians of North America also, however different the growth of their religious ideas has been from that of

[1] 'Brief Account of Joguth Chundra Gangooly, a Brahman of High Caste and a Convert to Christianity.' London, 1860.

their namesakes in the East.   The early missionaries among the Red Indians were struck by nothing so much as by their apparent pantheism, by their seeing the presence of the Divine everywhere, even in what were clearly the works of man. Thus Roger Williams related 'that when they talke amongst themselves of the English ships and great buildings, of the plowing of their Fields, and especially of Bookes and Letters, they will end thus: Manittôwock, "they are Gods," Cummanittôo, "you are a God."' He sees in these idioms an expression 'of the strong conviction naturall in the soule of man, that God is filling all things, and places, and that all Excellencies dwell in God, and proceed from him, and that they only are blessed who have that Jehovah for their portion.' It may have been so when Roger Williams wrote, but a scholarlike study of the North American languages such as has lately been inaugurated by a few American *savants*, shows that, if it was so, the equivocal character of language had more to do with producing this peculiar American pantheism than the independent evolution of thought. *Manito*, literally 'Manit,' plur. *manitóog* (see Trumbull, 'Transact. Am. Phil. Assoc.' i. p. 120), is no doubt the Indian name for their Supreme Spirit. Lahontaine defined it long ago as a name given by the savages ' to all that surpasses their understanding and proceeds from a cause that they cannot trace' ('Voyages,' Engl. ed. 1703, vol. ii. 29). But this Manit is not the name of the sky or the sun or any other physical phenomenon gradually developed into a bright god, like *Dyaus* or *Zeus*, and then generalised into a name of the Divine, like *deva* or *deus*. If we may trust the best students of the American languages the name of

Manit began with an abstract concept. It was formed
' by prefixing the indefinite or impersonal particle 'm
to the subjunctive participle (anit) of a verb which
signifies "to surpass," "to be more than." *Anue,* which
is an impersonal form of the same verb (in the indicat.
present), was the sign of the comparative degree, and
translated by "more," "rather."' As the word *Manit*,
however, besides being the name of the Highest God,
continued to be used in ordinary language in the sense
of excessive, extraordinary, wonderful, the missionaries
hearing the Indians at the apprehension of any ex-
cellency in men, women, birds, beasts, fish, etc., crying
out *Manitoo*, took it in the sense of 'it is a God.'
Possibly the two meanings of the word may have run
together in the minds of the Indians also, and, if so,
we should have here another instance of the influence
of language on thought, or, if you like, of petrified
on living thought, though in this case due, not to
polyonomy, but to homonymy. The result is the
same, but the steps which led to the expression 'this
is Manit' are different from the steps that led from
' dyaus,' sky, to our saying ' this is divine.'

Ancient language is a difficult instrument to handle,
particularly for religious purposes. It is impossible to
express abstract ideas except by metaphor, and it is
not too much to say that the whole dictionary of ancient
religion is made up of metaphors. With us these
metaphors are all forgotten. We speak of spirit without
thinking of breath, of heaven without thinking of the
sky, of pardon without thinking of a release, of revelation without thinking of a veil. But in ancient
language every one of these words, nay, every word
that does not refer to sensuous objects, is still in a

chrysalis stage: half material and half spiritual, and
rising and falling in its character according to the
varying capacities of speakers and hearers. Here is a
constant source of misunderstandings, many of which
have maintained their place in the religion and in the
mythology of the ancient world. There are two distinct tendencies to be observed in the growth of ancient
religion. There is, on the one side, the struggle of the
mind against the material character of language, a
constant attempt to strip words of their coarse covering, and fit them, by main force, for the purposes of
abstract thought. But there is, on the other side, a
constant relapse from the spiritual into the material,
and, strange to say, a predilection for the material
sense instead of the spiritual. This action and reaction
has been going on in the language of religion from the
earliest times, and it is at work even now.

It seems at first a fatal element in religion that it
cannot escape from this flux and reflux of human
thought, which is repeated at least once in every
generation between father and son, between mother
and daughter; but if we watch it more closely we
shall find, I think, that this flux and reflux constitutes
the very life of religion.

Place yourselves in the position of those who first
are said to have worshipped the sky. We say that
they worshipped the sky, or that the sky was their
god; and in one sense this is true, but in a sense very
different from that which is usually attached to such
statements. If we use 'god' in the sense which it
has now, then to say that the sky was their god is to
say what is simply impossible. Such a word as God,
in the sense in which we use it—such a word even

as *deus* and θεός, in Latin and Greek, or d e v a in Sanskrit, which could be used as a general predicate—did not and could not exist at that early time in the history of thought and speech. If we want to understand ancient religion, we must first try to understand ancient language.

Let us remember, then, that the first materials of language supply expressions for such impressions only as are received through the senses. If, therefore, there was a root meaning to burn, to be bright, to warm, such a root might supply a recognised name for the sun and for the sky.

But let us now imagine, as well as we can, the process which went on in the human mind before the name of sky could be torn away from its material object and be used as the name of something totally different from the sky. There was in the heart of man, from the very first, a feeling of incompleteness, of weakness, of dependence, whatever we like to call it in our abstract language. We can explain it as little as we can explain why the newborn child feels the cravings of hunger and thirst. But it was so from the first, and is so even now. Man knows not whence he comes and whither he goes. He looks for a guide, for a friend; he wearies for some one on whom he can rest; he wants something like a father in heaven. In addition to all the impressions which he received from the outer world, there was in the heart of man a stronger impulse from within — a sigh, a yearning, a call for something that should not come and go like everything else, that should be before, and after, and for ever, that should hold and support everything, that should make man feel at

home in this strange world. Before this vague
yearning could assume any definite shape it wanted a
name: it could not be fully grasped or clearly conceived except by naming it. But where to look for
a name? No doubt the storehouse of language was
there, but from every name that was tried the mind
of man shrank back because it did not fit, because
it seemed to fetter rather than to wing the thought
that fluttered within and called for light and freedom.

But when at last a name or even many names were
tried and chosen, let us see what took place, as far as
the mind of man was concerned. A certain satisfaction, no doubt, was gained by having a name or
several names, however imperfect; but these names,
like all other names, were but signs—poor, imperfect
signs; they were predicates, and very partial predicates, of various small portions only of that vague
and vast something which slumbered in the mind.
When the name of the brilliant sky had been chosen,
as it has been chosen at one time or other by nearly
every nation upon earth, was sky the full expression
of that within the mind which wanted expression?
Was the mind satisfied? Had the sky been recognised as its god? Far from it. People knew perfectly well what they meant by the visible sky; the
first man who, after looking everywhere for what he
wanted, and who at last in sheer exhaustion grasped
at the name of sky as better than nothing, knew but
too well that his success was after all a miserable
failure. The brilliant sky was, no doubt, the most
exalted, it was the only unchanging and infinite being
that had received a name, and that could lend its
name to that as yet unborn idea of the Infinite which

disquieted the human mind.   But let us only see
this clearly, that the man who chose that name
did not mean, could not have meant, that the visible
sky was all he wanted, that the blue canopy above
was his god.

And now observe what happens when the name
sky has thus been given and accepted.   The seeking
and finding of such a name, however imperfect, was the
act of a manly mind, of a poet, of a prophet, of a
patriarch, who could struggle, like another Jacob,
with the idea of God that was within him, till he had
conceived it, and brought it forth, and given it its
name.   But when that name had to be used with the
young and the aged, with silly children and doting
grandmothers, it was impossible to preserve it from
being misunderstood.   The first step downwards
would be to look upon the sky as the abode of that
Being which was called by the same name; the next
step would be to forget altogether what was behind
the name, and to implore the sky, the visible canopy
over our heads, to send rain, to protect the fields, the
cattle, and the corn, to give to man his daily bread.
Nay, very soon those who warned the world that it
was not the visible sky that was meant, but that
what was meant was something high above, deep
below, far away from the blue firmament, would be
looked upon either as dreamers whom no one could
understand, or as unbelievers who despised the sky,
the great benefactor of the world.   Lastly, many
things that were true of the visible sky would be
told of its divine namesake, and legends would spring
up, destroying every trace of the deity that once was
hidden beneath that ambiguous name.

I call this variety of acceptation, this misunderstanding, which is inevitable in ancient and also in
modern religion, the *dialectic growth and decay*, or, if
you like, the *dialectic life of religion*, and we shall see
again and again, how important it is in enabling us
to form a right estimate of religious language and
thought. The dialectic shades in the language of
religion are almost infinite; they explain the decay,
but they also account for the life of religion. You
may remember that Jacob Grimm, in one of his
poetical moods, explained the origin of High and Low
German, of Sanskrit and Prakrit, of Doric and Ionic,
by looking upon the high dialects as originally the
language of men, upon the low dialects as originally
the language of women and children. We can observe, I believe, the same parallel streams in the language of religion. There is a high and there is a low
dialect; there is a broad and there is a narrow dialect; there are dialects for men and dialects for children, for clergy and laity, for the noisy streets and
for the still and lonely chamber. And as the child on
growing up to manhood has to unlearn the language
of the nursery, its religion, too, has to be translated
from a feminine into a more masculine dialect. This
does not take place without a struggle, and it is this
constantly recurring struggle, this inextinguishable
desire to recover itself, which keeps religion from
utter stagnation. From first to last religion is oscil-
lating between these two opposite poles, and it is only
if the attraction of one of the two poles becomes too
strong, that the healthy movement ceases, and stagnation and decay set in. If religion cannot accommodate itself on the one side to the capacity of

children, or if on the other side it fails to satisfy the
requirements of men, it has lost its vitality, and it
becomes either mere superstition or mere philosophy.

If I have succeeded in expressing myself clearly, I
think you will understand in what sense it may be
said that there is truth in all religions, even in the
lowest. The intention which led to the first utterance of a name like sky, used no longer in its
material sense, but in a higher sense, was right. The
spirit was willing, but language was weak. The
mental process was not, as commonly supposed, an
identification of the definite idea of deity with sky.
Such a process is hardly conceivable. It was, on the
contrary, a first attempt at defining the indefinite impression of deity by a name that should approxi-
mately or metaphorically render at least one of its
most prominent features. The first framer of that
name of the deity, I repeat it again, could as little
have thought of the material heaven as we do when
we speak of the kingdom of heaven[1].

And now let us observe another feature of ancient
religion that has often been so startling, but which, if
we only remember what is the nature of ancient language, becomes likewise perfectly intelligible. It is
well known that ancient languages are particularly
rich in synonymes, or, to speak more correctly, that in
them the same object is called by many names—is, in
fact, *polyonymous*. While in modern languages most
objects have one name only, we find in ancient Sanskrit, in ancient Greek and Arabic, a large choice of
words for the same object. This is perfectly natural.

---

[1] Medhurst, 'Inquiry,' p. 20.

Each name could express one side only of whatever had to be named, and, not satisfied with one partial name, the early framers of language produced one name after the other, and after a time retained those which seemed most useful for special purposes. Thus, the sky might be called not only the brilliant, but the dark, the covering, the thundering, the rain-giving. This is the *polyonomy* of language, and it is what we are accustomed to call *polytheism* in religion. The same mental yearning which found its first satisfaction in using the name of the brilliant sky as an indication of the Divine, would soon grasp at other names of the sky, not expressive of brilliancy, and therefore more appropriate to a religious mood in which the Divine was conceived as dark, awful, all-powerful. Thus we find by the side of Dyaus, another name of the covering sky, Varuna, originally only another attempt at naming the Divine, but which, like the name of Dyaus, soon assumed a separate and independent existence.

And this is not all. The very imperfection of all the names that had been chosen, their very inadequacy to express the fulness and infinity of the Divine, would keep up the search for new names, till at last every part of nature in which an approach to the Divine could be discovered was chosen as a name of the Omnipresent. If the presence of the Divine was perceived in the strong wind, the strong wind became its name; if its presence was perceived in the earthquake and the fire, the earthquake and the fire became its names.

Do you still wonder at polytheism or at mythology? Why, they are inevitable. They are, if you

like, a *parler enfantin* of religion.   But the world has
its childhood, and when it was a child it spoke as a
child, it understood as a child, it thought as a child;
and, I say again, in that it spoke as a child its language was true, in that it believed as a child its
religion was true.   The fault rests with us, if we
insist on taking the language of children for the
language of men, if we attempt to translate literally
ancient into modern language, oriental into occidental
speech, poetry into prose[1].

It is perfectly true that at present few interpreters,
if any, would take such expressions as the head, the
face, the mouth, the lips, the breath of Jehovah in a
literal sense.

> Per questo la Scrittura condescende
> A vostra facultate, e piedi e mano
> Attribuisce a Dio, et altro intende[2].

But what does it mean, then, if we hear one of our
most honest and most learned theologians declare that
he can no longer read from the altar the words of the
Bible, 'God spake these words and said'? If we can
make allowance for mouth and lips and breath, we
can surely make the same allowance for words and
their utterance.   The language of antiquity is the
language of childhood: ay, and we ourselves, when
we try to reach the Infinite and the Divine by means

---

[1] 'An early Oriental historian does not write in the exact and accurate
style of a nineteenth century Occidental critic.'   Canon Rawlinson, in
the Lectures delivered under the auspices of the Christian Evidence
Society.

[2] Dante, 'Paradiso,' iv. 44-46.

of more abstract terms, are we even now better than children trying to place a ladder against the sky?

The *parler enfantin* in religion is not extinct; it never will be. Not only have some of the ancient childish religions been kept alive, as, for instance, the religion of India, which is to my mind like a half-fossilised megatherion walking about in the broad daylight of the nineteenth century; but in our own religion and in the language of the New Testament, there are many things which disclose their true meaning to those only who know what language is made of, who have not only ears to hear, but a heart to understand the real meaning of parables.

What I maintain, then, is this, that as we put the most charitable interpretation on the utterances of children, we ought to put the same charitable interpretation on the apparent absurdities, the follies, the errors, nay, even the horrors of ancient religion. When we read of Belus, the supreme god of the Babylonians, cutting off his head, that the blood flowing from it might be mixed with the dust out of which man was to be formed, this sounds horrible enough; but depend upon it what was originally intended by this myth was no more than this, that there is in man an element of Divine life: that 'we are also His blood, or His offspring.'

The same idea existed in the ancient religion of the Egyptians, for we read in the 17th chapter of their Ritual, that the Sun mutilated himself, and that from the stream of his blood he created all beings[1]. And

---

[1] Vicomte de Rougé, in 'Annales de Philosophie chrétienne,' Nov. 1869, p. 332.

the author of Genesis, too, when he wishes to express the same idea, can only use the same human and symbolical language; he can only say that 'God formed man from the dust of the ground, and breathed into his nostrils the breath of life.'

In Mexico, at the festival of Huitzilpochtli, an image of the god, made of the seeds of plants, and the blood of immolated children, was pierced by a priest with an arrow at the end of the ceremony. The king ate the heart, and the rest of the body was distributed among the congregation. This custom of eating the body of God, which can well be conceived symbolically, is apt to degenerate into crude fetishism, so that the faithful believes in the end that he really feeds on his God, not in the true, the spiritual, but in the false, the material, sense [1].

If we have once learnt to be charitable and reasonable in the interpretation of the sacred books of other religions, we shall more easily learn to be charitable and reasonable in the interpretation of our own. We shall no longer try to force a literal sense on words which, if interpreted literally, must lose their true and original purport, we shall no longer interpret the Law and the Prophets as if they had been written in the English of our own century, but read them in a truly historical spirit, prepared for many difficulties, undismayed by many contradictions, which, so far from disproving the authenticity, become to the historian of ancient language and ancient thought the strongest confirmatory evidence of the age, the genuineness, and the real truth of

[1] See Wundt, 'Vorlesungen über Menschen und Thierseele,' vol. ii. p. 262.

ancient sacred books. Let us but treat our own sacred books with neither more nor less mercy than the sacred books of any other nations, and they will soon regain that position and influence which they once possessed, but which the artificial and unhistorical theories of the last three centuries have well-nigh destroyed.

NOTES AND ILLUSTRATIONS

TO THE

INTRODUCTION TO THE SCIENCE OF RELIGION.

PAGE 17.

THE EMPEROR AKBAR.

As the Emperor Akbar may be considered the first who ventured on a comparative study of the religions of the world, the following extracts from the Ain i Akbari, the Muntakhab at Tawarikh, and the Dabistán, may be of interest at the present moment. They are taken from Dr. Blochmann's new translation of the Ain i Akbari, lately published at Calcutta, a most valuable contribution to the 'Bibliotheca Indica.' It is but seldom that we find in Eastern history an opportunity of confronting two independent witnesses, particularly contemporary witnesses, expressing their opinions of a still reigning Emperor. Abulfazl, the author of the Ain i Akbari, writes as the professed friend of Akbar, whose Vezier he was; Badáoní writes as the declared enemy of Abulfazl, and with an undisguised horror at Akbar's religious views. His work, the Muntakhab at Tawarikh, was kept secret, and was not published till the reign of Jahángír (Ain i Akbari, transl. by Blochmann, p. 104 note).

I first give some extracts from Abulfazl:

P

A'ÍN 77.

HIS MAJESTY AS THE SPIRITUAL GUIDE OF THE PEOPLE.

GOD, the Giver of intellect and the Creator of matter, forms mankind as He pleases, and gives to some comprehensiveness, and to others narrowness of disposition. Hence the origin of two opposite tendencies among men, one class of whom turn to religious (*dín*), and the other class to worldly thoughts (*dunyá*). Each of these two divisions select different leaders[1], and mutual repulsiveness grows to open rupture. It is then that men's blindness and silliness appear in their true light; it is then discovered how rarely mutual regard and charity are to be met with.

But have the religious and the worldly tendencies of men no common ground? Is there not everywhere the same enrapturing beauty[2] which beams forth from so many thousand hidden places? Broad indeed is the carpet[3] which God has spread, and beautiful the colours which He has given it.

The Lover and the Beloved are in reality one[4];
Idle talkers speak of the Brahmin as distinct from his idol.
There is but one lamp in this house, in the rays of which,
Wherever I look, a bright assembly meets me.

[1] As prophets, the leaders of the Church; and kings, the leaders of the State.

[2] God. He may be worshipped by the meditative, and by the active man. The former speculates on the essence of God, the latter rejoices in the beauty of the world, and does his duty as man. Both represent tendencies apparently antagonistic; but as both strive after God, there is a ground common to both. Hence mankind ought to learn that there is no real antagonism between *dín* and *dunyá*. Let men rally round Akbar, who joins Çufic depth to practical wisdom. By his example, he teaches men how to adore God in doing one's duties; his superhuman knowledge proves that the light of God dwells in him. The surest way of pleasing God is to obey the king.

[3] The world.

[4] These Çufic lines illustrate the idea that 'the same enrapturing beauty' is everywhere. God is everywhere, in everything: hence every-

One man thinks that by keeping his passions in subjection he worships God ; and another finds self-discipline in watching over the destinies of a nation. The religion of thousand others consists in clinging to an idea : they are happy in their sloth and unfitness of judging for themselves. But when the time of reflection comes, and men shake off the prejudices of their education, the threads of the web of religious blindness[1] break, and the eye sees the glory of harmoniousness.

But the ray of such wisdom does not light up every house, nor could every heart bear such knowledge. Again, although some are enlightened, many would observe silence from fear of fanatics, who lust for blood, but look like men. And should any one muster sufficient courage, and openly proclaim his enlightened thoughts, pious simpletons would call him a mad man, and throw him aside as of no account, whilst ill-starred wretches would at once think of heresy and atheism, and go about with the intention of killing him.

Whenever, from lucky circumstances, the time arrives that a nation learns to understand how to worship truth, the people will naturally look to their king, on account of the high position which he occupies, and expect him to be their spiritual leader as well : for a king possesses, independent of men, the ray of Divine wisdom, which banishes from his heart everything that is conflicting. A king will therefore sometimes observe the element of harmony in a multitude of

thing is God. Thus God, the Beloved, dwells in man, the lover, and both are one. Brahmin = man ; the idol = God; lamp = thought of God; house = man's heart. The thoughtful man sees everywhere ' the bright assemblage of God's works.'

[1] The text has *taqlid*, which means *to put a collar on one's own neck*, to follow another blindly, especially in religious matters. ' All things which refer to prophetship and revealed religion they [Abulfazl, Hakím Abulfath, &c.] called *taqlídiyát*, i. e. things against reason, because they put the basis of religion upon reason, not testimony. Besides, there came [during A. H. 983, or A. D. 1575] a great number of Portuguese, from whom they likewise picked up doctrines justifiable by reasoning.' ' Badáoní,' ii. p. 281.

things, or sometimes, reversely, a multitude of things in that which is apparently one; for he sits on the throne of distinction, and is thus equally removed from joy or sorrow.

Now this is the case with the monarch of the present age, and this book is a witness of it.

Men versed in foretelling the future, knew this when His Majesty was born[1], and together with all others that were cognizant of the secret, they have since been waiting in joyful expectation. His Majesty, however, wisely surrounded himself for a time with a veil, as if he were an outsider, or a stranger to their hopes. But can man counteract the will of God? His Majesty, at first, took all such by surprise as were wedded to the prejudices of the age; but he could not help revealing his intentions: they grew to maturity in spite of him, and are now fully known. He now is the spiritual guide of the nation, and sees in the performance of this duty a means of pleasing God. He has now opened the gate that leads to the right path, and satisfies the thirst of all that wander about panting for truth.

But whether he checks men in their desire of becoming disciples, or admits them at other times, he guides them in each case to the realm of bliss. Many sincere enquirers, from the mere light of his wisdom, or his holy breath, obtain a degree of awakening which other spiritual doctors could not produce by repeated fasting and prayers for forty days. Numbers of those who have renounced the world, as *Sannásis*,

---

[1] This is an allusion to the wonderful event which happened at the birth of the emperor. Akbar spoke: 'From Mirzá Sháh Muhammad, called Ghaznín Khán, son of Sháh Begkhán, who had the title of Daurán Khán, and was an Arghún by birth. The author heard him say at Láhor, in A. H. 1053, 'I asked Nawáb 'Azíz Kokah, who has the title of Khán i A'zam, whether the late emperor, like the Messiah, had really spoken with his august mother." He replied, "His mother told me, it was true."' *Dabistán ul Mazáhib*, Calcutta Edition, p. 390. Bombay edition, p. 260. The words which Christ spoke in the cradle, are given in the Qorán, Sur. 19, and in the spurious gospel of the 'Infancy of Christ,' pp. 5, 111.

Jogís, Sevrás, Qalandars, Hakíms, and *Çufís,* and thousands
of such as follow worldly pursuits, as soldiers, tradespeople,
mechanics, and husbandmen, have daily their eyes opened to
insight, or have the light of their knowledge increased. Men
of all nations, young and old, friends and strangers, the far
and the near, look upon offering a vow to His Majesty as the
means of solving all their difficulties, and bend down in
worship on obtaining their desire. Others again, from the
distance of their homes, or to avoid the crowds gathering
at Court, offer their vows in secret, and pass their lives in
grateful praises. But when His Majesty leaves Court, in
order to settle the affairs of a province, to conquer a kingdom,
or to enjoy the pleasures of the chase, there is not a hamlet,
a town, or a city, that does not send forth crowds of men and
women with vow-offerings in their hands, and prayers on their
lips, touching the ground with their foreheads, praising the
efficacy of their vows, or proclaiming the accounts of the
spiritual assistance received. Other multitudes ask for lasting bliss, for an upright heart, for advice how best to act,
for strength of the body, for enlightenment, for the birth of
a son, the reunion of friends, a long life, increase of wealth,
elevation in rank, and many other things. His Majesty, who
knows what is really good, gives satisfactory answers to
every one, and applies remedies to their religious perplexities.
Not a day passes but people bring cups of water to him,
beseeching him to breathe upon it. He who reads the letters
of the divine orders in the book of fate, on seeing the tidings
of hope, takes the water with his blessed hands, places it in
the rays of the world-illuminating sun, and fulfils the desire
of the suppliant. Many sick people[1] of broken hopes, whose

---

[1] 'He [Akbar] showed himself every morning at a window, in front
of which multitudes came and prostrated themselves; while women
brought their sick infants for his benediction, and offered presents on
their recovery.' From the account of the Goa Missionaries who came
to Akbar in 1595, in 'Murray's Discoveries in Asia,' ii. p. 96.

diseases the most eminent physicians pronounced incurable, have been restored to health by this divine means.

A more remarkable case is the following. A simple-minded recluse had cut off his tongue, and throwing it towards the threshold of the palace, said, 'If that certain blissful thought¹, which I just now have, has been put into my heart by God, my tongue will get well; for the sincerity of my belief must lead to a happy issue.' The day was not ended before he obtained his wish.

Those who are acquainted with the religious knowledge and the piety of His Majesty, will not attach any importance to some of his customs², remarkable as they may appear at first; and those who know His Majesty's charity and love of justice, do not even see anything remarkable in them. In the magnanimity of his heart, he never thinks of his perfection, though he is the ornament of the world. Hence he even keeps back many who declare themselves willing to become his disciples. He often says, 'Why should I claim to guide men, before I myself am guided?' But when a novice bears on his forehead the sign of earnestness of purpose, and he be daily enquiring more and more, His Majesty accepts him, and admits him on a Sunday, when the world-illuminating sun is in its highest splendour. Notwithstanding every strictness and reluctance shown by His Majesty in admitting novices, there are many thousands, men of all classes, who have cast over their shoulders the mantle

---

¹ His thought was this. If Akbar is a prophet, he must, from his supernatural wisdom, find out in what condition I am lying here.

² 'He [Akbar] showed, besides, no partiality to the Mahometans: and when in straits for money would even plunder the mosques to equip his cavalry. Yet there remained in the breast of the monarch a stronghold of idolatry, on which they [the Portuguese Missionaries] could never make any impression. Not only did he adore the sun, and make long prayers to it four times a day; he also held himself forth as an object of worship; and though exceedingly tolerant as to other modes of faith, never would admit of any encroachments on his own divinity.' 'Murray's Discoveries,' ii. p. 95.

of belief, and look upon their conversion to the New Faith as the means of obtaining every blessing.

At the above-mentioned time of everlasting auspiciousness, the novice with his turban in his hands, puts his head on the feet of His Majesty. This is symbolical[1], and expresses that the novice, guided by good fortune and the assistance of his good star, has cast aside[2] conceit and selfishness, the root of so many evils, offers his heart in worship, and now comes to enquire as to the means of obtaining everlasting life. His Majesty, the chosen one of God, then stretches out the hand of favour, raises up the suppliant, and replaces the turban on his head, meaning by these symbolical actions that he has raised up a man of pure intentions, who from seeming existence has now entered into real life. His Majesty then gives the novice the *Shaçt*[3], upon which is engraved 'the Great Name[4],' and His Majesty's symbolical motto, '*Allāhu Akbar.*' This teaches the novice the truth that

'*The pure Shaçt and the pure sight never err.*'

Seeing the wonderful habits of His Majesty, his sincere

---

[1] The text has *zabán i hál*, and a little lower down, *zabán i bezufāní. Zábán i hál*, or *symbolical* language, is opposed to *zabán i maqál*, spoken words.

[2] Or rather, *from his head*, as the text has, because the casting aside of selfishness is symbolically expressed by taking off the turban. To wear a turban is a distinction.

[3] *Shaçt* means *aim*; secondly *anything round*, either a ring, or a thread, as the Brahminical thread. Here a ring seems to be meant. Or it may be the likeness of the emperor which, according to Badáoní, the members wore on their turbans.

[4] The *Great Name* is a name of God. 'Some say, it is the word *Allah*; others say, it is *çamad*, the eternal; others, *alhayy*, the living; others, *alqayyúm*, the everlasting; others, *arrahmān arrahím*, the clement and merciful; others, *almuhaimin*, the protector.' *Ghiás.* 'Qází Hamíddudín of Nágor says, 'the Great Name is the word *Hú*, or He (God), because it has a reference to God's nature, as it shows that He has no other at His side. Again, the word *hú* is a root, not a derivative. All epithets of God are contained in it.' *Kashfullughát.*

attendants are guided, as circumstances require it; and from the wise counsels they receive, they soon state their wishes openly. They learn to satisfy their thirst in the spring of divine favour, and gain for their wisdom and motives renewed light. Others, according to their capacities, are taught wisdom in excellent advices.

But it is impossible while speaking of other matters besides, to give a full account of the manner in which His Majesty teaches wisdom, heals dangerous diseases, and applies remedies for the severest sufferings. Should my occupations allow sufficient leisure, and should another term of life be granted me, it is my intention to lay before the world a separate volume on this subject.

In another part of his work Abulfazl writes (Book I, Ain 18, p. 48):

His Majesty maintains that it is a religious duty and divine praise to worship fire and light; surly, ignorant men consider it forgetfulness of the Almighty, and fire-worship. But the deep-sighted know better. . . . There can be nothing improper in the veneration of that exalted element which is the source of man's existence, and of the duration of life; nor should base thoughts enter such a matter. . . . If light and fire did not exist, we should be destitute of food and medicines; the power of sight would be of no avail to the eyes. The fire of the sun is the torch of God's sovereignty.

And again (Book I, Ain 72, p. 154):

Ardently feeling after God, and searching for truth, His Majesty exercises upon himself both inward and outward austerities, though he occasionally joins public worship, in order to hush the slandering tongues of the bigots of the present age. But the great object of his life is the acquisition of that sound morality, the sublime loftiness of which captivates the hearts of thinking sages, and silences the taunts of zealots and sectarians.

The following is an account of Akbar's literary labours (Book I, Ain 34, p. 103):

His Majesty's library is divided into several parts; . . . prose books, poetical works, Hindi, Persian, Greek, Kashmirian, Arabic, are all separately placed. Experienced readers bring them daily and read them before His Majesty. He does not get tired of hearing a book over again, but listens to the reading of it with more interest.

Philologists are constantly engaged in translating Hindi, Greek, Arabic, and Persian books into other languages. Thus a part of the Zich i Jadíd i Mírzáí was translated under the superintendence of Amír Fathullah of Shiráz, and also the Kishnjóshí, the Gangádhar, the Mohesh Mahánand, from Hindi (Sanskrit) into Persian, according to the interpretation of the author of this book[1]. The Mahábhárat which belongs to the ancient books of Hindústán has likewise been translated, from Hindi into Persian, under the superintendence of Nagíb Khán, Mauláná 'Abdul Qádir of Badáon, and Shaik Sultán of Thanésar. . . . The same learned men translated into Persian the Rámáyan, likewise a book of ancient Hindustan, which contains the life of Rám Chandra, but is full of interesting points of philosophy. Hájí Ibráhím of Sirhind[2] translated into Persian the At'harban which, accord-

[1] This can hardly be quite right, for these names are the names of the assistants of Fathullah, viz. Kishan Jaïçí, Gangádhar, Mahaïs (Maheça). and Mahánand; see Garcin de Tassy, 'Histoire de la Littérature Hindouie.' M. M.

[2] Badáoní says 'that a learned Brahmin, Shaikh Bháwan, who had turned Muhammadan, was ordered to translate the Atharban for him, but that, as he could not translate all the passages, Shaikh Faizi and Hájí Ibráhím were commanded to translate the book. The latter, though willing, did not write anything. Among the precepts of the At'harban there is one which says that no man will be saved unless he read a certain passage. This passage contains many times the letter l, and resembles very much our Lá illah illallah. Besides, I found that a Hindú, under certain conditions, may eat cow flesh; and another, that

ing to Hindús, is one of the four divine books. The Líla-
watí, which is one of the most excellent works written by
Indian mathematicians on Arithmetic, lost its Hindú veil,
and received a Persian garb from the hand of my elder
brother, Shaikh 'Abdul Faiz i Faizí. At the command of His
Majesty, Mukammal Khán of Gujrát, translated into Persian
the Tájak, a well known work on Astronomy. . . . The
history of Kashmír, which extends over the last four thousand
years, has been translated from Kashmirian into Persian by
Mauláná Sháh Muhammad of Sháhábád. (It was rewritten
by Badáoní in an easier style.) . . . The Haribans, a book
containing the life of Krishna, was translated into Persian
by Mauláná Sherí. By order of His Majesty, the author of
this volume composed a new version of the Kalílah Damnah,
and published it under the title of 'Ayár Danish. . . . The
Hindi story of the Love of Nal and Daman has been metri-
cally translated by my brother, Shaikh Faizí.

We must now look at the other side of the picture, though,
I confess, that even the hostile statements of Badáoní and his
party only confirm the impression of Akbar's character produced by the friendly account of Abulfazl.

When speaking of Abulfazl, Badáoní says :

He lighted up the lamp of the Çabáhís, illustrating thereby
the story of the man who, because he did not know what to
do, took up a lamp in broad daylight, and representing himself as opposed to all sects, tied the girdle of infallibility
round his waist, according to the saying, ' He who forms an
opposition, gains power.' He laid before the emperor a

Hindús bury their dead, but do not burn them. With such passages
the Shaikh used to defeat other Brahmins in argument ; and they had
in fact led him to embrace Islám. Let us praise God for his conversion.' See also ' Lectures on the Scien e of Language,' vol. i.
p. 169.

commentary on the *A'yat ul-kursí*, which contained all subtleties of the Qorán; and though people said it had been written by his father, Abulfazl was much praised. The numerical value of the letters in the words *Tafsír i Akbarí* (Akbar's commentary) gives the date of composition [983]. But the emperor praised it, chiefly because he expected to find in Abulfazl a man capable of teaching the Mullás a lesson, whose pride certainly resembles that of Pharaoh, though this expectation was opposed to the confidence which His Majesty had placed in me.

The reason of Abulfazl's opinionativeness and pretensions to infallibility was this. At the time when it was customary to get hold of and kill such as tried to introduce innovations in religious matters (as had been the case with Mír Habshí and others), Shaikh 'Abdunnabí and Makhdúm ul mulk, and other learned men at court, unanimously represented to the emperor that Shaikh Mubárik also, in as far as he pretended to be *Mahdí*, belonged to the class of innovators, and was not only himself damned, but led others into damnation. Having obtained a sort of permission to remove him, they despatched police officers to bring him before the emperor. But when they found that the Shaikh, with his two sons, had concealed himself, they demolished the pulpit in his prayer-room. The Shaikh, at first, took refuge with Salím i Chishtí at Fathpúr, who then was in the height of his glory, and requested him to intercede for him. Shaikh Salím, however, sent him money by some of his disciples, and told him it would be better for him to go away to Gujrát. Seeing that Salím took no interest in him, Shaikh Mubárik applied to Mírzá 'Azíz Kokah [Akbar's foster-brother], who took occasion to praise to the emperor the Shaikh's learning and voluntary poverty, and the superior talents of his two sons, adding that Mubárik was a most trustworthy man, that he had never received lands as a present, and that he ['Azíz] could really not see why the Shaikh was so much persecuted. The emperor at last gave up all thoughts of killing the Shaikh. In a short time matters took a more favourable turn; and Abulfazl, when once in favour with the emperor (officious as he was, and time-serving, openly faithless, continually studying His Majesty's whims, a flatterer beyond all bounds) took every opportunity of reviling in the most shameful way that sect whose labours and motives have been so little appreciated[1], and became the cause not only of the extirpation of these experienced people, but also of the ruin of all servants of God, especially of Shaikhs, pious men, of the helpless, and the orphans, whose livings and grants he cut down.

Then follows Badáoní's account of the origin of the religious and philosophical disputations at the emperor's court :

During the year 983 A.H., many places of worship were built at the command of His Majesty. The cause was this. For many years previous to 983, the emperor had gained in succession remarkable and decisive victories. The empire had grown in extent from day to day; everything turned out well, and no opponent was left in the whole world. His Majesty had thus leisure to come into nearer contact with ascetics and the disciples of the Mu'íniyyah sect, and passed much of his time in discussing the word of God (Qorán), and the word of the prophet (the *Hadís*, or Tradition). Questions of Çúfism, scientific discussions, enquiries into Philosophy and Law, were the order of the day. His Majesty passed whole nights in thoughts of God: he continually occupied himself with pronouncing the names *Yá hú* and *Yá hádí*, which had been mentioned to him[2], and his heart was full of reverence

---

[1] Badáoní belonged to the believers in the approach of the Millennium. A few years later, Akbar used Mahdawí rumours for his own purposes; *vide* below. The extract shows that there existed, before 982, heretical innovators, whom the emperor allowed to be persecuted. Matters soon took a different turn.

[2] By some ascetic. *Yá hú* means O He (God), and *Yá hádí*, O

for Him who is the true Giver. From a feeling of thankfulness for his past successes, he would sit many a morning alone in prayer and melancholy, on a large flat stone of an old building which lay near the palace in a lonely spot, with his head bent over his chest, and gathering the bliss of early hours.

For these discussions, which were held every Thursday[1] night, His Majesty invited the Sayyids, Shaikhs, 'Ulamás, and grandees, by turn. But as the guests generally commenced to quarrel about their places, and the order of precedence, His Majesty ordered that the grandees should sit on the east side ; the Sayyids on the west side ; the 'Ulamás to the south ; and the Shaikhs to the north. The emperor then used to go from one side to the other, and make his enquiries . . ., when all at once, one night, the vein of the neck of the 'Ulamás of the age swelled up, and a horrid noise and confusion ensued. His Majesty got very angry at their rude behaviour, and said to me [Badáoní], 'In future report any of the 'Ulamás that cannot behave and talks nonsense, and I shall make him leave the hall.' I gently said to Áçaf Khán, 'If I were to carry out this order, most of the 'Ulamás would have to leave,' when His Majesty suddenly asked what I had said. On hearing my answer he was highly pleased, and mentioned my remark to those sitting near him.

At one of the above-mentioned meetings, His Majesty asked how many *freeborn* women a man was legally allowed to marry (by *nikáh*). The lawyers answered that four was the limit fixed by the prophet. The emperor thereupon remarked that from the time he had come of age, he had not restricted himself to that number, and in justice to his wives, of whom he had a large number, both freeborn and slaves, he

---

Guide. The frequent repetition of such names is a means of knowledge. Some faqírs repeat them several thousand times during a night.

[1] The text has *Shab i Jum'ah*, the night of Friday ; but as Muhammadans commence the day at sunset, it is our *Thursday* night.

now wanted to know what remedy the law provided for his case. Most expressed their opinions, when the emperor remarked that Shaikh 'Abdunnabí had once told him that one of the Mujtahids had had as many as nine wives. Some of the 'Ulamás present replied that the Mujtahid alluded to was Ibn Abí Laila; and that some had even allowed eighteen from a too literal translation of the Qorán verse (Qor. Sur. IV. 3), 'Marry whatever women ye like, two and two[1], and three and three, and four and four;' but this was improper. His Majesty then sent a message to Shaikh 'Abdunnabí, who replied that he had merely wished to point out to Akbar that a difference of opinion existed on this point among lawyers, but that he had not given a *fatwa*, in order to legalize irregular marriage proceedings. This annoyed His Majesty very much. 'The Shaikh,' he said, 'told me at that time a very different thing from what he now tells me.' He never forgot this.

After much discussion on this point, the 'Ulamás, having collected every tradition on the subject, decreed, *first*, that by *Mut'ah* [not by *nikáh*] a man might marry any number of wives he pleased; and *secondly*, that *Mut'ah* marriages were allowed by Imám Málik. The Shí'ahs, as was well known, loved children born in *Mut'ah* wedlock more than those born by *nikáh* wives, contrary to the Sunnís and the Ahl i Jamá'at.

On the latter point also the discussion got rather lively, and I would refer the reader to my work entitled *Najáturra-shíd*, in which the subject is briefly discussed. But to make things worse, Naqíb Khán fetched a copy of the *Muwatta*

---

[1] Thus they got 2 + 2, 3 + 3, 4 + 4 = 18. But the passage is usually translated, 'Marry whatever women ye like, two, or three, or four.' The Mujtahid who took nine unto himself, translated ' two + three + four,' = 9. The question of the emperor was most ticklish, because, if the lawyers adhered to the number four, which they could not well avoid, the *harámzádagí* of Akbar's *freeborn* princesses was acknowledged.

of Imám Málik, and pointed to a tradition in the book, which Imám had cited as a proof against the legality of *Mut'ah* marriages.

Another night, Qází Ya'qúb, Shaikh Abulfazl, Hájí Ibráhím, and a few others were invited to meet His Majesty in the house near the *Anúptaláo* tank. Shaikh Abulfazl had been selected as the opponent, and laid before the emperor several traditions regarding *Mut'ah* marriages, which his father (Shaikh Mubárik) had collected, and the discussion commenced. His Majesty then asked me, what my opinion was on this subject. I said, 'The conclusion which must be drawn from so many contradictory traditions and sectarian customs, is this:—Imám Málik and the Shí'ahs are unanimous in looking upon *Mut'ah* marriages as legal; Imám Sháfi'í and the Great Imám (Hanífah) look upon *Mut'ah* marriages as illegal. But, should at any time a Qází of the Málikí sect decide that *Mut'ah* is legal, it is legal, according to the common belief, even for Sháfi'ís and Hanafís. Every other opinion on this subject is idle talk.' This pleased His Majesty very much.

The emperor then said, 'I herewith appoint the Málikí Qází Husain 'Arab as the Qází before whom I lay this case concerning my wives, and you, Ya'qúb, are from to-day suspended.' This was immediately obeyed, and Qází Hasan, on the spot, gave a decree which made *Mut'ah* marriages legal.

The veteran lawyers, as Makhdúm ul mulk, Qází Ya'qúb, and others, made very long faces at these proceedings.

This was the commencement of 'their sere and yellow leaf.'

The result was that, a few days later, Maulúná Jaláluddín of Multán, a profound and learned man, whose grant had been transferred, was ordered from Ágrah (to Fathpúr Síkrí,) and appointed Qází of the realm. Qází Ya'qúb was sent to Gaur as District Qází.

From this day henceforth, 'the road of opposition and difference in opinion' lay open, and remained so till His Majesty
was appointed Mujtahid of the empire.

During this year [983], there arrived Hakím Abulfath,
Hakím Humáyún (who subsequently changed his name to
Humáyún Qulí, and lastly to Hakím Humám), and Núruddín,
who as poet is known under the name of *Qarárí*. They
were brothers, and came from Gílán, near the Caspian Sea.
The eldest brother, whose manners and address were exceed-
ing winning, obtained in a short time great ascendency over
the emperor; he flattered him openly, adapted himself to
every change in the religious ideas of His Majesty, or even
went in advance of them, and thus became in a short time a
most intimate friend of Akbar.

Soon after there came from Persia Mullá Muhammad of
Yazd, who got the nickname of Yazídí, and attaching himself to the emperor, commenced openly to revile the *Çahábah*
(persons who knew Muhammad, except the twelve Imáms),
told queer stories about them, and tried hard to make the
emperor a Shí'ah. But he was soon left behind by Bír Bar
—that bastard!—and by Shaikh Abulfazl, and Hakím Abulfath, who successfully turned the emperor from the Islám,
and led him to reject inspiration, prophetship, the miracles
of the prophet and of the saints, and even the whole law, so
that I could no longer bear their company.

At the same time, His Majesty ordered Qází Jaláluddín
and several 'Ulamás to write a commentary on the Qorán;
but this led to great rows among them.

Soon after, the observance of the five prayers and the fasts,
and the belief in every thing connected with the prophet,
were put down as *taqlídí*, or religious blindness, and man's
reason was acknowledged to be the basis of all religion.
Portuguese priests also came frequently; and His Majesty
enquired into the articles of their belief which are based
upon reason.

His Majesty till now [986] had shown every sincerity, and was diligently searching for truth. But his education had been much neglected ; and surrounded as he was by men of low and heretical principles, he had been forced to doubt the truth of the Islám. Falling from one perplexity into the other, he lost sight of his real object, the search of truth ; and when the strong embankment of our clear law and our excellent faith had once been broken through, His Majesty grew colder and colder, till after the short space of five or six years not a trace of Muhammadan feeling was left in his heart. Matters then became very different.

The following are the principal reasons which led His Majesty from the right path. I shall not give all, but only some, according to the proverb, 'That which is small, guides to that which is great, and a sign of fear in a man points him out as the culprit.'

The principal reason is the large number of learned men of all denominations and sects that came from various countries to court, and received personal interviews. Night and day people did nothing but inquire and investigate; profound points of science, the subtleties of revelation, the curiosities of history, the wonders of nature, of which large volumes could only give a summary abstract, were ever spoken of. His Majesty collected the opinions of every one, especially of such as were not Muhammadans, retaining whatever he approved of, and rejecting everything which was against his disposition, and ran counter to his wishes. From his earliest childhood to his manhood, and from his manhood to old age, His Majesty has passed through the most various phases and through all sorts of religious practices and sectarian beliefs, and has collected everything which people can find in books, with a talent of selection peculiar to him, and a spirit of inquiry opposed to every [Islámitic] principle. Thus a faith based on some elementary principles traced itself on the mirror of his heart, and as the result of all the influences

which were brought to bear on His Majesty, there grew
gradually, as the outline on a stone, the conviction in his
heart that there *were sensible men in all religions, and ab-
stemious thinkers, and men endowed with miraculous powers,
among all nations.*   If some true knowledge was thus everywhere to be found, why should truth be confined to one religion, or a creed like the Islám, which was comparatively
new, and scarcely a thousand years old? why should one
sect assert what another denies? and why should one claim
a preference without having superiority conferred on itself?

Moreover Sumanís[1] and Brahmins managed to get frequent
private interviews with His Majesty.   As they surpass other
learned men in their treatises on morals, and on physical
and religious sciences, and reach a high degree in their
knowledge of the future, in spiritual power and human perfection, they brought proofs, based on reason and testimony,
for the truth of their own, and the fallacies of other religions,
and inculcated their doctrines so firmly, and so skilfully
represented things as quite self-evident which require consideration, that no man, by expressing his doubts, could now
raise a doubt in His Majesty, even if mountains were to
crumble to dust, or the heavens were to tear asunder.

Hence His Majesty cast aside the Islámitic revelations
regarding resurrection, the day of judgment, and the details
connected with it, as also all ordinances based on the tradition of our prophet.   He listened to every abuse which
the courtiers heaped on our glorious and pure faith, which
can be so easily followed; and eagerly seizing such oppor-
tunities, he showed, in words and gestures, his satisfaction at
the treatment which his original religion received at their
hands.

[1] Explained in Arab. Dictionaries as a sect in Sind who believe in
the transmigration of souls (*tanásukh*). Akbar, as will be seen from the
following, was convinced of the transmigration of souls, and therefore
rejected the doctrine of resurrection.
   [Is not Sumaní here meant for Samana, i. e. *Sramana*?—M. M.

How wise was the advice which the guardian gave a lovely being,

'Do not smile at every face, as the rose does at every zephyr [1].'

When it was too late to profit by the lesson,

She could but frown, and hang down the head.

For some time His Majesty called a Brahmin, whose name was Puzukhotam [2], author of a commentary on the . . . [3], whom he asked to invent particular Sanskrit names for all things in existence. At other times, a Brahmin of the name of Debí was pulled up the wall of the castle [4], sitting on a *chárpái*, till he arrived near a balcony where the emperor used to sleep. Whilst thus suspended, he instructed His Majesty in the secrets and legends of Hinduism, in the manner of worshipping idols, the fire, the sun and stars, and of revering the chief gods of these unbelievers, as Brahma, Mahádev, Bishn, Kishn, Rám, and Mahámáí, who are supposed to have been men, but very likely never existed, though some, in their idle belief, look upon them as gods, and others as angels. His Majesty, on hearing further how much the people of the country prized their institutions, commenced to look upon them with affection. The doctrine of the transmigration of souls especially took a deep root in his heart, and he approved of the saying, 'There is no religion in which the doctrine of transmigration has not taken firm root.' Insincere flatterers composed treatises, in order to fix the evidence for this doctrine; and as His Majesty relished inquiries into the sects of these infidels (who cannot be counted, so numerous they are,

[1] Just as Akbar liked the zephyr of inquiry into other religious systems. But zephyrs are also destructive; they scatter the petals of the rose.

[2] [Probably Purushottama.—M. M.]

[3] The text has a few unintelligible words.

[4] Perhaps in order not to get polluted, or because the balcony belonged to the Harem.

and who have no end of revealed books, but nevertheless, do not belong to the *Ahl i Kitáb* (Jews, Christians, and Muhammadans), not a day passed, but a new fruit of this loathsome tree ripened into existence.

Sometimes again, it was *Shaikh Tájuddín* of Dihlí, who had to attend the emperor. This Shaikh is the son of Shaikh Zakariyá of Adjodhan. The principal 'Ulamás of the age call him *Tájul' árifín*, or crown of the Çúfís. He had learned under Shaikh Zamán of Pánípat, author of a commentary on the Lawáih, and of other very excellent works, was in Çúfism and pantheism second only to Shaikh Ibn 'Arabí, and had written a comprehensive commentary on the *Nuzhat ularwáh*. Like the preceding he was drawn up the wall of the castle. His Majesty listened whole nights to his Çúfic trifles. As the Shaikh was not overstrict [1] in acting according to our religious law, he spoke a great deal of the pantheistic presence, which idle Çúfís will talk about, and which generally leads them to denial of the law and open heresy. He also introduced polemic matters, as the ultimate salvation by faith of Pharaoh—God's curse be upon him!—which he mentioned in the *Fuçúç ulhikam* [2], or the excellence of hope over fear [3], and many other things to which men incline from weakness of disposition, unmindful of cogent reasons, or distinct religious commands, to the contrary. The Shaikh is therefore one of the principal culprits, who weakened His Majesty's faith in the orders of our religion. He also said that infidels would,

---

[1] As long as a Çúfí conforms to the Qorán, he is *shar'í;* but when he feels that he has drawn nearer to God, and does no longer require the ordinances of the *profanum vulgus*, he is *dzád*, free, and becomes a heretic.

[2] Pharaoh claimed divinity, and is therefore *mal'ún*, accursed by God. But according to some books, and among them the Fuçúç, Pharaoh repented in the moment of death, and acknowledged Moses a true prophet.

[3] The Islám says, *Alimán baina-l khaufi warrijá,* 'Faith stands *between* fear and hope.' Hence it is sin to fear God's wrath more than to hope for God's mercy ; and so reversely.

of course, be kept for ever in hell, but it was not likely, nor could it be proved, *that the punishment in hell was eternal.* His explanation of some verses of the Qorán, or of the tradition of our prophet, were often far-fetched. Besides, he mentions that the phrase *'Insán i kámil* (perfect man) referred to the ruler of the age, from which he inferred that the nature of a king was holy. In this way, he said many agreeable things to the emperor, rarely expressing the proper meaning, but rather the opposite of what he knew to be correct. Even the *sijdah* (prostration), which people mildly call *zamínbos* (kissing the ground), he allowed to be due to the Insán i kámil; he looked upon the respect due to the king as a religious command, and called the face of the king *Ka'bah i Murádát*, the sanctum of desires, and *Qiblah i Hájat*, the cynosure of necessities. Such blasphemies [1] other people supported by quoting stories of no credit, and by referring to the practice followed by disciples of some heads of Indian sects.

Learned monks also came from Europe, who go by the name of *Pádre* [2]. They have an infallible head, called *Pápá*. He can change any religious ordinances as he may think advisable, and kings have to submit to his authority. These monks brought the gospel, and mentioned to the emperor their proofs for the Trinity. His Majesty firmly believed in the truth of the Christian religion, and wishing to spread the doctrines of Jesus, ordered Prince Murád [3] to take a few

[1] As the *zamínbos*, or the use of holy names as *Ka'bah* (the temple at Makkah) or *qiblah* (Makkah), in as far as people turn to it their face when praying.

[2] Rodolpho Aquaviva, called by Abulfazl, Pádrí Radalf, Antonio de Monserrato, Francisco Enriques.

[3] Prince Murád was then about eight years old. Jahángír (Salím) was born on Wednesday, the 17th Rabí'ulawwal 977. Three months after him, his sister *Shahzádah Khánum* was born; and after her (perhaps in the year 978) *Sháh Murád*, who got the nickname of *Pahári*, as he was born in the hills of Fathpúr Síkrí. Dányál was

lessons in Christianity by way of auspiciousness, and charged Abulfazl to translate the Gospel. Instead of the usual *Bismilláh-irrahman-irrahím*[1], the following lines were used—

> *Ai nám i tu Jesus o Kiristo*
>
> (O thou whose names are Jesus and Christ)

which means, 'O thou whose name is gracious and blessed;' Shaikh Faizí added another half, in order to complete the verse

> *Subhánaka lá siwáka Yá hú.*

(We praise Thee, there is no one besides Thee, O God!)

These accursed monks applied the description of cursed Satan, and of his qualities, to Muhammad, the best of all prophets—God's blessings rest on him and his whole house! —a thing which even devils would not do.

Bír Bar also impressed upon the emperor that the sun was the primary origin of everything. The ripening of the grain on the fields, of fruits and vegetables, the illumination of the universe, and the lives of men, depended upon the sun. Hence it was but proper to worship and reverence this luminary; and people in praying should face towards the place where he rises, instead of turning to the quarter where he sets. For similar reasons, said Bír Bar, should men pay regard to fire and water, stones, trees, and other forms of

---

born in Ajmír during the night between Tuesday and Wednesday, the 10th Jumádalawwal 979.

[1] The formula ' *Bismilláh, &c.*' is said by every schoolboy before he commences to read from his text book.

The words *Ai nám i tu Jesus o Kiristo* are taken from the Dabistán; the edition of Badáoní has *Ai námí wai zhazho Kiristo*, which, though correct in metre (*vide* my 'Prosody of the Persians,' p. 33, No. 32), is improbable. The formula as given in the Dabistán has a common Masnawí metre (*vide* my 'Prosody,' p. 33, No. 31), and spells *Jesus* ديزز *dezuz*. The verse as given by H. H. Wilson ('Works,' ii. p. 387) has no metre.

existence, even to cows and their dung, to the mark on the forehead and the Brahminical thread.

Philosophers and learned men who had been at Court, but were in disgrace, made themselves busy in bringing proofs. They said, the sun was 'the greatest light,' the origin of royal power.

Fire-worshippers also had come from Nausárí in Gujrát, and proved to His Majesty the truth of Zoroaster's doctrines. They called fire-worship 'the great worship,' and impressed the emperor so favourably, that he learned from them the religious terms and rites of the old Pársís, and ordered Abulfazl to make arrangements, that sacred fire should be kept burning at Court by day and by night, according to the custom of the ancient Persian kings, in whose fire-temples it had been continually burning; for fire was one of the manifestations of God, and 'a ray of His rays.'

His Majesty, from his youth, had also been accustomed to celebrate the *Hom* (a kind of fire-worship), from his affection towards the Hindu princesses of his Harem.

From the New Year's day of the twenty-fifth year of his reign [988], His Majesty openly worshipped the sun and the fire by prostrations; and the courtiers were ordered to rise, when the candles and lamps were lighted in the palace. On the festival of the eighth day of Virgo, he put on the mark on the forehead, like a Hindu, and appeared in the Audience Hall, when several Brahmins tied, by way of auspiciousness, a string with jewels on it round his hands, whilst the grandees countenanced these proceedings by bringing, according to their circumstances, pearls and jewels as presents. The custom of Rák'hí (or tying pieces of clothes round the wrists as amulets) became quite common.

When orders, in opposition to the Islám, were quoted by people of other religions, they were looked upon by His Majesty as convincing, whilst Hinduism is in reality a religion in which every order is nonsense. The Originator of our belief, the Arabian Saints, all were said to be adulterers, and highway robbers, and all the Muhammadans were declared worthy of reproof, till at length His Majesty belonged to those of whom the Qorán says (Sur. 61, 8): 'They seek to extinguish God's light with their mouths: but God will perfect his light, though the infidels be averse thereto.' In fact matters went so far, that proofs were no longer required when anything connected with the Islám was to be abolished.

After Makhdúm ul mulk and Shaikh 'Abdunnabí had left for Makkah (987), the emperor examined people about the creation of the Qorán, elicited their belief, or otherwise, in revelation, and raised doubts in them regarding all things connected with the prophet and the imáms. He distinctly denied the existence of *Jins*, of angels, and of all other beings of the invisible world, as well as the miracles of the prophet and the saints; he rejected the successive testimony of the witnesses of our faith, the proofs for the truths of the Qorán as far as they agree with man's reason, the existence of the soul after the dissolution of the body, and future rewards and punishments in as far as they differed from metempsychosis.

In this year, Shaikh Mubárik of Nágor said in the presence of the emperor of Bír Bar, 'Just as there are interpolations in your holy books, so there are many in ours (Qorán); hence it is impossible to trust either.'

Some shameless and ill-starred wretches also asked His Majesty, why, at the approaching close of the Millennium, he did not make use of the sword, 'the most convincing proof,' as Sháh Ismá'il of Persia had done. But His Majesty, at last, was convinced that confidence in him as a leader was a matter of time and good counsel, and did not require the sword. And indeed, if His Majesty, in setting up his claims, and making his innovations, had spent a little money, he would have easily got most of the courtiers, and much more the vulgar, into his devilish nets.

At a council meeting for renovating the religion of the empire, Rájah Bhagawán said, 'I would willingly believe that Hindus and Musalmáns have each a bad religion; but only tell us where the new sect is, and what opinion they hold, so that I may believe.' His Majesty reflected a little, and ceased to urge the Rájah. But the alteration of the orders of our glorious faith was continued.

During those days also the public prayers and the *azán*, which was chanted five times a day for assembly to prayer in the statehall, were abolished. Names like *Ahmad, Muhammad, Muçtafa*, &c., became offensive to His Majesty, who thereby wished to please the infidels outside, and the princesses inside, the Harem, till, after some time, those courtiers who had such names, changed them; and names as *Yár Muhammad, Muhammad Khán*, were altered to *Rahmat*. To call such ill-starred wretches by the name of our blessed prophet would indeed be wrong, and there was not only room for improvement by altering their names, but it was even necessary to change them, according to the proverb, 'It is wrong to put fine jewels on the neck of a pig.'

In *Rabí'ussání* 990, Mír Fathullah came from the Dak'hin. * * * * As he had been an immediate pupil of Mír Ghiásuddín Mançúr of Shíráz, who had not been overstrict in religious matters, His Majesty thought that Fathullah would only be too glad to enter into his religious scheme. But Fathullah was such a stanch Shí'ah, and at the same time such a worldly office-hunter, and such a worshipper of mammon and of the nobility, that he would not give up a jot of the tittles of bigoted Shí'ism. Even in the statehall he said, with the greatest composure, his Shí'ah prayers—a thing which no one else would have dared to do. His Majesty, therefore, put him among the class of the bigots; but he connived at his practices, because he thought it desirable to encourage a man of such attainments and practical knowledge. Once the emperor, in Fathullah's presence [1], said to Bír Baŗ, 'I really wonder how any one in his senses can believe that a man, whose body has a certain weight, could, in the space of a moment, leave his bed, go up to heaven, there have 90,000 conversations with God, and yet on his return find his bed still warm?' So also was the splitting of the moon ridiculed. 'Why,' said His Majesty, lifting up one foot, 'it is really impossible for me to lift up the other foot! What silly stories men will believe.' And that wretch (Bír Baŗ) and some other wretches—whose names be forgotten—said, 'Yea, we believe! Yea, we trust!' This great foot-experiment was repeated over and over again. But Fathullah—His Majesty had been every moment looking at him, because he wanted him to say something; for he was a new-comer— looked straight before himself, and did not utter a syllable, though he was all ear.

Lastly, a few passages from the Dabistán [2].

Salámullah also said that God's Representative (Akbar) had often wept and said, 'O that my body were larger than all bodies together, so that the people of the world could feed on it without hurting other living animals!'

A sign of the sagacity of this king is this, that he employed in his service people of all classes, Jews, Persians, Túránís, &c., because one class of people, if employed to the exclusion

---

[1] As Fathullah was a good mechanic, Akbar thought that by referring to the weight of a man, and the following experiment with his foot, he would induce Fathullah to make a remark on the prophet's ascension (mi'ráj).

[2] The Dabistán, ascribed to Mohsan Fáni, who lived in the 17th century, during the reign of the Emperor Jehangír (1605-1628), Shah Jehan (1628-1659), and Aurengzeb (1659-1707). English translation by A. Troyer, Paris, 1843.

of others, would cause rebellions, as in the case of the Uzbaks and Qizilbáshes (Persians), who used to dethrone their kings. Hence Sháh 'Abbás, son of Sultán Khudábandah i Çafawí, imitated the practice of Akbar, and favoured the Gurjís (Georgians). Akbar paid likewise no regard to hereditary power, or genealogy and fame, but favoured those whom he thought to excel in knowledge and manners.

PAGE 40.

ON THE LANGUAGES OF AFRICA.

THE following review of Professor Lepsius' 'Nubische Grammatik' (*Times*, 29 Dec. 1880), gives an account of that scholar's latest views on the languages and population of Africa.

Whatever may have been written of late about the decadence of the German Universities, and particularly that of Berlin, the stars that once gave lustre to that name have not yet set, nor does it seem, to judge from late publications, that they have lost their former brilliancy. There are not many Universities in any country that count among their professors so many stars of the first magnitude as Berlin; and, what is most extraordinary, though men like Lepsius, Mommsen, E. Curtius, Zeller, Helmholtz, to speak of the Philosophical Faculty only, have all passed the meridian of life, their power of work, and of creative work, too, seems undiminished. Professor Lepsius is 70 years old, yet he has just brought out a work which would have taxed to the utmost the powers of younger men, and which is full, not only of facts carefully collected, but of theories that will startle many of his readers, and set them thinking and, we hope, working. In publishing his long-expected 'Nubian Grammar,' a volume of more than 600 pages, Professor Lepsius has added an Introduction which, though smaller in extent, is by far the weightiest portion of the book. It gives the results of his long-continued studies of all, or nearly all, the languages of Africa, and lays down at the same time general principles which affect the highest interests of the science of language. While most comparative philologists just now are absorbed in *minutiae* concerning the character and possible dialectic varieties of single vowels and consonants, Professor Lepsius draws in bold strokes the broad outlines of a history of language running through 4000 or 5000 years, and covering the whole continent of Africa and the neighbouring coast of Asia. As the admirers of Gerard Douw shake their heads at the vast canvas covered by Paolo Veronese, we can well understand that scholars engaged in the question whether the Aryan language possessed originally four or five different a's should turn away with a kind of shudder from pages in which languages which share hardly one single word in common, and agree grammatically in nothing but the fact that they distinguish the two genders of nouns are classed as of common origin. Fortunately, there is room both for Gerard Douws and Paolo Veroneses in the science of language; nay, in the interest of that science it is sincerely to be wished that both styles should always be cultivated side by side. There is plenty of rough work to be done among the unexplored languages of the world, and for that work the keen, far-reaching eye of the hunter is far more essential than the concentrated intensity of the linguistic microscopist.

While the latest researches in African philology had tended to the admission of an ever-increasing number of independent families of speech, Professor Lepsius, in a true Darwinian spirit, starts from the fundamental principle that there is but one aboriginal African language, and that the large number of local dialects scattered over the African continent is due to development, to a struggle for life against foreign intruders and the survival of the fittest. Before he attempts to establish this fact he has first to clear the ground of a number of what he considers prejudices which impede the progress both of linguistic and anthropological research.

Race and speech, he holds, must in some remote period have been identical. But that period is far beyond the reach of historical knowledge, and during what we call historic, and even pre-historic ages, languages and races have been destroyed, revived, and mixed up to such an extent that the two can no longer be used as commensurate terms. Races and languages must be classified independently of each other, and the classifications hitherto proposed, both by comparative anatomists and comparative philologists, are altogether inadequate. Dolichocephalic and brachycephalic tribes, for instance, are found among all races, nor are the peculiarities of the hair, even if they had been more carefully ascertained, which, as Professor Lepsius shows, they have not, a sufficient foundation for a truly scientific classification. Friedrich Müller and Häckel, relying on trichological and glottological indications, have lately proposed a division of the human race into 12 races, and of language into 100 families. But Lepsius shows the insecurity of the ground on which they rest, by proving, for instance, on the authority of A. B. Meyer, the absence of *Büschelhaar* among the Papuas, and the complete divergence of the grammars of the Hottentots and Papuas, which Friedrich Müller felt inclined to refer to one and the same class (pp. x., lxxi.).

According to Lepsius there is physically but one negro type, varying in shades of colour, according to fixed thermal lines, generally dolichocephalic, prognathic, with eyes widely distant, noses flat, lips full, hair woolly and crisp, and everywhere distinguished by a marked proclivity of gait. Bushmen and Hottentots are not excluded from this general definition, and all local peculiarities of the autochthonic tribes of Africa are explained as mere varieties. Instead of the ordinary division of African races into (1) the Northern and blackest tribes; (2) the Pul and Nuba tribes, scattered among the former; (3) the Kafir or Bântu tribes, south of the Equator; (4) the Hottentots and Bushmen (even these two being treated as totally distinct by certain ethnologists), Professor Lepsius admits of three varieties only in one and the same original negro type—viz. (1) the Northern negroes; (2) the Southern or Bântu negroes; (3) the Cape negroes. He then groups all African languages also into three zones—(1) the Southern, south of the Equator, the Bântu dialects, explored chiefly on the west and east coasts, but probably stretching across the whole continent, comprising the Hereró, Pongue, Fernando Po, Kafir ('Osa and Zulu), Tshuana (Soto and Rolon), Suahili, &c.; (2) the Northern zone, between the Equator and Sahara, and east as far as the Nile, comprising Efik, Ibo, Yoruba, Ewe, Akra or Ga, Otyi, Kru, Vei (Mande), Temne, Bullom, Wolof, Fula, Sonrhai, Kanuri, Teda (Tibu), Logone, Wandala, Bagirmi, Mâba, Konjâra, Umâle, Dinka, Shilluk, Bongo, Bari, Oigob, Nuba, and Barea; (3) the Hamitic zone, including the extinct Egyptian and Coptic, the Libyan dialects, such as Tuareg (Kabyl and Amasheg), Hausa, the Kushitic or Ethiopian languages, including the Beja dialects, the Soho, Falasha, Agau, Galla, Dankali, and Somali. The Hottentot and Bushman languages are referred to the same zone.

The Hamitic languages comprised in the third zone, the Egyptian, Libyan, and Kushitic, are considered by Lepsius as alien to Africa. They are all intruders from the East, though reaching Africa at different times and by different roads. The true aboriginal nucleus of African speech is contained in the first zone, and represented by that class of languages which, on account of their strongly marked grammatical character, has been called the Bântu family. Professor Lepsius attempts to show that the languages of the Northern zone are modifications of the same type which is represented in the Southern zone, these modifications being chiefly due to contact and more or less violent friction with languages belonging to the Hamitic zone, and, to a certain extent, with Semitic languages also.

This is an enormous undertaking, and Professor Lepsius would probably be the first to admit that, in the present imperfect state of our knowledge of many of these languages, his views are liable in the future to considerable modification. Still, as an attempt to show how much change is possible in a language without making it lose its own identity, his remarks deserve very careful consideration. The problem which he has discussed is of fundamental importance, and nowhere, perhaps, could it have been watched and tested to greater advantage than in the conflict between the Bântu and Hamitic families of speech, which differ from each other in many of the most essential points of grammatical articulation. To mention only a few, the Bântu languages are prefixing, the Hamitic suffixing, showing different angles of mental vision which it would seem impossible to bring together into the same focus. Bântu grammar admits of no gender, or, we should rather say, of no gender to denote sex; Hamitic grammar does. On this Professor Lepsius, following in the main the late Dr. Bleek, lays great stress, and he expresses his strong belief in an original Turanianism (p. xxiv.), out of which the Semitic, Hamitic, and Japhetic families of speech arose, all retaining the common feature of marking the feminine by a suffix, which in the Hamitic and Semitic families is the same, the 't,' while the Japhetic family replaced it by a variety of new terminations. What Professor Lepsius attempts to show is that the traces of gender or suffixes, and other grammatical features quite repugnant to the genius of the Bântu languages, can be explained by the greater or lesser amount of contact of the original African race with Hamitic and, in some cases, with Semitic neighbours. Even when every distinctive feature seems to be erased, Professor Lepsius is not disheartened, and he marks the foreign character of a new grammatical expedient with the same confidence with which an archæologist discovers the restored portions of an ancient statue. It would seem, if this view of the formation of the Northern African languages is right, that the grammatical structure of a language could no longer be held so inaccessible to foreign influences as all philosophic students of language have hitherto believed. Yet this is not quite so. On the contrary, the fact that these foreign influences can be detected as foreign and the outward changes accounted for as mere adaptations to outward necessities, shows that the science of language can and ought to distinguish between these new shoots and the old stem which, however barren in appearance, yet remains the only source of life, both for the new and the old growth. In fact, the problem of dialectic growth, which has hitherto been so strangely neglected by students of language, meets us on every page of this work, and not only as a theory, but in all its practical aspects. 'If you think my admissions with regard to the ancient changes of language too violent,' Professor Lepsius seems to say, 'look around you and see what is taking place under your very eyes, if you have but eyes to see. In and about Kordofan (p. xx.), where the dialects lie about piecemeal, the inhabitants of one mountain peak do not understand those of another, but learn to understand with great facility estranged or really strange tribes that have settled among them for a short time only.' This receptivity of language, and more particularly of the language of savage and nomadic tribes, for foreign influences is illustrated again and again in the course of Professor Lepsius's arguments. The power of mimicry is far greater among lower than among higher tribes, and it extends in the case of language even to purely grammatical turns. There are limits, however, even to this, and in one case, that of the Hausa language, Professor Lepsius is driven to admit that it cannot be classed as a Bântu or prefixing dialect modified by Hamitic neighbours, but that it is really a Hamitic, more especially a Libyan language, surrounded and modified by Bântu speech (p. xlix.)

By a similar process of reasoning he excludes the Hottentot language also from the African family, properly so called, and brings these people in the south in connexion with the Kushites in the north, from whom they were separated by the pressure of Bântu tribes, recovering the eastern territory that had for a time been wrested from them by Kushite invaders.

Startling as such a theory will appear, it is hardly less so than the view which Professor Lepsius takes of the language to which he has devoted his special attention, the Nubian. This language, spoken on the Nile, in the very midst of a Kushitic population, is, nevertheless, treated by him, not as Kushitic, but as Bântu, and the Nubian *physique*, though by a long continued intercourse hardly distinguishable in many places from the Egyptian, is traced back to its original African type among South Nubian tribes. On our maps Nubia generally extends south from the first cataract over the whole breadth between the Nile and the Red Sea as far as Habesh, south east beyond Chartum, south and south-west along the White Nile to the Bahr-el-Gazâl. Lepsius, though admitting the presence of scattered Nubian tribes in the south, more particularly about Kordofan and the neighbouring hills, fixes on the Nile as the natural frontier between the true Nubian, sometimes, though wrongly, called Berber, in the west, and Kushitic tribes coming from the east, these being represented by the modern Bejas as their most advanced post. What gives an additional interest to these Nubian tribes is that they alone among African races have something like a history, to be read on the monuments of their neighbours, the Egyptians. The Egyptian monuments distinguish from the earliest times between the red or brown Southern race and the negroes, who are called Nahasi. Among these the Uaua occupy a prominent place so far back as the third millennium before our era, and they are identified by Lepsius with the Nubians. Whether the so-called Nubian inscriptions which are found scattered over the country oc-

cupied by Nubian tribes, and beyond, so far as the confluence
of the White and the Blue Nile, are of Nubian or Kushite
origin has never been determined. These inscriptions have
their own alphabet, running from right to left, and considering that the words are divided, as they are in the
cuneiform inscriptions of Persia, there is no reason why we
should despair of seeing them deciphered before long. Professor Lepsius thinks that they are not Nubian, that is to
say, not negro, but Kushitic, and that the key to be applied
to their interpretation should be looked for in the Beja, and
not in the Nubian language.

Having once entered upon these remote periods of ethnic
rather than political history, Professor Lepsius adds a most
interesting chapter on another ancient race, the Kushites,
called in hieroglyphics, Kash or Kish. These Kushites are
separated from Egypt proper by the old intrusive negro
population, and, though closely connected with the Hamitic
occupants of the Nile valley, they had migrated, so Professor
Lepsius thinks, from Arabia by sea, without passing through
Egypt. Their original home was in Asia, and thence they
moved on in parallel columns with the ancestors of the
Egyptians and Libyans towards the west, followed after a
time by their old neighbours, the Semites. They occupied
the south of Arabia, and then passed on to the opposite coast
of Africa. They thus became the first great maritime
nation, extending their navigations over the Red Sea, the
Persian Gulf, and the Indian Ocean; they were, in fact,
according to Lepsius, the real ancestors of the Phœnicians.
The Phœnicians on the Mediterranean coast, though they
had adopted a Semitic language, were known to Herodotus
as emigrants from the coasts of the Red Sea, and in the
Bible the Canaanites are mentioned among the sons of
Kush; while in Egyptian monuments the Southern Kushites,
both on the African and Arabian coasts, are known by the
name of Puna—i. e. Pœni and Phœnicians, the red sailors of

the Red Sea, as distinguished from the Kefa, the Phœnician sailors of the Mediterranean. In Greek mythology Kepheus is used synonymously with Phœnix, the husband of Kassiopeia, the daughter of Arabos. These Kefa races, originally Kushitic, are traced by Professor Lepsius in Kepheis, the old name of Æthiopia, and in the Æthiopian Kephenes of Babylon, a town founded by Nimrod, the Kushite, 'the beginning of whose kingdom was Babel, and Erech, and Accad, and Calneh in the land of Shinar.' The Chaldæans of Babylon are called Kephenes by Hellanicus, while Kush (Ethiopia), compassed by the Gihon, must be in Mesopotamia, where Herodotus, too, knows of the country of the Kissians.

After thus tracing the presence of the Kushites in Asia, Arabia, Ethiopia, and Phœnicia, Professor Lepsius takes another step, and boldly declares the civilization of Babylon as the work of Kushite colonists, who carried the seeds of Egyptian culture back from Africa to Asia. This fact is represented in the legend of Oannes, the fishman—i. e. the sailor, from the Red Sea, who taught the Babylonians the arts of a civilized life. Rejecting as altogether fanciful the theory of a Turanian or Accadian civilization anterior to that of Babylon, Professor Lepsius holds that the hieroglyphics from which the cuneiform alphabets are derived were Egyptian, that the Babylonian astronomy was Egyptian, the Babylonian measures Egyptian, the Babylonian architecture Egyptian, their temples, pyramids, obelisks, all imperfect imitations of Egyptian models. Here the gauntlet has been thrown down to nearly the whole army of Babylonian scholars, and we may look forward before long to a lively combat between them and their bold assailant. It is a pity that Professor Lepsius should not have entered more fully into the grounds on which he bases his denial of an early Turanian or Accadian civilization in Mesopotamia. In fact, his Introduction, extending to 126 pages, contains materials that might have sufficed for many volumes. Many volumes have been written on the origin of the Hyksos, yet Professor Lepsius in only a few pages tries to decide the question, and makes them Kushites from Arabia. He speaks of the migrations, the inroads, the repulses, and the alliances of those early nations as if they had happened but yesterday, instead of four or five thousand years ago. He places implicit confidence in fragmentary notices which agree with his theories, sometimes forgetting the old rule that we should never be so much on our guard as when we meet with unexpected confirmations of our favourite notions. But, with all these reservations, we cannot but think that in this Introduction to his Nubian Grammar Professor Lepsius has given a new impulse, not only to African philology, but to a reconsideration of some of the most interesting problems of ancient ethnology, tradition, and history. That all his views will stand the test of time who would venture to say? One hundred years hence, ay, even much sooner it may be, the Nubian inscriptions, when deciphered, may tell a very different story of the colonization of the Upper Nile valley from that which Professor Lepsius has constructed out of Egyptian and Babylonian documents, Greek legends, and African grammars. The researches of Dr. Theophilus Hahn and Miss Lloyd on the Hottentot and Bushman dialects may supersede those of Dr. Bleek, and Livingstones and Nachtigalls of the future may discover remnants of African populations more ancient than any we know of at present. African philology and ethnology are in no danger as yet of becoming stationary, and those who are interested in them must be prepared to unlearn and to learn many things from year to year. This is exactly as it ought to be. Healthy life is impossible without a constant throwing off of what has been exhausted, and scientific progress is impossible without our leaving behind those that came before us, even though they were giants in their days. The bane of scientific life is to rest and be satisfied, and even a wrong theory is sometimes better than no theory at all. Professor

Lepsius might have repeated the old song of African philology, and no doubt he would have been applauded on all sides. Having thrown a firebrand into the peaceful kraal of African scholars, he will be attacked on all sides, criticized, and roundly abused. But he is old enough to know that what is true of private life holds true also of scientific life, 'Woe unto you when all men shall speak well of you! for so did their fathers to the false prophets.'

VEDIC LITERATURE.

The following Statistics on the Vedic Literature were communicated to the Asiatic Society of Bengal by Mr. J. Muir, 1846.

Name of Veda.	Name of Sakha.	Name and Extent of Sanhita in slokas or lines of 32 syllables each.	Name and Extent of Brâhmana.	Name of Commentator.	Extent of Commentary.	Remarks.
Rig-veda	1. Sâkala	12,000	Aitareya-Brâh. 5,000 in 8 pañgikas (sic)	On Sanhitâ, Mâdhava; On Brâhm., Mâdhava	100,000; 20,000	
	2. Bâshkala; 3. Sânkhâyana	... ... each 12,000	... ... each 5,000	Unknown	.'.	Not read at Benares.
White Yagur-veda	1. Mâdhyandina	Vâgasaneyi-S. 4,000	Satapatha, 14 kândas, 24,000	On Sanhitâ, Maht-dhara, and Uvata; On Brâhm., Mâdhava	12,000; 15,000; 60,000	There is also a commentary on the Brâhmana by Harihara-svâmin.
	2. Kânva	4,000	24,000	On Sanhitâ, Mâdhava; On Brâhm., Mâdhava	12,000; 55,000	
Black Yagur-veda	Taittirîya	Âpastamba-S. 9,000	5,000	On Sanhitâ, Mâdhava; On Brâhm., Mâdhava	30,000; 15,000	
Sâma-veda	Kauthuma	Khândasî, I Part, 2,000; Uttara-Sanhitâ, II Part, 3,000	8 Brâhmanas, 8,000	On Sanhitâ, Mâdhava; On Brâhm., Mâdhava	16,000; 25,000	Not read at Benares. Differs in accentuation only from the Kauthumas. The Brâhmanas is said to be different.
	Rânâyana	... ...	... ...	... ...	...	
Atharva-veda	Saunaka	10,000	Gopatha-Br. 6,000	On Sanhitâ, Mâdhava(?); On Brâhm., Mâdhava	80,000; 20,000	Mâdhava is called Vidyâranya, at another period of his life.

PAGE 66.

ON POLYNESIAN MYTHOLOGY.

EXTRACTS from an Introduction to the Rev. W. W. Gill's 'Myths and Songs from the South Pacific :'—

If new minerals, plants, or animals are discovered, if strange petrifactions are brought to light, if flints or other stone weapons are dredged up, or works of art disinterred, even if a hitherto unknown language is rendered accessible for the first time, no one, I think, who is acquainted with the scientific problems of our age, would ask what their importance consists in, or what they are good for. Whether they are products of nature or works of man, if only there is no doubt as to their genuineness, they claim and most readily receive the attention, not only of the learned, but also of the intelligent public at large.

Now, what are these Myths and Songs which Mr. W. W. Gill has brought home from Mangaia, but antiquities, preserved for hundreds, it may be for thousands of years, showing us, far better than any stone weapons or stone idols, the growth of the human mind during a period which, as yet, is full of the most perplexing problems to the psychologist, the historian, and the theologian? The only hope of our ever unravelling the perplexities of that mythological period, or that mythopœic phase of the human intellect, lies in our gaining access to every kind of collateral evidence. We know that mythopœic period among the Aryan and Semitic races, but we know it from a distance only, and where are we to look now for living myths and legends, except among those who still think and speak mythologically, who are, in fact, at the present moment what the Hindus were before the collection of their sacred hymns, and the Greeks long before the days of Homer? To find ourselves among a people who really believe in gods and heroes and ancestral spirits, who still offer human sacrifices, who in some cases devour their human victims, or, at all events, burn the flesh of animals on their altars, trusting that the scent will be sweet to the nostrils of their gods, is as if the zoologist could spend a few days among the megatheria, or the botanist among the waving ferns of the forests, buried beneath our feet. So much is written just now, and has been written during the last fifty years, on human archæology, on the growth and progress of the intellect, on the origin of religion, on the first beginnings of social institutions; so many theories have been started, so many generalizations put forward with perfect confidence, that one might almost imagine that all the evidence was before us, and no more new light could be expected from anywhere. But the very contrary is the case. There are many regions still to be explored, there are many facts, now put forward as certain, which require the most careful inspection, and as we read again and again the minute descriptions of the journey which man is supposed to have made from station to station, from his childhood to his manhood, or, it may be, his old age, it is difficult to resist a feeling of amazement, and to suppress at almost every page the exclamation, Wait! wait!

There are the two antagonistic schools, each holding its tenets with a kind of religious fervour—the one believing in a descending, the other in an ascending, development of the human race; the one asserting that the history of the human mind begins of necessity with a state of purity and simplicity which gradually gives way to corruption, perversity, and savagery; the other maintaining, with equal confidence, that the first human beings could not have been more than one step above the animals, and that their whole history is one of progress towards higher perfection.

With regard to the beginnings of religion, the one school holds to a primitive suspicion of something that is beyond —call it supernatural, transcendent, infinite, or divine. It considers a silent walking across this *jhúla*[1] of life, with eyes fixed on high, as a more perfect realisation of primitive religion than singing of Vedic hymns, offering of Jewish sacrifices, or the most elaborate creeds and articles. The other begins with the purely animal and passive nature of man, and tries to show how the repeated impressions of the world in which he lived, drove him to fetishism, whatever that may mean, to ancestor-worship, to a worship of nature, of trees and serpents, of mountains and rivers, of clouds and meteors, of sun and moon and stars, and the

[1] 'So, on the 12th of August, we made the steep ascent to the village of Namgea, and from there to a very unpleasant *jhúla*, which crosses the foaming torrent of the Sutlej. In this part of the Himálaya, and, indeed, on to Kashmír, these bridges are constructed of twigs, chiefly from birch trees or bushes, twisted together. Two thick ropes of these twigs, about the size of a man's thigh, or a little larger, are stretched across the river, at a distance of about six to four feet from each other, and a similar rope runs between them, three or four feet lower, being connected with the upper ropes by more slender ropes, also usually of birch twigs twisted together, but sometimes of grass, and occurring at an interval of about five feet from each other. The unpleasantness of a *jhúla* is that the passenger has no proper hold of the upper ropes, which are too thick and rough to be grasped by the hand; and that, at the extremities, they are so far apart that it is difficult to have any hold of both at the same time; while the danger is increased by the bend or hang of the *jhúla*, which is much lower in the middle than at its ends. He has also to stoop painfully in order to move along it, and it is seldom safe for him to rest his feet on the lower rope, except where it is supported from the upper ropes by the transverse ones. To fall into the raging torrent underneath would be almost certain destruction. The high wind which usually prevails in the Himálaya during the day makes the whole structure swing about frightfully. In the middle of the bridge there is a cross-bar of wood (to keep the two upper ropes separate) which has to be stepped over; and it is not customary to repair a *jhúla* until some one falls through it, and so gives practical demonstration that it is in rather a rotten condition.'—Andrew Wilson, 'The Abode of Snow,' p. 197.

vault of heaven, and at last, by what is called a natural mistake, of One who dwells in heaven above.

There is some truth in every one of these views; but they become untrue by being generalized. The time has not come yet, it probably never will come, when we shall be able to assert anything about the real beginnings of religion in general. We know a little here, a little there, but whatever we know of early religion, we always see that it presupposes vast periods of a still earlier development.

Some people imagine that fetishism, at all events, presupposes nothing: they would probably not hesitate to ascribe to some of the higher animals the faculty of fetish-worship. But few words are so devoid of scientific precision as *fetishism*, a term first rendered popular by the writings of De Brosses. Let us suppose that it means a kind of temporary worship of any material object which the fancy may happen to select, as a tree, a stone, a post, an animal :— can that be called a primitive form of religion? First of all, religion is one thing, worship another, and the two are by no means necessarily connected. But, even if they were, what is the meaning of worship paid to a stone, but the outward sign of a pre-existent belief that this stone is more than a stone, something supernatural, it may be something divine, so that the ideas of the supernatural and the divine, instead of growing out of fetishism, are generally, if not always, presupposed by it? The same applies to ancestor-worship, which often presupposes the conceptions of immortality and of the ideal unity of a family, and in many cases implies a belief that the spirits of the departed are worthy to share the honours paid to divine beings.

To maintain that all religion begins with fetishism, all mythology with ancestor-worship, is simply untrue, as far as our present knowledge goes. There is fetishism, there is ancestor-worship, there is nature-worship, whether of trees or serpents, of mountains or rivers, of clouds and meteors,

of sun and moon and stars, and the vault of heaven; there
is all this, and there is much more than all this, wherever
we can watch the early growth of religious ideas: but, what
we have to learn is, first of all, to distinguish, to study each
religion, each mythology, each form of worship by itself, to
watch them during successive periods of their growth and
decay, to follow them through different strata of society, and
before all, to have each of them, as much as possible, studied
in their own language.

If language is the realization of thought and feeling, the
importance of a knowledge of the language for a correct
appreciation of what it was meant to convey in the expression of religious thought and feeling, requires no proof.
I have often insisted on this, and I have tried to show—
whether successfully or not, let others judge—that much of
what seems at first irrational and inexplicable in mythology,
and in religion also, can be explained by the influence which
language exercises on thought. I have never said that the
whole of mythology can be explained in that way, that all
that seems irrational is due to a misunderstanding, or that
all mythology is a disease of language. Some parts of
mythology I have proved to be soluble by means of linguistic
tests, but mythology as a whole I have always represented
as a complete period of thought, inevitable, I believe, in the
development of human thought, and comprehending all and
everything that at a given time can fall within the horizon
of the human mind. The Nemesis of disproportion seems to
haunt all new discoveries. Parts of mythology are religious,
parts of mythology are historical, parts of mythology are
metaphysical, parts of mythology are poetical; but mythology
as a whole is neither religion, nor history, nor philosophy, nor
poetry. It comprehends all these together under that peculiar form of expression which is natural and intelligible at
a certain stage, or at certain recurring stages in the development of thought and speech, but which, after becoming

traditional, becomes frequently unnatural and unintelligible. In the same manner nature-worship, tree-worship, serpent-worship, ancestor-worship, god-worship, hero-worship, fetishism, all are parts of religion, but none of these by itself can explain the origin or growth of religion, which comprehends all these and many more elements in the various phases of its growth.

If anything can help to impress upon students of religion and mythology the necessity of caution, the advantage of special research, and, above all, the necessity of a scholarlike treatment, it is a book like that of Mr. Gill,—an account of a religion and mythology which were still living in the island of Mangaia [1], when Mr. Gill went there as a missionary twenty-two years ago, and which, as they died away before his eyes, he carefully described to us from what he saw himself, from what the last depositaries of the old faith told him, and from what was recorded of it in sacred songs, which he gives us in the original, with literal translations.

It is true that the religion and mythology of the Polynesian race have often been treated before, but one of their greatest charms consists in the very fact that we possess them in so many forms. Each island has, so to say, its own religious and mythological dialect, and though there is much that is common to all, and must therefore be old, there is at the same time much local and individual variety. Again, the great advantage of Mr. Gill's collection is that Mangaia has kept itself freer from foreign influences than almost any other of the Polynesian islands. 'The isolation of the Hervey Islanders,' he says, ' was in favour of the purity of their traditions, and the extreme jealousy with which they were guarded was rather an advantage than otherwise.'

---

[1] Mangaia belongs to the Hervey Group, a small cluster of islands in the South Pacific, lying between the 19° and 22° parallels of S. latitude and 157° and 160° of W. longitude.

When we find strange coincidences between the legends of Mangaia and Jewish, Christian, or classical stories, we need not suspect that former European travellers had dropped the germs of them, or that missionaries had given, unconsciously, their own colouring to them.   Mr. Gill has been specially on the guard against this and other sources of error.   'Whilst collecting my myths,' he says, 'I put away from me all classical mythology, being afraid that unconsciously I might mould these Polynesian stories into similarity with those of Greece and Rome.'

On my making inquiries whether the Polynesian tradition about Eve (Ivi) (on which see my Selected Essays, vol. II. p. 456), was to be found in Mangaia, Mr. Gill informed me that it was not, and that he strongly suspected its European origin.   The elements of the story may have previously existed, and we see some traces of it in the account of the creation current in Mangaia, but Mr. Gill suspects that some of the mutineers of the *Bounty* may have told the natives the Bible story, and that it became incorporated with their own notions.

The jawbone, too, with which we are told that Maui, the great solar hero of the Polynesians, destroyed his enemies, is absent in Mangaia.   When I inquired about it, Mr. Gill informed me that he never heard of it in the Hervey Group in connection with Maui.

Such things are extremely important for a proper treatment of mythology.   I hold no longer to the rule that when two mythologies agree in what is irrational or foolish, they must have had the same origin, or must have come into contact with each other at some period of their history. If there was a reason for the jawbone to be used as a weapon in one country, the same reason may have existed in another.   But, even if there was no reason, a fact that happened or was imagined to have happened in one place may surely have happened or have been imagined to have happened in another.

At first, no doubt, we feel startled by such coincidences ; and that they often offer a *primâ facie* presumption in favour of a common origin cannot be denied. But as we read on from one mythology to another, our sensitiveness with regard to these coincidences becomes blunted, and we feel hardened against appeals which are founded exclusively on such evidence.

At first sight, what can be more startling than to see the interior of the world, the invisible or nether world, the Hades of the Mangaians, called *Avaiki*, Avîki, lit. the lower region, being the name of one of the lower regions, both among Brahmans and Buddhists ? But we have only to look around, and we find that in Tahitian the name for Hades is *Hawai'i*, in New Zealand *Hawaiki*, and more originally, I suppose, *Sawaiki ;* so that the similarity between the Sanskrit and Polynesian words vanishes very quickly.

That the name of the Sun-god in Mangaia is *Ra* has been pointed out as a strange coincidence with Egypt; but more really important is the story of Ra being made captive, as reminding us of similar solar legends in Greece, Germany, Peru, and elsewhere [1].

Who can read the Mangaian story of Ina (the moon) and her mortal lover, who, as he grew old and infirm, had to be sent back to the earth to end his days there, without thinking of Selene and Endymion, of Eos and Tithonos ?

Who again, if acquainted with the Vedic myth of the *Maruts* [2], the strikers, the Storm-gods, and their gradual change into the Roman god of war, Mars, can fail to see the same transition of thought in several of the gods of the storms, of war and destruction among the Polynesians, though here again the similarity in the name of *Maru* is purely accidental.

[1] 'Chips from a German Workshop.' Second edition, vol. ii. p. 116.
[2] Rig-Veda-Sanhita, The Sacred Hymns of the Brahmans. Translated by F. Max Müller. Vol. i. Hymns to the Maruts, or the Storm-Gods. London, Trübner & Co., 1869.

In some of the Polynesian islands the Deluge is said to have lasted exactly forty days. This, no doubt, is startling. It may be the result of missionary influence. But, even if it were not, the coincidence between the Polynesian and the Jewish accounts on that one point may be either purely accidental, or may be founded on rude meteorological calculations which we have not yet detected. I do not like to quote coincidences from American traditions, because we know that we are never safe there against Spanish by-notes; otherwise the account of the Toltec deluge, and the statement that the mountains were covered to the depth of 'fifteen cubics,' might be quoted as another undesigned coincidence [1]. According to the Chimalpopoca MS., the Creator produced His work in successive epochs, man being made on the seventh day from dust and ashes. Why, we may ask, on the seventh day? But others, without even insisting on the peculiar character of the seventh number, may simply ask, Why not? There is much similarity between the Hindú account of the Deluge and the Jewish; but no one who has read the numerous accounts of a deluge in other parts of the world, would feel much surprised at this. At all events, if we admitted a common origin of the two, or an actual borrowing, then to explain the differences between them would be extremely difficult. The only startling coincidence is, that in India the flood is said to begin on the seventh day after it had been announced to Manu. Considering, however, that the seventh day is mentioned in the 'Bhâgavata-Purâna' only, I feel inclined to look upon it as merely accidental. It might, no doubt, have been borrowed from Jewish or even Mohammedan sources; but how can we imagine any reason why so unmeaning a fact should have been taken over, while on so many other points, where there was every temptation to borrow, nothing was done to assimilate the two accounts, or to remove features of which, at that time, the Hindus

---

[1] Bancroft, 'Native Races,' vol. v. p. 20.

might well be supposed to have been ashamed? I mention all this for the sole purpose of preaching patience and caution; and I preach it against myself quite as much as against others, as a warning against exclusive theories.

On every page of these Mangaian legends there is evidence that many of them owe their origin to language, whether we adopt the theory that the Mangaians played on their words, or that their words played on the Mangaians. Mr. Gill himself fully admits this; but to say that the whole of the Mangaian mythology and theology owed its origin to the oxydizing process to which language is exposed in every country, would be to mistake the rust for the iron.

One great temptation against which we must guard in studying mythology, is to look upon everything that has an abstract or philosophical character as late or secondary. It may be so, and, in many cases, we know it is so, but it does not follow that it is so by necessity. One of the chief sources of mythology is the indistinct yearning after causes, an impulse to explain what is visible by what is not visible, an attempt to go beyond the horizon of human experience. Among the Aryan nations the answers given to the first questionings of the human mind seem to have assumed from the first a more concrete character, and only after the sky, and the sun, and the moon, and the dawn, and the winds had been conceived as the givers and makers of all things, do we hear of attempts to go beyond to the conception of more abstract powers. But even among some of the Aryan nations, and particularly in India, it is by no means certain that the more philosophical conception of the supernatural did not find expression from the very beginning, that the two streams of mythological thought, the metaphysical and physical, did not run parallel for a long time, till in the end the metaphysical developed into philosophy, while the physical supplied the materials for religion and superstition.

If we come fresh from Aryan mythology to that of Mangaia, and read that the Universe (Avaiki), in the form of cocoa-nut shell, rests on a thick stem, gradually tapering to a point, and that this point is conceived as a demon, without human form, and that its name *Te-aka-ia-roê* signifies the Root of all Existence, we imagine ourselves in the Brâhmaṇas and Upanishads. Likewise, when we read that above this extreme point there is another demon called *Te-tangaengaie*, which means *Breathing*, and then again another called *Te-manava-roa*, which means *The Long-lived*, all this seems abstract, speculative, systematical, or late. But is it so? Do we know that it is so, and that it could not be otherwise?

Let us go a step further. As we advance into the interior of the cocoa-nut shell, we meet at the very bottom with an old woman, a demon of flesh and blood, called *Vari-ma-te-takave*. What is the meaning of her name? We are told, *The very Beginning*, or literally *The Beginning and the Bottom*. This sounds again abstract enough. But she herself is no mere abstraction. She plucks a bit of her right side, and it became the First Man. Many stories are told about that First Man. He is half man, half fish; his one eye was human, the other a fish-eye; his right side was furnished with an arm, the left with a fin. He had one proper foot, and half a fish tail. He had, as we shall see, brothers, and became in fact a purely legendary character. Yet he was clearly in the beginning a nominal concept of the sky. His name is *Avatea* or *Vatea*, and that still means Noon. And now the legend tells that *Vatea* had two magnificent eyes, rarely visible at the same time. In general, whilst one, called by the mortals the Sun, is seen here in this upper world, the other eye, called by men the Moon, shines in Avaiki. Of course this is not the only myth. In another myth the sun and moon are not the eyes of Vatea, but themselves living beings, and no one is offended by such contradictions. They are all true alike, as long as people were able to understand them, and when they ceased to be intelligible they became sacred.

With all these uncertainties before us, with the ground shaking under our feet, who would venture to erect at present complete systematic theories of mythology or religion? Let any one who thinks that all religion begins with fetishism, all worship with ancestor-worship, or that the whole of mythology everywhere can be explained as a disease of language, try his hand on this short account of the beliefs and traditions of Mangaia; and if he finds that he fails to bring even so small a segment of the world's religion and mythology into the narrow circle of his own system, let him pause before he ventures to lay down rules as to how man, on ascending from a lower or descending from a higher state, must have spoken, must have believed, must have worshipped. If Mr. Gill's book were to produce no other effect but this, it would have proved one of the most useful works at the present moment. But it contains much that in itself will deeply interest all those who have learned to sympathize with the childhood of the world, and have not forgotten that the child is the father of the man; much that will startle those who think that metaphysical conceptions are incompatible with downright savagery; much also that will comfort those who hold that God has not left Himself without a witness, even among the lowest outcasts of the human race.

PAGE 128.

ON THE CHINESE NAME FOR GOD.

The old controversy whether *Tî* in Chinese should be translated by God, and whether God should be translated by *Tî*, was revived in 1880 by some of the Bishops and Missionaries in China, who addressed the following letter to me.

SHANGHAI, CHINA, *June 25,* 1880.

SIR,—We, the undersigned missionaries labouring among the Chinese, have had brought under our notice the volume on the Chinese religion which forms one of the series you are now editing under the general title of 'The Sacred Books of the East.'

We fully agree with your prefatory statement—'that much of the value and utility of the series must depend on the absence of any colour borrowed from theory or prejudice,' and we therefore deplore the fact that in the important volume alluded to there has been, as we conceive, a forgetfulness of the principle which was laid down at the outset. We refer to the meaning which has in this book throughout been attached to the term 'Shang-ti,' so frequently found in the Chinese classics.

You can be no stranger to the fact that a controversy has long existed among Chinese scholars as to who or what is meant by the term or title 'Shang-ti.' Some hold that it designates the God of the Christian Scriptures, while others feel themselves utterly unable to accept it in such a sense. Whatever the rights of this question are, the controversy is a great fact and ought not to be ignored. It arose, as is

well known, among the early Roman Catholic missionaries in
China, and a like contention exists at the present day among
the different Protestant missionaries. It cannot be said that
there has been any lack of scholarship in the discussion of
this question. Both views have been well represented from
time to time, first among Roman Catholic missionaries, and
latterly among Protestant missionaries, by men whose Chinese
as well as general scholarship is undoubted. We ne.d but
mention the names of the early Jesuit missionaries, Matteo
Ricci on one side and Longobardi on the other, and the
Protestant missionaries, Dr. Medhurst, Dr. Legge, Dr. Edkins,
and Dr. Chalmers on one side, and Bishop Boone, Dr. Bridgman, and Dr. Williams on the other. To the last three should
be added, though of the Greek Church, the distinguished
name of the late Archimandrite Palladius, so well known as
one of the most profound Chinese scholars.

Considering, then, that the question has been agitated
among all classes of Christian missionaries for nearly 300
years, our complaint is, that in a book containing a translation of the Chinese classics intended for English readers,
and brought out with your *imprimatur*, the term 'Shang-ti'
has been, not translated, as it might have been, by such a
phrase as 'Supreme Ruler' or 'Supreme Emperor,' or 'Ruler
(or Emperor) on high,' or transferred, as has been done
indeed in some passages of the same book, with the term
'Ti,' in either of which cases no fault could have been found,
but interpreted as the God of revelation—the view which the
eminent translator, Dr. Legge, so strenuously advocated while
in China as a missionary. That is, he sets forth his own
private view by substituting 'God' for 'Shang-ti' wherever
it occurs in the classics; whereas this has been denied by
persons as thoroughly qualified as himself to form a judgment
on the subject. His reaffirmation of his reasons for this view
in the addition to the preface made in the present volume
does not make his translation of 'Shang-ti' any the less

a serious departure from the principle laid down in your preface.

Moreover, this is not merely a literary—it is a missionary question. Many who have read or will read the book exercise strong influence from England and other countries, directly or indirectly, on Christian missions in China, and it is exceedingly important that their minds should be kept free from prejudice on one side or the other, seeing they have no means of examining or determining upon the question for themselves. Such a book as Dr. Legge's is to them, so long as the controversy is undecided, simply misleading.

We respectfully urge that, in editing it, the balance between the two parties in a difficult and still open contention should have been held with a steady hand, and express our regret that the book referred to, though brought out with the statement of so admirable a principle, of avoidance of all colouring, is, nevertheless, of a distinctly partisan character, inasmuch as by its interpretation of 'Shang-ti' it is the exponent of the view of a very small number even of those who prefer to use 'Shang-ti' to make known the true God to the Chinese; for of those who use the term, very few agree with Dr. Legge in the opinion that 'Shang-ti' of the Chinese classics is the same as 'Jehovah' of the Christian Scriptures.

It is on this account that we venture to address you. Were you less enlightened and liberal than you are, we might conclude by asking you to pardon us for addressing you; but we do not do so, as we are assured that your fearless and uncompromising love of truth will induce you to hail with satisfaction any suggestion which may remove from a volume with your name on the title-page the faintest trace of one-sidedness.

We have the honour to be, Sir,
Your faithful and obedient servants,

Thos. M'Clatchie, M.A., Canon of St. John's Cathedral, Hongkong, and of the Cathedral of the Holy Trinity, Shanghae, 1844.

MATTHEW L. YATES, D.D., 1847.
EDWARD C. LORD, M.A., D.D., 1847.
FREDERICK F. GOUGH, M.A., 1850.
A. P. HAPPER, 1844.
R. NELSON, D.D., 1851.
J. S. BURDON, Bishop of Victoria, Hongkong, 1853.
JOHN L. NEVINS, D.D., 1854.
T. P. CRAWFORD, D.D., 1852.
H. BLODGET, D.D., 1854.
SAMUEL I. J. SCHERESCHEWSKY, Missionary Bishop of the American
    Episcopal Church, Shanghai, 1859.
ELLIOT H. THOMPSON, 1859.
CHARLES HENRY BUTCHER, D.D., 1864.
WM. J. BOONE, M.A., 1869.
HUNTER CORBETT, M.A., 1863.
CHAS. R. MILLS, M.A., 1857.
JOHN WHERRY, M.A., 1864.
JAMES BATES, 1867.
L. D. CHAPIN, 1863.
CHAUNCEY GOODRICH, 1865.
C. A. STANLEY, 1862.
J. A. LEYENBERGER, 1866.
HENRY V. NOYES, 1866.

To this letter I returned the following answer :—

Gentlemen,—I have taken some time to consider what
answer I should return to the letter which you addressed to
me as editor of 'The Sacred Books of the East,' and in which
you complain that, in the translation of the Shu-king and
Shih-king by Professor Legge, the names Ti and Shang-ti
should have been rendered by ' God.' You call my attention
to the controversy which has been carried on for 300 years,
and is still kept up to the present day among the missionaries
in China, as to what is the nearest equivalent to be found in
the Chinese language for expressing God. You remind me
that Ti and Shang-ti were rejected by Papal authority, and
have been accepted among Protestant missionaries by one
party only, and you remark that, even those who in rendering
the Scriptures into Chinese are willing, in the absence of a

better name, to accept Ti or Shang-ti for God, would shrink
from translating these terms by God when they occur in the
writings of Confucius.   As Professor Legge, during his long
stay in China, has been one of the most strenuous defenders
of the name Shang-ti as the best rendering of God in Chinese,
you complain that he should have taken advantage of his
position, as one of my fellow-workers in the translation of 'The
Sacred Books of the East,' and have translated Shang-ti,
whenever it occurs in the Shu-king and Shih-king, by God,
expressing, at the same time, his conviction that 'the Ti and
Shang-ti of the Chinese classics is God, our God, the true
God.' You also blame me, as editor of 'The Sacred Books of
the East,' for not having held with a steady hand the balance
between the two parties in a difficult and still open contention,
particularly as I had promised that these translations, offered
to the public under the auspices of the University of Oxford,
should be complete, trustworthy, and readable; and you call
on me to repair the injustice which has been done to those
who differ from Dr. Legge in his views on the true meaning
of the words Ti and Shang-ti.

Allow me to state, in reply to your letter, that, so far as
the so-called 'Term Question' is concerned, I had, nearly
thirty years ago (*Edinburgh Review*, October, 1852), expressed
my conviction that it would be impossible to find in Chinese
a more adequate rendering of God than Shang-ti.   On that
point, therefore, I could hardly claim now to be an impartial
judge.

But this, as you yourselves admit, is not really the question which concerns the translator or the editor of 'The
Sacred Books of the East.' The question on which, with
the assistance of my learned friend, Dr. Legge, I was called
upon to form an opinion when examining his translation of
the Shu-king and Shih-king, forming the third volume of
my series, was whether Ti and Shang-ti, when they occur
in Chinese, should be rendered in English by God.   On this

point, I readily admit, it is by no means easy to give a decisive answer. In fact, I can well understand why many missionaries in China should have hesitated to identify the Shang-ti of the Confucians with the God they come to preach, and all I can do is to try to explain to you why, in spite of all objections, I myself agree with Dr. Legge in accepting Shang-ti, when it occurs in the ancient Scriptures of the Chinese, as a name intended for the true God.

There are, perhaps, passages in the sacred texts of the Chinese in which Shang-ti is spoken of in what we should call mythological language, language, in our opinion, inapplicable to the Supreme Ruler of the Universe. But does it follow, therefore, that the Chinese, when they formed the name of Shang-ti, did not mean the true God, or that the best among them had never had any idea of the true God? You know far better than I do that there must be in the prayers and creeds of all religions a compromise between the language of the wise and the foolish, the old and the young, and that the sacred texts of no nation, not even those of Jews and Christians, are entirely free from childlike, helpless, poetical, and what are called mythological expressions. There is, perhaps, no better name for God than Father, and there are few religions in which that name has not been used; yet, in order to render that name applicable to God, we must take out of it almost everything it implies in ordinary usage. Our own word God was borrowed by our ancestors from heathen temples, and the names for God used by the Romanic nations come from *deus*, Sanskrit *deva*, which *deva* is a mere derivation of *div*, the sky.

And, if we are not to translate Shang-ti by God, what are we to do? You would not say that the Chinese, alone of all nations on earth, had never any word for God at all, for you yourselves say that they deified the sky, and how could people deify the sky or anything else without possessing an idea and a word for deity?

You suggest that either the name Shang-ti should have been left untranslated, or that it should have been rendered by Supreme Ruler. If the first expedient had been adopted, all readers unacquainted with Chinese would have taken Shang-ti for a proper name, such as Jupiter, while Dr. Legge, whose Chinese scholarship you do not call in question, states that it 'never became with the people a proper name like the Zeus of the Greeks' (Preface, p. xxv.). If, on the contrary, Shang-ti had been rendered by Supreme Ruler, as was done by Medhurst, or by *le Seigneur* and *le Souverain Maître*, as was done by Gaubil, would these expressions have evoked in the minds of European readers any conception different from that of God, the true God?

How could missionaries in China, if they are willing to translate Shang-ti by Supreme Ruler, continue to represent Him as a false God, or, at all events, as not quite true? Are there any who still believe in the actual existence of false gods, or of gods not quite true? Do they believe that Bel, or Jupiter, or Varuna, or Shang-ti were so many individual beings existing by the side of Jehovah? They were, if you like, false, or, at least, imperfect names of God; but never the names of false or imperfect gods.

I have tried to show in all my writings on language, mythology, or religion, and more especially in my Hibbert lecture 'On the origin and growth of religion, as illustrated by the religions of India,' how we ought to read in the manifold names of the Deity, preserved to us in the ancient languages of the world, the gradual growth of human thought and human language in their endeavour to find better and better names for what after all admits of no name. What an ancient Christian martyr said, ὁ θεὸς ὄνομα οὐκ ἔχει, 'God has no name,' is true, in one sense; but from an historical point of view, we should, I think, be equally right if we called God πολλῶν ὀνομάτων μορφὴ μία, 'of many names the one person.'

Some of these names may seem to us very objectionable, but not all; and I confess I could never help admiring the bold language of an ancient Sanskrit poet who introduces Bhagavat, his own supreme God, saying, 'Even those who worship idols, worship me.'

If we are so hard on the Chinese, and tell them that their word Shang-ti cannot be used as the name of the true God, because it is used synonymously with tien, which means the sky, what shall we say when they point to such verses in the New Testament as Luke xv. 21, 'I have sinned against heaven, and in thy sight, and am no more worthy to be called thy son'? And if we are offended by every anthropomorphic expression in the sacred writings of non-Christian races, how is it that we can bear so well with the language of the Old Testament, in reading of 'the Lord God walking in the garden in the cool of the day'? Do the words of Dante—

'Per questo la Scrittura condescende
A vostra facultate, e piedi e mano
Attribuisce a Dio, et altro intende,'

apply to our Scriptures only? Should we not apply them even in a far more generous spirit to the scriptures of the Chinese, the Hindus, the Persians, the Mohammedans? It was, I need hardly tell you, one of the chief objects for which I undertook the publication of 'The Sacred Books of the East,' to show, as St. Augustine said, that there is no religion without some truth in it, and particularly to make missionaries see that, hidden beneath a fearful amount of rubbish, and worse than rubbish, there are grains of gold to be found in every book that has once been called sacred by human lips. Nothing, I confess, has rejoiced me so much as when I heard the other day an excellent missionary tell me, 'You have shown us that the heathen religions are not the work of the devil; and you have taught us to look first of all for what the heathen religions share with us in common, and to make that the foundation of our labour.' Surely the name for God in Chinese, or in any other language, unless it is simply intolerable, should be treated by missionaries with the greatest reverence. Let them slowly and gently cut down the rank growth of mythology that has choked so many of the names of God; but let them be careful lest, in tearing up the roots, they kill the stem on which alone their new grafts can live and thrive. Let them follow, in fact, in the footsteps of the boldest and greatest missionary the world has ever seen, who at Athens did not break the altar of the unknown God, but said, 'Whom ye ignorantly worship, Him declare I unto you.'

These are, in a few words, the reasons which made me not only approve of Professor Legge's translation of 'Shang-ti,' when it occurs in the Shu-king and Shih-king, by 'God,' but sincerely rejoice at it. Nor do I think that, in adopting the course we thought right to adopt, either he or I took an unfair advantage of those who, on conscientious grounds, differ from us. If this translation of 'Shang-ti' by 'God' had been inserted in 'The Sacred Books of the East' without any warning to the reader, I should plead guilty for myself, and I could well understand in that case the remonstrances of those who all their lives have been opposing Dr. Legge in his views on Chinese religion. But when there is in the preface, from page xxiii. to xxix., a clear explanation of the reasons which induced Dr. Legge to render 'Shang-ti' by 'God,' when the translations of that name proposed by other Chinese scholars are clearly set forth and examined, and when the translator is prepared to take upon himself the full responsibility of that rendering which he personally considers the only true one, surely there is no solid foundation for the charge of *mala fides*, either against Dr. Legge or against myself. I need hardly say, therefore, in conclusion, that it would be a great satisfaction to myself, and, I have no doubt, to Dr. Legge also, if after having read my explanations, and the pamphlet which Dr. Legge has addressed to me

('Letter to Professor F. Max Müller, chiefly on the translation into English of the Chinese terms Ti and Shang-ti,'
by James Legge, Professor of the Chinese Language in the
University of Oxford; Trübner, 1880), and which by this
time has, no doubt, reached you, you should think it right to
withdraw the charges which you have brought against us.

I have the honour to be, Gentlemen,

Your obedient servant,

F. MAX MÜLLER.

OXFORD, *Dec.* 19.

A more elaborate answer was written by Dr. Legge himself,
and published as 'A Letter to Professor Max Müller, chiefly
on the translation into English of the Chinese terms Ti and
Shang-Ti,' London, Trübner, 1880.

I here subjoin an article from the pen of the great Chinese
scholar, John Chalmers, published in a Hong-Kong paper,
28 Dec. 1880, and not easily accessible to European scholars.

THE INTERMINABLE QUESTION.

The Interminable Question is about a word for the Deity
in Chinese. There are three views held by powerful sections
of the Missionary army, whom, for brevity, we will designate
the Romanists, the Reformers, and the Rumpers. 1. The
view of the first is negative. 'There is,' they say, 'no word
for God in Chinese, we must make one. We make the expression Heaven-Lord (天主 T'ien Chu) to stand for
God.' This is the Catholic faith as decreed by the Pope
some two hundred years ago. 2. The Reformers hold that
the Chinese word for God is 帝 Ti, or 上帝 Shang-ti,
and that the word which the people use for their objects of
worship generally means *ghosts*. This party includes *all*
Germans, *all* English and Scotch Presbyterians, *all* Wes-

leyans, and *all* London Missionaries. 3. The third party, on the contrary, say that Ti or Shang-ti means *the Firmament deified,* and that the word which the Romanists and Reformers generally agree in translating *ghosts* or *spirits,* means *gods* and *God.* Therefore they use the latter word, which is 神 shan. I call these last Rumpers because they are a diminished body, now much in need of a Cromwell. A few follow them from various unsettled sections. And the most unsettled section of all is the Church of England. Taken collectively 'the Church' may be said to hold out her arms lovingly to embrace us all; but taken individually her members are at war one with another.

The doctrine of *Shan,* held by the Rumpers, has been refuted again and again. But they never seem to know that they are beaten. So long ago as 1876, I published, in a Pamphlet on the subject, twenty-five sentences from good native authors to shew that the '*shan*' of a man means his spirit or ghost, and not his god. In consequence of that publication, a certain person calling himself 'Inquirer' sent an article to the *Chinese Recorder,* in which he said his teacher had 'quite providentially' found one passage in which 'my *shan*' did not mean 'my ghost' but 'my god.' It turned out, however, that the phrase meant only the ghosts of my ancestors; as one might speak of 'Hamlet's ghost,' meaning the ghost of his father which he saw. When Inquirer's first article appeared I thought I could discover in it the style of a well-known Doctor, and sent a note congratulating him on having said some true things, but the Doctor replied that he did 'not claim the honor.' Who Inquirer is, therefore, remains to me a profound mystery, and if I say anything hard about him he must not suppose that I am personally acquainted with him at all. He has for some time past been writing to the *Chinese Recorder* rambling, irrelevant, and unreadable articles, which have done little or no harm and less good. The last, which appeared in the number for May and June 1880, in the form of a letter to Professor Max Müller, is to my mind the feeblest of all. It was with some surprise therefore that I learnt a few mails ago that Professor Müller, to whom it was addressed, and Professor Legge, against whom it was directed, were preparing to do battle with Inquirer, as if he were a foeman worthy of their steel. This nobody calling himself Inquirer, who has shown himself utterly incapable of dealing with any philological subject, and who does not know the difference between the subject and the predicate of a sentence, now undertakes to be the *instructor* of Professor Max Müller, and to charge Professor Legge with 'a crime as well as a blunder,' because forsooth he had grieved the narrow souls of Inquirer and his friends by thinking and saying in plain English that, when Confucius spoke of 'sinning against Heaven,' and said 'Heaven knows me,' Confucius meant 'God.' Inquirer thinks Confucius' words should be explained to mean 'sinning against *the Firmament deified*,' and '*the Firmament deified* knows me.' Heaven in Chinese, he thinks, has always this peculiar meaning, and any one who honestly believes otherwise, or supposes it possible that the heathen Chinese might have meant *the* Supreme Being, is guilty of a crime. Therefore he urges upon Professor Max Müller the stern and solemn duty of suppressing Dr. Legge. Dr. Legge has now answered for himself in a printed letter, which will soon be in the hands of all whom it concerns. But my reason for referring to this subject at all now is another fact which has come to my knowledge within the last few days, that certain persons of the Rump party and certain adherents of the Romanists have taken to imitating Inquirer's example of writing letters to Professor Max Müller and others, in a less open way, seeking to convey the impression that Dr. Legge is all but singular in his views about the Chinese Heaven and Shang-ti; in order I believe to prejudice the minds of men of influence at home against the uniform usage and opinion of the Reformers, and give them the impression that we are *hors de combat.* Two or three known men, and a score of unknown, have conspired together to do this thing, without consulting the large and respectable body of their brethren who not only honour and esteem the good and great man who holds the Chair of Chinese at Oxford, but feel under an everlasting obligation to him for leading them so wisely and heroically in the slippery paths of Chinese philology. I appeal to an impartial public whether such tactics are fair either to us and to him, or to the cause of truth. Why was not an opportunity given to the other side to state their views? Why was it said, as I understand it was said, in communications sent home, that we are but one or two, that we can be counted, in the words of Inquirer, ' on the fingers of one hand,' or in fact that we are not worth counting? Why, above all, could not these men let the Interminable Question rest, when it seemed, on the surface at least, to be at rest; or, if they must move, why trouble the waters from beneath in this clandestine manner? I wish this bit of information to meet the eyes of the Reforming Community, without delay, that they may be prepared to act promptly if need be. At the same time, I am fully persuaded that an appeal to Max Müller and men of his stamp will in the end lead to a result which the appellants do not anticipate; and while sorry for them, I rejoice in spirit.

JOHN CHALMERS.

HONGKONG, *Dec.* 28, 1880.

MYTHOLOGY AMONG THE HOTTENTOTS.

In a book just published under the title of *Tsuni-||goam,
the Supreme Being of the Khoi-khoi*, Dr. Theophilus Hahn
has collected the most curious fragments of the religion and
mythology of the Hottentot tribes, and made for the first
time a bold attempt at supplying a truly scientific explanation of the myths and legends of savage races.

The name *Hottentot*, or *Hüttentüt*, was given by the Dutch
to the yellowish race of men with whom they became first
acquainted near the Cape of Good Hope. Dapper, in 1670,
writes that the name was given by the Dutch to the natives
on account of the curious clicks and harsh sounds in their
language, and that the same word is applied in Dutch to
one who stammers and stutters. In the *Idioticon Hambur-
gense* (1755) *Hüttentüth* is given as a term of reproach for
a physician, our quack. These so-called Hottentots, however, call themselves by a much grander name, *Khoi-khoi*, i.e.
men of men; and they draw a sharp line between themselves and the Bushmen (Boŝjesmen), whom they call *Sâ-n*,
and reckon as lower almost than dogs. Nevertheless Dr.
Hahn is convinced that the Khoi-khoi and the Sâ were
originally one race, and spoke originally one language, but
while the former led a pastoral and agricultural life, the
latter always remained hunters. Such is the influence of
life on language, that while all the Khoi-khoi tribes can,
to a certain extent, converse together, the dialects of the Sâ

T

or Bushmen differ widely from each other, and the tribes speaking them have long ceased to be mutually intelligible. Dr. Hahn states that in the Khoi-khoi idioms the root is monosyllabic and ends in a vowel, the grammatical articulation taking place by means of pronominal suffixes. The Sâ dialects, on the contrary, have no such formative elements, their roots seem often polysyllabic, and the whole language bears clear traces of violent phonetic decay and grammatical confusion. Yet Dr. Hahn feels convinced that the language of the Sâ or Bushmen stands to that of the Khoi-khoi in the same relation as English does to Sanskrit—a comparison, we venture to think, not very flattering to the English. The Khoi-khoi have a very perfect decimal system of numbers, while the Bushmen have long been quoted as having no numerals at all, beyond two or three. Dr. Hahn, however, discovered among the Ai-Bushmen numerals up to twenty. The Khoi-khoi have the curious system of calling all sons after their mother, all daughters after their father. The eldest daughter was highly respected, and the milking of the cows was entirely left to her. It is well known that in Sanskrit also the daughter is called *duhitar*, the milker, from *duh*, to milk, the Greek θυγάτηρ, and our own *daughter*. Dr. Hahn quotes a little song addressed to the eldest daughter :

My lioness,
Art thou afraid that I shall bewitch thee?
Thou milkest the cow with a soft hand.
Bite me (*i.e.* kiss me) !
Pour for me milk !
My lioness,
Great man's daughter.

Dr. Hahn gives many more illustrations of the daily life, the customs, social distinctions, occupations, and amusements

of the Khoi-khoi, or Hottentots, and certainly, amongst
much that seems strange and even repulsive, he discloses
many sweet and redeeming features in their wild character.
So it always is and will be, when a man who can speak the
language of so-called savages watches their daily life, and is
able to observe their real motives for good or evil.   In this
respect also the Chair of South African Philology at Cape
Town will, it is to be hoped, bear good fruit.   It will excite
not only a scientific, a philological, or craniological interest
in the yellow and black races who are brought in daily contact with their white rulers, but it will show that, in spite
of many differences, there is a common ground between them
and ourselves.   They have a religion, less dogmatic than
ours, but often, it seems, marvellously practical.   They
have traditions, legends, poetry, they have refined feelings
and a warm heart.   If Dr. Hahn in his lectures succeeds
in exciting some kindly sympathies among his hearers for
Hottentots, Bushmen, or Kafirs, the liberality of the Cape
Parliament in endowing his Chair will have been well be-
stowed, and will be amply repaid in the future.

The first instalment of Dr. Hahn's labours will, however,
be of interest, not at the Cape only, but in every University
of Europe.   It is, in fact, a most valuable contribution to
the comparative study of religion and mythology.   It has
often been urged against these new sciences that they confine
themselves too exclusively to the mythologies of civilised
nations, the Aryan and Semitic, and thus leave out of account the majority of the human race, the illiterate and so-
called savage tribes of Asia, Africa, America, and Polynesia.
It is easy to understand why this should be so.   Comparative
mythology and, still more, comparative theology are of

very recent date; and when a beginning has to be made, when an entirely new mine has to be opened, the work, if it is to be well done, must at first be confined within very narrow limits. If comparative philologists had waited till they had mastered the languages of the whole world, if comparative mythologists had suppressed their theories till they could prove their applicability to the mythology of every savage tribe, we should be now where we were a hundred years ago. It is far more easy to ask for what is impossible than to do what is possible. No doubt there is the danger of premature generalisation; and after having discovered how one family of languages grew up, or how the mythologies of the best known nations came to be what they are, scholars are apt to speak of the origin and growth of language and mythology in general, as if their own theories must be applicable to all, or as if no new facts could possibly modify those theories. This danger, however, is not so great as it may seem. Scholars know perfectly well how far the shafts have been run, and how wide the safe levels extend. Though they do not always say so, they always have the proviso in their mind, 'so far as we know at present;' and the world at large, even without being expressly told so, is not likely to forget the same caution, influenced, as most people really are, not by their own judgment, but by that of men who have a personal knowledge both of the mine and of the miners whom they are asked to trust.

There is another reason why comparative philology, and still more comparative mythology, has hitherto been confined to a rather narrow field. Comparative mythology is chiefly studied by two classes—by scholars and by anthropologists. Now the true scholar who knows the intricacies

of a few languages, who is aware of the traps he has to avoid
in exploring their history, who in fact has burnt his fingers
again and again when dealing with Greek, and Latin, and
Sanskrit, shrinks by a kind of instinct from materials which
crumble away as soon as critical scholarship attempts to
impart to them a certain cohesion and polish.   These
materials are often supplied by travellers ignorant of the
language, by missionaries strongly biassed in one direction
or the other, or by natives who hardly understood the
questions they were asked to answer. A very useful collection was made some time ago by Mr. Tylor to show the
untrustworthiness of the accounts of most travellers and
missionaries, when they give us their impressions of the
languages, religions, and traditions of races among whom
they lived for a longer or shorter time. The same people
who by one missionary are said to worship either one or
many gods, are declared by another to have no idea and no
name of a Divine Being.   But, what is stranger still, even
the same person sometimes makes two equally confident
assertions which flatly contradict each other. Thus Sparrman (see Hahn, p. 46) is very doubtful in one place whether
the Hottentots believe in a Supreme Being, and tells us that
the Khoi-khoi themselves declared that they were too stupid
to understand anything, and never heard of a Supreme
Being.   In another place, however, the same Sparrman
argues that the Khoi-khoi *must* believe in a supreme, but
very powerful and fiendish Being, from whom they expect
rain, thunder, lightning, cold, &c.   Liechtenstein, again,
while denying that there is any trace of religious worship
among the Khosa Kafirs, admits that they believe in a
Supreme Being who created the world, though, if we are to

believe Van der Kamp (died about 1811), they have no name for such a Being. Such a worship of a nameless God would seem to show us the highest ideal of spiritual religion, realised among one of the lowest races of mankind!

In Greece, where we have a language that has been carefully studied for centuries, and a literature clearly and fully reflecting the thoughts of a whole nation, the true scholar constantly doubts as to the exact meaning of a word, hesitates as to its real etymology, and confesses his ignorance of the original character of many a Homeric god or hero. How, then, can he be expected to work with any kind of confidence or pleasure on materials such as are mostly put before him in studying the mythologies of savage nations? They may be delightful for dabbling and making mud-pies, but they are quite useless for making bricks. In Greek, or Latin, or Sanskrit, when all seemed certain, the length of a vowel, or the change of an accent, has often upset the most carefully elaborated theories. And here the student is to pronounce an opinion on the real meaning of legendary personages, the names of which he can hardly spell or pronounce, much less analyse or understand. This is the real reason why the best comparative mythologists have preferred to work on Aryan mythology, particularly when there is so much in it still untouched and unexplored, instead of applying their solvents to the folklore of savage tribes, however attractive the subject may seem. The time will come, they say, when the dialects of the Hottentots, the Fijians, or Weddahs, will be known far more accurately than at present, when scholars will be able to tell us what is possible and what is not in the dialectic changes of their words, and when the phonetic laws which regulate the changes of their vowels

and consonants will be understood as well as those of
Sanskrit or Zend. Then, and not till then, will it be time
to inquire into the prehistoric antecedents of these languages
and religions, with some hope of our catching a few glimpses
of the thoughts and intentions which influenced their first
formation and development.

Dr. Hahn's book shows that such a hope has been realised
sooner than we had any right to expect, with regard to one
savage race at least, the Khoi-khoi. Accounts of their religion and mythology were scattered about in various books.
These have been carefully collected by Dr. Hahn and printed
in his second chapter, enriched and improved by what he has
been able to collect himself. But this is not all. To a man
brought up among the Khoi-khoi, the names of their gods
and heroes were not mere names. They conveyed a meaning
to him, and encouraged him to apply to their decipherment
the same process which has proved so successful in unlocking
the mysteries of Aryan mythology. He knows what is possible and what is not in the etymological analysis of African
names; and the fact that he often speaks with hesitation as
to the real etymology of a word, so far from discrediting his
results, shows only that he has a grammatical conscience, the
sine quâ non of all mythological research.

And what are his results? Certainly comparative mythology could not have wished for a greater triumph than
what has come so unexpectedly from the first scientific
analysis of the mythology of one of the lowest races of
mankind. The mythology of the savage races—which, as
agriologists confidently maintained, would sooner or later
upset the whole system of comparative mythology—the first
time that it is taken up in a truly scholarlike spirit, seems to

bless that system altogether. Almost every principle it has been contending for during the last twenty years is here confirmed. Most of the Hottentot myths are solar or celestial. This may seem of less importance at the present moment, when the opposition to the solar theory has gradually died away, crushed, as it were, by the evidence that has been pouring in simultaneously in support of it from Egypt, from Babylonia, from Polynesian, from American, and from African tribes. But what is far more curious is, that among the Khoi-khoi, too, we see how what is called the irrational element in mythology is due to a misunderstanding of ancient names, and how, so far from real events being turned into myths, myths have there, too, been turned into accounts of real events.

The name of the Supreme Being among the Khoi-khoi is Tsui || Goab, the two strokes before the G indicating the lateral click, which, however, in future we must dispense with. Tsuni-||goam, the name given in the title of the book, is the reconstructed original of the same name. This name, as written down by travellers and missionaries, differs considerably, yet there seems no doubt that forms such as Tiqua, Thuickwe, Tuiqua, Tigoa, Tanquoa, Tsoi Koap, Tshu Koab, Tsu-goam, are all meant for the same being, namely our Tsui-||goab.

At first missionaries could hardly bring themselves to believe that the Khoi-khoi had any religion at all. Peter Kolb, in the beginning of the last century, quotes Saar, an officer of the Dutch Government, who says :—

‘ One does not know what kind of religion they have ; but early, *when the day dawns*, they assemble and take each other by the hands and dance, and call out in their language towards the heavens.   From this one may conclude that they must have some idea of the Godhead.'

He quotes Father Tachard, who recorded his conviction that, 'although these people know nothing of the creation of the world or of the Trinity in the Godhead, they pray to a God.'

The missionary Böving, a contemporary of Kolb, says:—

There are some *rudera*, and traces of an idea (perception) of a God.   For they know, at least the more intelligent among them, that there is a God, who has made the earth and heavens, who causes thunder and rain, and who gives them food and skins for clothing, so that also of them may be said what St. Paul says, Rom. i. 19.

Kolb's own experience runs thus: 'It is obvious that all Hottentots believe' in a God, they know him and confess it; to him they ascribe the work of creation, and they maintain that he still rules over everything, and that he gives life to everything.   On the whole he is possessed of such high qualities that they could not well describe him. . . . .'

One of the first who mentioned the name of Tsui-goab, as the chief god of the Khoi-khoi, was the missionary George Schmidt, sent to the Cape by the Moravian Mission in 1737.

'At the return of the Pleiades (he writes), these natives celebrate an anniversary.   As soon as these stars appear above the eastern horizon, mothers will lift their little ones on their arms, and, running up to elevated spots, will show to them those friendly stars, and teach them to stretch their little hands towards them.   The people of a kraal will assemble to dance and to sing, according to the old custom of their ancestors.'

The chorus always sings: 'O Tiqua, our Father above our heads, give rain to us, that the fruits (bulbs, &c.), uientjes, may ripen, and that we may have plenty of food; send us a good year.'

The *Tiqua* here mentioned is a corruption of Tsui-goab, and in another place George Schmidt calls him Tui'qua. That the Khoi-khoi continued to use this word as the name of their Supreme Being is best shown by the translation of the New Testament into the Namaqua dialect, made by Schmelen, a missionary of the London Missionary Society, of which I possess a copy, perhaps the only one in England. He was married to a Hottentot woman, and learned to speak the language well. The name which he uses for God is Tsoeikwap, *i.e.* Tsui-goab, while he calls the devil Kauaap, *i.e.* Gaüäb or Gaunab. Dr. Moffat, while travelling among the same Namaquas, heard them call God Tsui-kuap or Uti-kuap; and the same name still continues even among Christian converts, though they are now taught to call God *Elob,* a corruption of *Elohim.* If, for instance, they suddenly exclaim, 'Good God!' they do not say 'Elob,' but 'Tsu-goatse;' and if they swear or call God to witness, they always use the same old name (p. 62).

Most valuable are some of the hymns which Dr. Hahn has collected from the mouth of the people. They seem to carry us back into the midst of the Vedic hymns, and show that those Aryan hymns are, after all, not so very different from the simple utterances of savages. Dr. Hahn gives us the following translation of one sacred hymn, addressed to Tsui-goab (p. 58):—

Thou, oh Tsui-goa,
Thou Father of Fathers,
Thou art (our) Father!
Let stream the thunder-cloud!
Let our flocks live, please!
Let us also live!
I am very weak indeed
From thirst,
From hunger.
Oh, that I may eat the fruits of the field!
Art thou then not our Father,
The Father of Fathers,
Thou, Tsui-goa!
Oh, that we may praise thee,
That we may give thee in return,
Thou Father of Fathers,
Thou, oh Lord,
Thou, oh Tsui-goa.

After this we shall be better able to understand the original character of this Hottentot Indra or Zeus, and be able to interpret without difficulty some at least of the acounts given both of his doings and of his misdoings. Dr. Hahn records the following conversation which he had with an old Namaqua :—

Very heavy thunder-clouds (he writes p. 64), were towering above the horizon. We both looked with great enjoyment towards the clouds, calculating that in a few hours' time the whole country ought to swim in water. 'Ah,' he said, 'there comes Tsui-goab in his old manner, as he used to do in the times of my grandfathers. You will see to-day rain, and very soon the country will be covered by ' *Tusib.*' I asked him what he meant by '*Tusib.*' He answered: 'When the first green grass and herbs come after the rain, and in the morning you see that green shining colour spread over the country, we say: *Tusib covers the earth.*'

This reminded us of 2 Samuel xxiii. 4: 'And he shall be as the light of the morning, when the sun riseth, even a morning without clouds; as the tender grass springing out of the earth by *clear shining after rain*, or by the *splendour of the rain.*'

Here we see the natural and poetical aspect of Tsui-goab. But Dr. Hahn gives us an opportunity of watching the practical influence also which a belief in Tsui-goab still exercises on the people. He was himself travelling in Namaqua-land, and wishing to go to a mission station (p. 63).

The distance (he writes) to our next water was calculated three days' hard riding with the ox-wagon. We, however, had made the calculation without the host, because, after three days, we found ourselves still another twelve hours from the water. We had only for ourselves a little water in a cask, which, however, was almost consumed. In the night before the fourth day we lost our road, and it was only after some hours that we discovered our mistake. If we had to pass another twenty-four hours like this, not one of us would have seen the next day. Even in the night the air appeared to come from a hot oven. I scolded the guide, a raw heathen from the Habobe tribe, angrily for his carelessness, and asked: 'What have you done? to-morrow we shall be eaten by the jackals and vultures. Who will now help us out of this trouble?'

The man coolly answered: 'Tsui-goab will help us.'

I: 'What nonsense! you and your Tsui-goab are both stupid fools!'

He: 'Truly, master, he will help.'

In the morning, about nine o'clock, we reached the water. After we had quenched our thirst, and were relishing a cup of coffee and a pipe, and talking over our troubles, my guide said laughingly: 'My dear master, yesterday you would almost have killed me, but the Lord refused you (to do so); but have you now convinced yourself that the Lord has helped?'

So far, all that is told us about Tsui-goab is intelligible, and offers striking points of similarity with the thoughts and expressions of other more civilised nations who, like the Khoi-khoi, and perhaps neither sooner nor later, discovered in the great celestial phenomena, and more particularly in the constant manifestation of the power of the sun and its influence on the life of nature and of man, the first indications of higher and supernatural powers, whom they called by names applicable originally to natural phenomena only. Nothing can be more natural, or, we might say, more human, than the way in which the Khoi-khoi speak of Tsui-goab, always supposing that Tsui-goab was originally a name of the sky, or of the rising sun, or of the pouring rain, or of the thunder. All these names would easily find their common focus in a so-called solar or celestial deity, in a Jupiter, or a Varuna, or an Indra, or a Thor, and the smallest knowledge of the mythological language of the ancient world would suffice to enable us to understand their legends, such as they are told us by Dr. Hahn and his predecessors.

But we now come to the irrational element in these legends. The very same Tsui-goab, the god of the sky, the sun, the rain, the thunder—the Supreme Being, in fact, of the Khoi-khoi—is the subject of the strangest stories. He is said to have been originally, and not many generations back, a quack doctor with a broken knee. Appleyard, for instance, in his Kafir grammar, tells us 'that the Hottentot Tsoei-koap is known to the Kafirs under the name of *u-Tixo*, and that this name means the *Wounded Knee*, and was originally applied to a doctor or sorcerer of considerable notoriety and skill among the Hottentots or Namaquas some generations

back, in consequence of his having received some injury to
his knee.   Having been held in high repute for extraordinary
powers during life, he was invoked, even after death, as one
who could still relieve and protect, and hence in process of
time he became nearest in idea to their first conception of
God.'

The same story is told again and again with but slight
variations.   Dr. Moffat, in his *Missionary Labours and
Scenes in South Africa*, writes:—

In my journey to the back parts of Great Namaqualand I
met with an aged sorcerer or doctor, who stated that he had
always understood that Tsui-goab was a notable warrior of
great physical strength; that in a desperate struggle with
another chieftain he received *a wound in the knee;* but,
having vanquished his enemy, his name was lost in the
mighty combat which rendered the nation independent; for
no one could conquer the Tsui-goab (wounded knee).   When
I referred to the import of the word, ' *one who inflicts pain,*'
or *a sore knee*, manifesting my surprise that they should give
such a name to their Creator and Benefactor, he replied in a
way that induced a belief that he applied the term to what
we should call the devil, or to death itself; adding, that he
thought death, or the power of causing death, was very sore
indeed.

Dr. Hahn heard the following account from an old Habobe-
Nama:—

Tsui-goab was a powerful chief of the Khoikhoi; in fact,
he was the first Khoikhoib, from whom all the Khoikhoi
tribes took their origin.   But Tsui-goab was not his original
name.   This Tsui-goab went to war with another chief
Gaunab, because the latter always killed great numbers of
Tsui-goab's people.   In this fight, however, Tsui-goab was

repeatedly overpowered by Gaunab, but in every battle the former grew stronger; and at last he was so strong and big that he easily destroyed Gaunab, by giving him one blow behind the ear.   While Gaunab was expiring he gave his enemy a blow on the knee.   Since that day the conqueror of Gaunab received the name Tsui-goab, '*sore knee*' or '*wounded knee.*'   Henceforth he could not walk properly, because he was lame.   He could do wonderful things, which no other man could do, because he was very wise.   He could tell what would happen in future times.   He died several times, and several times he rose again.   And whenever he came back to us, there were great feastings and rejoicings.   Milk was brought from every kraal, and fat cows and fat ewes were slaughtered.   Tsui-goab gave every man plenty of cattle and sheep, because he was very rich.   He gives rain, he makes the clouds, he lives in the clouds, and he makes our cows and sheep fruitful.   Tsui-goab lives in a beautiful heaven; and Gaunab lives in a dark heaven, quite separate from the heaven of Tsui-goab.

Here, then, we have what has been called the irrational element in mythology.   No one is surprised at legends which give a more or less metaphorical or poetical version of natural phenomena, or express, in a somewhat exaggerated form, moral, philosophical, or religious ideas shared in common by the whole human race.   What makes mythology mythological, in the true sense of the word, is what is utterly unintelligible, absurd, strange, or miraculous.   We listen to all that is told us about Tsui-goab, and can to a certain extent enter into it. But when we are told that the Khoi-khoi believed their Supreme God to have been originally a weak-kneed quack, we pause, and say, surely this requires an explanation.

There are only two systems possible in which the irrational

element in mythology can be accounted for. One school takes
the irrational as a matter of fact; and if we read that Daphne
fled before Phoibos and was changed into a laurel tree, that
school would say that there probably was a young lady called
Aurora, like, for instance, Aurora Königsmark; that a young
man called Robin, or, possibly, a man with red hair, pursued
her, and that she hid behind a laurel tree that happened to
be there. This was the theory of Euhemeros, re-established
by the famous Abbé Banier, and not quite extinct even now.
According to another school, the irrational element in
mythology is inevitable, and due to the influence of language
on thought, so that many of the legends of gods and heroes
may be rendered intelligible, if only we can discover the
original meaning of their proper names. The followers of
this school try to show that Daphne, the name of the laurel
tree, was an old name for the Dawn, and that Phoibos was
one of the many names of the sun, who pursued the dawn,
till she vanished before his rays. Of these two schools, the
former has always appealed to the mythologies of savage
nations as showing that gods and heroes were originally
human beings, worshipped, after their death, as ancestors and
as gods; while the latter has confined itself chiefly to an etymological analysis of mythological names in Greek, Latin,
Sanskrit, and other languages, such as had been sufficiently
studied to admit of a scientific grammatical and etymological
treatment.

Now these legends of the Hottentots about Tsui-goab, the
weak-kneed doctor, seemed to supply the strongest evidence
in support of Abbé Banier's theory. What could be clearer
than that the Hottentots worshipped as their Supreme Being
a human being, in fact, an old medicine man with a lame

knee, who, either for his bravery in battle, or for his medical skill, had been raised after death to the dignity of a god? Here surely, it might be said, so far from natural phenomena becoming personified and deified, we see that the ancient pantheon consists clearly of human ancestors, their very names being those which they bore while walking on earth.

Before entering on an etymological interpretation of the 'sore knee' of Tsui-goab, we have still to say a few words on another system of mythological interpretation which we thought was only a revival of the views of Euhemeros and of the Abbé Banier, but which we are assured rests on a different basis, namely, the system put forward by Mr. Herbert Spencer in his interesting volume of *Principles of Sociology.*

Knowing how difficult it is to represent a theory, which one considers utterly untenable, with perfect accuracy and fairness, we feel obliged to give the *ipsissima verba* of the eminent Sociologist—though even then we are afraid we shall hardly escape the suspicion of having wilfully mutilated his statements, which, of course, it is impossible to reprint completely within the narrow limits of a Review.

Mr. Herbert Spencer tells us (*Principles of Sociology,* p. 390),

that the mythologists hold that the powers of Nature, at first conceived and worshipped as impersonal, come to be personalised, because of certain characters in the words applied to them; and that the legends concerning the persons identified with these natural powers arise afterwards.

'Mythologist' is a very vague term, and it would, indeed, be difficult to prove that no person who could claim such a title had ever given utterance to the opinions just stated. But the science of mythology, as it is now represented by many writers in England, France, Italy, Germany, proposes the very opposite view. It holds that the conception of *impersonal* powers is always later than that of *personal* powers, and that, in an early stage of thought and language, such distinction had not yet been made; while the idea of worshipping impersonal powers belongs to the very latest stage of mental development, if, in fact, it has ever been held in that crude form at all.

But however unfair and inaccurate the representation may be which Mr. Herbert Spencer gives of that view of mythology of which he does not approve, the explanation which he gives of his own view may safely be accepted as correctly stated, if we state it in his own words :—-

Contrariwise [he says], the view here held is that the human personality is the primary element; that the identification of this with some natural power or object is due to identity of name ; and that the worship of this natural power thus arises secondarily.

Let us at once take an instance, and compare the view put forward by the science of mythology with that propounded by Mr. Herbert Spencer.

The comparative mythologist would say that, in accordance with the laws which govern the growth of human thought and language, it was inevitable that our earliest ancestors should think and say, 'The Sun dies,' or 'the Sun is killed by the Night,' a saying which has been varied in a thousand different ways in all the mythologies of the world, ending generally in a story of a bright being, divine, half-divine, or human, who was killed by a dark enemy. Mr. Herbert Spencer says No; quite the contrary. There probably was a man who was called Sun. Why not? many people are called Sun, Sonne, Soleil, even now. That person died; and, again, what can be more natural? Or he was actually killed by another person, who might have been called Black or Night. After his death, Mr. Sun would become an ancestor and be worshipped as such, or he might even become a god, if gods existed—though one hardly knows how they could have come into existence. Then, as Mr. Sun or St. Sun was worshipped, the identity of his name with the sun would naturally lead in the end to the transference of a worship and legends, intended for Mr. Sun or St. Sun, to the impersonal sun seen in the sky. Lest we should be supposed to have given an absurd aspect to this new method of mythological interpretation, we must quote in full. Mr. Herbert Spencer gives (p. 390) an imaginary myth as follows:—

All winter the beautiful Sunshine, pursued by the dark Storm, was ever hiding herself, now behind the clouds, now below the mountains. She could not steal forth from her concealment for more than a short time without being again chased with swift footsteps and loud threatening noise, and had quickly to retreat. After many moons, however, the Storm, chasing less furiously, and seeing her more clearly, became gentler; and Sunshine, gaining courage, from time to time remained longer visible. Storm failing to capture by pursuit, and softened by her charms, made milder advances. Finally came their union. Then the earth rejoiced in the moist warmth; and from them were born plants which covered its surface, and made it gay with flowers. But every autumn Storm begins to frown and growl; Sunshine flies from him; and the pursuit begins again.

This myth is not very like a real old Aryan myth, as every practised student of mythology will at once perceive, the idea of a union between the Sun, as a woman, and the Stormwind, as a man, being somewhat unnatural. But letting that pass, we shall now listen to Mr. Herbert Spencer's further speculations :—

Supposing (he says) the Tasmanians had been found by us in a semi-civilized state with a developed mythology containing some such legend as this, the unhesitating interpretation put upon it, after the method now accepted, would be that the observed effects of mingled sunshine and storm were thus figuratively expressed, and that the ultimate representation of Sunshine and Storm, as persons who once lived on the earth, was due to the natural mythopœic tendency, which took its direction from the genders of the words.

Certainly this would be the interpretation of comparative mythologists, only with this reservation, that they would not call the language figurative—if that term implies anything intentional and artificial—but natural and inevitable; and that the difference of gender would be with them concomitant rather with mythic thought than productive of it.

Now let us hear what interpretation Mr. Herbert Spencer would put on such a myth (p. 391):—

As already shown (he writes), birth-names among un-civilized races, taken from the incidents of the moment, often refer to the time of day and the weather. Among such which Mason enumerates, as given by the Karens, are 'Evening,' 'Moon-rising,' etc. There is, therefore, nothing anomalous or exceptional in the fact that 'Ploo-ra-na-loo-na,' meaning Sunshine, is the name of a Tasmanian woman; nor is there anything exceptional in the fact that among the neighbouring Australians 'Hail,' 'Thunder,' and 'Wind' occur as names.

The inference here drawn, therefore, harmonising with all preceding inferences, is that the initial step in the genesis of such a myth would be the existence of human beings named Storm and Sunshine, that from the confusion inevitably arising in tradition between them and the natural agents having the same names, would result this personalising of these natural agents, and the according to them human origins and human adventures: the legend, once having thus germinated, being, in successive generations, elaborated and moulded into fitness with the phenomena.

Let us now apply this sociological interpretation to the myth of Tsui-goab, and we can hardly wrong Mr. Herbert Spencer in supposing that he would readily accept the tradition that there was once upon a time a Hottentot doctor who by some accident had injured his knee, and who after his death was worshipped as an ancestor, till he became the Supreme Being, and was invoked as such to send the thunder-cloud, to protect the flocks, and to let the fruits of the earth grow and abound. He might even go a step further, and compare the struggle of Tsui-goab and Gaunab, and the lame knee of one of the combatants, with similar legends elsewhere. Mr. Herbert Spencer, though he warns us that it is perilous to compare other religions with our own, does not shrink from such perils. Thus he writes (*Principles of Sociology*, p. 434):—

On reading that when the Spaniards arrived in Mexico, the natives, thinking them gods, offered up human beings to them, it is allowable to ask whether the ideas and motives of these people were analogous to those of the Scandinavian king On, when he immolated his son to Odin; but it is not allowable to ask whether like ideas and motives prompted Abraham's intention to sacrifice Isaac. The fact that Dr.

Barth was taken by the Fulahs for their god, Fete, may probably raise the question whether, if there had arisen a quarrel between his party and the Fulahs in which he was worsted by one of their chiefs, there might not have grown up a legend akin to that which tells how the god Ares was worsted by Diomede ; but it is highly improper to raise the question whether the story of Jacob's prolonged struggle with the Lord had an origin of allied kind.   Here, however, pursuing the methods of science, and disregarding foregone conclusions, we must deal with the Hebrew conception in the same manner as with all others; and must ask whether it had not a kindred genesis.

Where is the danger that Mr. Spencer apprehends ?   No question would seem more innocent than that which he asks, and we may be perfectly certain that if there were the slightest presumptive evidence, no one would be burnt, or even black-balled at a club, for asking it.   It comes simply to this, whether he who wrestled with Jacob was a man like Dr. Barth, called El, or whether the Jews ever thought that he was ; and, if Mr. Herbert Spencer can really produce any evidence on that point, then no doubt the similarity between the sore knee of Tsui-goab after his fight with Gaunab, and the hollow of Jacob's thigh being out of joint after his struggle, would considerably strengthen his position, and show that such accidents will happen at all times and in all places.

But let us now hear what Dr. Hahn has to say.   He, too, like most people who have written on this curious story of Tsui-goab[1], was much puzzled why the Khoi-khoi should

[1] See Bleek, 'Comparative Grammar of the South African Languages,' 1862, §§ 395-397.

have changed a lame old doctor into their Supreme Being.
'Lame Knee' is certainly the meaning of his name, and no
native seems to have a doubt about it, as little as the ancient
Hindus doubted that their god Savitri, the sun, had an
artificial hand made of precious gold. The first question which
Dr. Hahn asks is, What is the etymology, *i. e.* what is the
historical origin, of the name? And he finds that *goa-b* is
derived from a root *goa*, to walk, to approach. From it is
formed *goa-b*, meaning, as a verb, coming he, *i. e.* he comes,
and, as a substantive, the comer, the approaching one. This
goab, meaning originally the goer, was used for knee. But
the same *goab* has a second meaning also, viz. the day, and,
more particularly, the approaching day. Thus *goara* means,
the day dawns. The same root *goa* produced several other
words besides; but we need not dwell on them at present,
beyond calling attention to the striking similarity between
the derivation of special words from general roots in the
Khoi-khoi language and in Sanskrit.

If, then, *goab* may mean morning, what does *Tsu* mean?
Its general meaning is sore; but it can also mean bloody,
red-coloured, just as *ava*, red, meant originally bloody in
Khoi-khoi. That names of colour are derived from the
colour of wounds is well known to scholars[1]. But if there
were any doubt as to *tsu* having had the meaning of red, how
could we account for tsu-xu-b, a name for night? The verb
xu means to go away, tsu-xu-b therefore means 'tsu-gone
away-he.' Here the translation, 'the Sore-on is gone away,'
would have no meaning at all, while 'the Red one is gone
away,' is a perfectly intelligible name of the night.

---

[1] See 'Hibbert Lectures,' 2nd ed. p. 42.

If, then, Tsui-goab, which is now taken in the sense of sore knee, may have meant originally red dawn or morning, might not that name and that concept lend themselves more naturally to become the name of the Supreme Being than a lame-kneed doctor? Was not *Dyaus*, the bright sky, and is not *Dieu* still the name of the Supreme Being?

But let us now look at the legends told of Tsui-goab by the Africans themselves, to see whether they fit the old doctor better, or the rising sun, the giver of light and life. They say that Tsui-goab comes from the East (p. 134). The Koras, as Dr. Hahn informs us, believe that Tsui-goab lives in the red heaven, while his enemy Gaunab lives in the black heaven (p. 126). When the day dawns, the Khoi-khoi go and pray with the face turned to the east: 'Oh, Tsui-goa, All Father.'

The Khoi-khoi believe that this Tsui-goab is the avenger. Thus they say (p. 62): 'Oh, Tsu-goa, thou alone knowest that I am without guilt;' or, 'Do what you think, but you will know Tsui-goab;' *i.e.* he will find you out and punish you, just as Saranyû, the dawn, in the Veda, becomes the Greek Erinnys.

The principal enemy of Tsui-goab is Gauṛab, and Gaunab means the destroyer, who sends sleep and death, and whom Dr. Hahn identifies with the dark night.

Tsui-goab, then, the red dawn, but also the Father of Fathers, became, as was natural with people whose religion was full of ancestor-worship, the ancestor of the Khoi-khoi. He was worshipped as a being who had formerly lived on earth, who had a wife and a son, and performed many valiant deeds. The greatest of his deeds, performed every morning or every year, was his struggle with Gaunab, the dark; and what was more natural, when mothers and grandmothers were asked to talk about Tsui-goab, particularly when *tsui* had ceased to mean red, and *goab* was at all events more familiar in the sense of knee than in that of dawn—what was more natural than that his name 'sore knee' should give rise to questions and ready answers ?

Other names shared the same fate. *Nanub*, meaning the streaming thunder-cloud, became a god or an ancestor, and sometimes meant the same as Tsui-goab. *Gurub*, thunder, not an imitative word, but derived from *gu*, to cover, was intended at first for the covering cloud and darkness (Sanskrit v*ri*tra), but soon assumed the same kind of personality as Nanub and Tsui-goab. All three are asked to give rain, and the other gifts which men ask from the powers above. Gurub is asked more particularly not to scold, Tsui-goab to give rain and food. If Tsui-goab was an old doctor, Gurub (Thunder) must have been another Hottentot, and Nanub (Cloud) another Bushman.

No one can deny that, as Mr. Herbert Spencer tells us, people are sometimes called Thunder and Lightning, Dawn and Cloud ; and as reality is stranger than fiction, these persons, before they were changed into gods, may have met with such strange accidents as are recorded in the mythologies both of civilized and uncivilized races. Scholars and anthropologists must choose between the two systems of explaining the irrational in mythology; but it seems to us that Dr. Hahn's book will always form a very heavy weight in the scale of the scholars.

SACRED BOOKS OF THE EAST,

TRANSLATED, WITH INTRODUCTIONS AND NOTES,

BY VARIOUS ORIENTAL SCHOLARS,

AND EDITED BY

F. MAX MÜLLER.

APART from the interest which the Sacred Books of all religions possess in the eyes of the theologian, and, more particularly, of the missionary, to whom an accurate knowledge of them is as indispensable as a knowledge of the enemy's country is to a general, these works have of late assumed a new importance, as viewed in the character of ancient historical documents. In every country where Sacred Books have been preserved, whether by oral tradition or by writing, they are the oldest records, and mark the beginning of what may be called documentary, in opposition to purely traditional, history.

There is nothing more ancient in India than the Vedas; and, if we except the Vedas and the literature connected with them, there is again no literary work in India which, so far as we know at present, can with certainty be referred to an earlier date than that of the Sacred Canon of the Buddhists. Whatever age we may assign to the various portions of the Avesta and to their final arrangement, there is no book in the Persian language of greater antiquity than the Sacred Books of the followers of Zarathustra, nay even than their translation in Pehlevi. There may have been an extensive ancient literature in China long before Kung-fu-tze and Lao-tze, but among all that was rescued and preserved of it, the five King and the four Shu claim again the highest antiquity. As to the Qur'ân, it is known to be the fountain-head both of the religion and of the literature of the Arabs.

This being the case, it was but natural that the attention of the historian should of late have been more strongly attracted by these Sacred Books, as likely to afford most valuable information, not only on the religion, but also on the moral sentiments, the social institutions, the legal maxims of some of the most important nations of antiquity. There are not many nations that have preserved sacred writings, and most of those that have been preserved have but lately become accessible to us in their original form, through the rapid advance of Oriental scholarship in Europe. Neither Greeks, nor Romans, nor Germans, nor Celts, nor Slaves have left us anything that deserves the name of Sacred Books. The Homeric Poems are national Epics, like the Râmâyana, and the Nibelunge ; the Homeric Hymns have never received that general recognition or sanction which alone can impart to the poetical effusions of personal piety the sacred or canonical character which is the distinguishing feature of the Vedic Hymns. The sacred literature of the early inhabitants of Italy seems to have been of a liturgical rather than of a purely religious kind, and whatever the Celts, the Germans, the Slaves may have possessed of sacred traditions about their gods and heroes, having been handed down by oral tradition chiefly, has perished beyond all hope of recovery. Some portions of the Eddas alone give us an idea of what the religious and heroic poetry of the Scandinavians may have been. The Egyptians possessed Sacred Books, and some of them, such as the Book of the Dead, have come down to us in various forms. In Babylon and Assyria, too, important fragments of what may be called a Sacred Literature have lately come to light. The interpretation, however, of these Hieroglyphic and Cuneiform texts is as yet so difficult that, for the present, they are of interest to the scholar only, and hardly available for historical purposes.

Leaving out of consideration the Jewish and Christian Scriptures, it appears that the only great and original religions which profess to be founded on Sacred Books, and have preserved them in manuscript, are:—

1. The religion of the Brahmans.
2. The religion of the followers of Buddha.
3. The religion of the followers of Gina.
4. The religion of the followers of Zarathustra.
5. The religion of the followers of Kung-fu-tze.
6. The religion of the followers of Lao-tze.
7. The religion of the followers of Mohammed.

A desire for a trustworthy translation of the Sacred Books of these Eastern religions has often been expressed. Several have been translated into English, French, German, or Latin, but in some cases these translations are difficult to procure, in others they are loaded with notes and commentaries, which are intended for students by profession only. Oriental scholars have been blamed for not having as yet supplied a want so generally felt, and so frequently expressed, of a complete, trustworthy, and readable translation of the principal Sacred Books of the Eastern Religions. The reasons, however, why hitherto they have shrunk from such an undertaking are clear enough. The difficulties in many cases of giving complete translations, and not selections only, are very great. There is still much work to be done in a critical restoration of the original texts, in an examination of their grammar and metres, and in determining the exact meaning of many words and passages. That kind of work is naturally far more attractive to scholars than a mere translation, particularly when they cannot but feel that, with the progress of our knowledge, many a passage which now seems clear and easy, may, on being re-examined, assume a new import. Thus while scholars, who are most competent to undertake a translation, prefer to devote their time to more special researches, the work of a complete translation is deferred to the future, and historians are left under the impression that Oriental scholarship is still in so unsatisfactory a state as to make any reliance on translations of the Veda, the Avesta, or the Tao-te-king, extremely hazardous.

It is clear, therefore, that a translation of the principal Sacred Books of the East can be carried out only at a certain sacrifice. Scholars must leave for a time their own special researches in order to render the general results already obtained accessible to the public at large. And even then, really useful results can be achieved *viribus unitis* only. If four of the best Egyptologists have to combine in order to produce a satisfactory edition and translation of one of the

Sacred Books of ancient Egypt, the Book of the Dead, a much larger number of Oriental scholars will be required for translating the Sacred Books of the Brahmans, the Buddhists, the Gainas, the Zoroastrians, the followers of Kung-fu-tze, Lao-tze, and Mohammed.

Lastly, there was the most serious difficulty of all, a difficulty which no scholar could remove, viz. the difficulty of finding the funds necessary for carrying out so large an undertaking. No doubt there exists at present a very keen interest in questions connected with the origin, the growth, and decay of religion. But much of that interest is theoretic rather than historical. How people might or could or should have elaborated religious ideas, is a topic most warmly discussed among psychologists and theologians, but a study of the documents, in which alone the actual growth of religious thought can be traced, is much neglected. A faithful, unvarnished prose translation of the Sacred Books of India, Persia, China, and Arabia, though it may interest careful students, will never, I fear, excite a wide-spread interest, or command a circulation large enough to make it a matter of private enterprise and commercial speculation.

No doubt there is much in these old books that is startling by its very simplicity and truth, much that is elevated and elevating, much that is beautiful and sublime; but people who have vague ideas of primeval wisdom and the splendour of Eastern poetry will soon find themselves grievously disappointed. It cannot be too strongly stated, that the chief, and, in many cases, the only interest of the Sacred Books of the East is historical; that much in them is extremely childish, tedious, if not repulsive; and that no one but the historian will be able to understand the important lessons which they teach.   It would have been impossible to undertake a translation even of the most important only of the Sacred Books of the East, without the support of an Academy or a University which recognises the necessity of rendering these works more generally accessible, on the same grounds on which it recognises the duty of collecting and exhibiting in Museums the petrifactions of bygone ages, little concerned whether the public admires the beauty of fossilised plants and broken skeletons, as long as hard-working students find there some light for reading once more the darker pages in the history of the earth.

Having been so fortunate as to secure that support, having also received promises of assistance from some of the best Oriental scholars in England and India, I hope I shall be able, after the necessary preparations are completed, to publish about three volumes of translations every year, selecting from the stores of the seven so-called 'Book-religions' those works which at present can be translated, and which are most likely to prove useful. All translations will be made from the original texts, and where good translations exist already, they will be carefully revised by competent scholars.   Such is the bulk of the religious literature of the Brahmans and the Buddhists, that to attempt a complete translation would be far beyond the powers of one generation of scholars.   Still, if the interest in the work itself should continue, there is no reason why this series of translations should not be carried on, even after those who commenced it shall have ceased from their labours.

What I contemplate at present, and I am afraid at my time of life even this may seem too sanguine, is no more than a Series of twenty-four volumes, the publication of which will probably extend over eight years.   In this Series I hope to comprehend the following books, though I do not pledge myself to adhere strictly to this outline :—

   1. From among the Sacred Books of the Brahmans I hope to give a translation of the Hymns of the Rig-Veda.   While I shall continue my translation of selected hymns of that Veda, a *traduction raisonnée* which is intended for Sanskrit scholars only, on the same principles which I have followed in the first volume [1], explaining every word and sentence that seems to require elucidation, and carefully examining the opinions of previous commentators, both native and European, I intend to contribute a freer translation of the hymns to this Series, with a few explanatory notes only, such as are absolutely necessary to enable readers who are unacquainted with Sanskrit to understand the thoughts of the Vedic poets.   The translation of perhaps another Samhitâ, one or two of the Brâhmanas, or portions of them, will have to be included in our Series, as well as the principal Upanishads, theosophic treatises of great interest and beauty.   There is every prospect of an early appearance of a translation of the Bhagavadgîtâ, of the most important among the sacred Law-books, and of one at least of the Purânas.

   2. The Sacred Books of the Buddhists will be translated chiefly from the two original collections, the Southern in Pâli, the Northern in Sanskrit.   Here the selection will, no doubt, be most difficult.   Among the first books to be

---

[1] 'Rig-Veda-Sanhitâ, The Sacred Hymns of the Brahmans,' translated and explained by F. Max Müller. Vol. I. Hymns to the Maruts or the Storm-Gods : London, 1869.

published will be, I hope, Sûtras from the Dîgha Nikâya, a part of the Vinaya-piṭaka, the Dhammapada, the Divyâvadâna, the Lalita-Vistara, or legendary life of Buddha.

3. The Sacred Books of the Zoroastrians lie within a smaller compass, but they will require fuller notes and commentaries in order to make a translation intelligible and useful.

4. The books which enjoy the highest authority with the followers of Kung-fu-tze are the King and the Shû. Of the former the Shû King or Book of History; the Odes of the Temple and the Altar, and other pieces illustrating the ancient religious views and practices of the Chinese, in the Shih King, or Book of Poetry; the Yî King; the Li Ki; and the Hsiâo King or Classic of Filial Piety, will all be given, it is hoped, entire. Of the latter, the series will contain the Chung Yung, or Doctrine of the Mean; the Ta Hioh, or Great Learning; all Confucius' utterances in the Lun Yu or Confucian Analects, which are of a religious nature and refer to the principles of his moral system; and Măng-tze's Doctrine of the goodness of Human Nature.

5. For the system of Lao-tze we require only a translation of the Tao-te-king with some of its commentaries, and, it may be, an authoritative work to illustrate the actual operation of its principles.

6. For Islam, all that is essential is a trustworthy translation of the Qur'ân.

It will be my endeavour to divide the twenty-four volumes which are contemplated in this Series as equally as possible between the seven religions. But much must depend on the assistance which I receive from Oriental scholars, and also on the interest and the wishes of the public.

The foll w'ng are the names of the scholars who have promised to supply translations :

BEAL S
BHANDARKAR, R G.
BUHLER, G
COWELL, E B
DARMESTETER, J.
EGGELING, J.

FAUSBOLL, V
JACOBI, H.
J LLY, J
KERN, H.
LEGGE, J
MAX MULLER, F

OLDENBERG H.
PALMER E H
RHYS DAVIDS, T W
TELANG, K T.
WEST, E W.

OXFORD, *October*, 1876

LETTER TO THE VERY REV. THE DEAN OF CHRIST CHURCH.

OXF RD, *March* 18, 1882.

MY DEAR DEAN,

When, in the year 1875, I received an invitation from the Austrian Government to transfer my services to Vienna, and to publish there, under the auspices of the Imperial Academy, a Series of Translations of the Sacred Books of the East, it was, I believe, mainly due to your kind exertions that the University invited me to stay at Oxford, and to carry out the same undertaking here, substituting only English for German in the translations which I had originally contemplated   I then submitted to you, and through you to the Delegates of the Clarendon Press and the Secretary of State for India, a general outline of the translations which, if only I could secure the co-operation of Oriental scholars in England, I hoped to bring out in a series of twenty-four volumes.   This was in October 1876, and as the time is now approaching when this Series ought to be finished, viz. in October 1884, I think I ought to render, through you, to the

Delegates of the Clarendon Press and the Secretary of State for India, an account of my stewardship.

There was in the beginning, as it could hardly have been otherwise, considerable delay. The help of really competent scholars had to be secured, and some time had to elapse before they could prepare their translations. The first volume therefore could not be published before 1879, and now in 1882 the number of volumes published amounts to fourteen only. It would be too long to explain to you all the causes of delay. I lost by death the valuable assistance of Professor Childers, who had undertaken the translation of important parts of the Buddhist Canon. Illness prevented Professors Cowell and Pischel, and likewise Dr. Rajendralal Mitra from fulfilling their promises, while similar causes delayed very considerably the work entrusted to Professor Bhandarkar, Rev. S. Beal, Professor Jacobi, Professor Kielhorn, and Mr. K. T. Telang.

Under these circumstances the execution of the work I had undertaken became, at one time, extremely precarious, and I had to apply for assistance to other scholars in order not to disappoint the Delegates of the Press and the Indian Government. That assistance was readily granted, and I have now the satisfaction of informing you that I still hope to be able to fulfil all I had promised, and to fulfil it within the stipulated time.

Fourteen volumes are now finished, eight more are in the Press, and the translation of the remaining two volumes is sufficiently advanced to be ready by October 1884.

Looking at the work that has been done and will be done by the end of 1884, it may be seen that all the great religions of the East have been fairly represented, although twenty-four volumes cannot possibly give an adequate idea even of the more important only among the Sacred Books of the East; meaning by Sacred Books none but those that have received some kind of canonical sanction.

For the ancient *Vedic Religion* there will be, in the present Series, two or three volumes of Upanishads, two or three volumes of the Brâhmana of the Yagur-veda, and one volume of Grihya Sûtras on domestic ceremonies. Regret has been expressed at the non-appearance of a translation of the Rig-veda, but no one who is in the least acquainted with the present state of Vedic studies would fail to perceive the cause of this. People write and speak as if there were no translations of the Rig-veda. We possess five translations of the Rig-veda, one in French, two in English, and two in German. Of these the French translation is purely tentative. The English translation by Professor Wilson follows the commentary of Sâyana, as published by myself, and represents the native or traditional interpretation of the Vedic hymns. The German metrical version by Grassmann marked at the time a real progress, but has now been left behind by the prose translation of Professor Ludwig. The English translation, now publishing at Calcutta, is eclectic, sometimes following native, sometimes European authorities. For those who can read modern Sanskrit there are in addition Sâyana's translation published by me, and the translation now publishing at Benares by Dayananda Sarasvati. What I consider a translation of the Rig-veda *ought* to be, I have shown in one small volume, published in 1869 containing an interpretation, with its full justification, of twelve hymns only. What prevented me from continuing this translation was ill health, and the warning it gave me that I ought to finish some other work before it was too late. In the meantime it has become quite clear, chiefly through the labours of Ludwig and Bergaigne, that, before any new translation of the Rig-veda is undertaken, we must have a translation of the Yagur-veda, which contains the key to many allusions to ceremonial subjects occurring in the Rig-veda. Such a translation of the hymns of the Yagur-veda has long been promised by Professor Weber; while a translation of the Brâhmana of that Veda has been undertaken by Professor Eggeling, and will appear in our Series of Sacred Books. Though I feel deeply sensible therefore of the compliment paid to me by so many scholars in asking me to publish a new translation of the Rig-veda, I think they will agree with me that the time for a new translation has hardly come, while I may add that there are others quite as competent as myself for undertaking so laborious a task.

I felt at the same time that there was other work connected with the Vedas which would at present be far more useful, and I therefore undertook a translation of the Upanishads, works which, in the actual state of Sanskrit scholarship, seem to me to deserve the most careful study, as embodying, if I am not mistaken, the first germs of Buddhism in its historical development out of Brahmanism. It required, no doubt, some courage to begin the Series of the Sacred Books of the East with the Upanishads, partly on account of their obscurity and the repellent character of some of them, partly on account of the many difficulties which still beset a translation of these works, particularly in the Âranyaka portions, which had deterred all former translators. If, as has been pointed out, my translation often differs so widely from previous translations as to seem hardly based on the same original text, this is chiefly due to my keeping myself as much as possible independent of native commentators, who, though indispensable and extremely useful, are so much under the spell of the later systematic Vedânta philosophy, as often to do violence to the simpler thoughts of ancient poets and philosophers.

In the *ancient Law-books* we shall have fulfilled nearly all that was promised, chiefly owing to the excellent work done for us by Professors Bühler and Jolly. Their translations have opened an entirely new mine of ancient literature, and there has been an unanimous verdict as to the real benefit which they have conferred by their work both on the students of the ancient and on the administrators of the modern laws of India.

We have been less fortunate with the *metrical Law-books*, but there is every reason to hope that the series will not be closed without containing translations of Manu and Yâgñavalkya by Professor Bühler.

In the *later Brahmanical* literature we owe to Mr. Telang a careful translation, not only of the Bhagavadgîtâ, as promised by him, but likewise of the Anugîtâ and the Sanatsugâtîya.

The almost fatal illness of Dr. Rajendralal Mitra obliged me for a time to give up the idea of a translation of one of the Purânas. Professor Bhandarkar has now declared his willingness to undertake a translation of that Purâna which, by common consent, was pointed out as at present the most important, viz. the Vâyu-purâna. No one would have thanked us for a translation of the Bhâgavata-purâna, which, though very popular, is known to be very modern, and has been translated into French by Burnouf, a translation to be continued and finished under the auspices of the French Government by M. Hauvette-Besnault; while of the Vishnu-purâna we have Wilson's translation, lately re-edited by Dr. Fitz-Edward Hall. Whether this translation of the Vâyu-purâna is to be published, will depend on the decision of the Delegates.

Buddhism has of late occupied so large a share of public interest that we thought it right to have it presented as fully as possible in its different phases. The severe loss inflicted on our undertaking by the death of Professor Childers has been remedied by the ready help of Mr. T. W. Rhys Davids, Professor Fausboll, and Professor Oldenberg. We have published a volume of Suttas, the Dhammapada, and the extremely important Sutta Nipâta. There will be a complete translation of the Mahâvagga and *K*ullavagga, the canonical books on Buddhist Discipline. The first volume of these is ready, and two more will finish this interesting portion of the Sacred Canon of Ceylon.

Of *Sanskrit documents* illustrative of Northern Buddhism there will be a translation by Professor Kern of the 'Lotus of the Good Law,' and possibly a volume of miscellaneous translations treating of the Amitâbha Buddhism of China and Japan.

The Rev. S. Beal was long prevented by illness from finishing his promised translation of the most ancient Life of Buddha in Chinese, but his version of the Fo sho-hing-tsan-king is now passing through the Press, and will be finished, it is hoped, before the end of this year.

Professor Jacobi had undertaken to supply translations of some of the sacred books of the *G*ainas, and though the difficulties, chiefly arising from the imperfections of the MSS, have delayed his work, one volume at least of his translation will form part, we hope, of our Series.

With regard to the *Parsi Religion* M Darmesteter's translation of the *Vendidâd*, published in the fourth volume of our
Series, has attracted general attention among Zend scholars;
and though it has given rise to controversies, it has received
the highest praise even from those who differed most widely
from the translator's principles. Such controversies are not
only unavoidable in the interpretation of ancient texts, but
are really most desirable and most useful for the advancement
of Oriental scholarship. We may expect at least one more
volume from the pen of our distinguished *collaborateur*.

The later *Parsi* or *Pahlavi* literature has found its first
successful interpreter in Mr. E. W. West, and no contribution
has been more gratefully received by Oriental scholars than
his translations of the Bundahis, Bahman Yast, and Shâyast lâ-
Shâyast   The second volume, now in the Press, will contain
the Dâdistân î Dînîk, and possibly the Mainyô Khard.

Professor Palmer's translation of the *Qur'ân* lies finished
before us in two volumes, and seems to have raised quite a
new interest in a work which was often supposed to be
unreadable except in Arabic.

As to the works of Confucius and Lao tze it was well known
that they were in the very best hands   Professor Legge's
translation of the Shû King, Shih King, and Hsiâo King has
proved acceptable to scholars both in Europe and in China,
and his forthcoming translation of the Yî King is looked
forward to with the highest interest.

With regard to myself I think I may say that I have tried
to fulfil my duties as Editor to the best of my power and
judgment.   I have been blamed, I know, for not making this
Series of Sacred Books more attractive and more popular, but
to do so would have been incompatible with the very object

I had in view in publishing these translations. I thought the time had come when the ancient religions of the East should be studied in their own canonical texts, and that an end should thus be put to the vague assertions as to their nature and character, whether coming from the admirers or the detractors of those ancient creeds. To have left out what seems tedious and repulsive in them would have been to my mind simply dishonest, and I could have been no party to such an undertaking. The translations, as here published, are historical documents that cannot be tampered with without destroying their value altogether. It is for the historian to find out what is good and what is bad in them, and I still believe that he who has eyes to see will recognise that there are nuggets of gold to be found in these ancient books, all the more precious because hidden under so much rubbish, that is, under so much *detritus* of early thought.

When in 1876 I undertook to bring out this Series of Sacred Books, I hardly thought that I could look forward to more than eight years of work. Still as I have been spared, and do not yet feel quite *senio confectus*, I am willing to work on as long as I can. If, therefore, the Delegates of the Press and the Secretary of State for India are satisfied with what I have hitherto done, I am at their service for whatever may remain to me of active life.

I remain, my dear Dean,

Yours very truly and gratefully,

F. MAX MÜLLER.

The 17 Volumes already published contain :—

Vol. I. THE UPANISHADS. Part I. The *Kʰândogya*-upani-
shad, The Talavakâra-upanishad, The Aitareya-âra*ny*aka,
The Kaushîtaki-brâhma*n*a-upanishad, and The Vâ*g*asaneyi-
sa*m*hitâ-upanishad. Translated by F. MAX MÜLLER. 8vo.
pp. ci, and 320.

Vol. II. THE SACRED LAWS OF THE ÂRYAS, as taught in
the Schools of Âpastamba, Gautama, Vâsish*tʰa*, and Baud-
hâya*na*. Part I. Âpastamba and Gautama. Translated
by GEORG BÜHLER. 8vo. pp. lvii, and 312.

Vol. III. THE SACRED BOOKS OF CHINA. The Texts of
Confucianism. Part I. The Shû King, The religious
portions of the Shih King, The Hsiâo King. Translated
by JAMES LEGGE. 8vo. pp. xxx, and 492.

Vol. IV. THE ZEND-AVESTA. Part I. The Vendîdâd. Translated by JAMES DARMESTETER. 8vo. pp. cii, and 240.

Vol. V. PAHLAVI TEXTS. Part I. The Bundahis, Bahman
Ya*st*, and Shâyast-lâ-Shâyast. Translated by E. W. WEST.
8vo. pp. lxxiv, and 438.

Vol. VI and IX. THE QUR'ÂN. Translated by E. H. PALMER.
8vo. Part I. Chapters I–XVI. pp. cxviii, and 268. Part II.
Chapters XVII–CXIV. pp. x, and 362.

Vol. VII. THE INSTITUTES OF VISH*N*U. Translated by JULIUS
JOLLY. 8vo. pp. xxxvii, and 316.

Vol. VIII. THE BHAGAVADGÎTÂ, WITH THE SANATSU*G*ÂTÎYA,
AND THE ANUGÎTÂ. Translated by KÂSHINÂTH TRIMBÂK
TELANG. 8vo. pp. 446.

Vol. X. THE DHAMMAPADA. A Collection of Verses. Being
one of the Canonical Books of the Buddhists. Translated
from Pâli by F. MAX MÜLLER. 8vo. pp. lv, and 99.

The following Volumes are in the Press:—

Vol. XIX. The Fo-Sho-Hing-Tsan-King. Translated by Samuel Beal.

Vol. XX. The Vâyu-Purâna. Translated by R. G. Bhandarkar.

Vol. XXI. The Saddharma-Pundarîka. Translated by H. Kern.

Vol. XXII. The Âkârânga-Sûtra. Translated by H. Jacobi.

Vol. XXIII. The Zend-Avesta. Part II. The Yasts. Translated by James Darmesteter.

INDEX.

Bournouf, 27, 28.
Böving on the Khoi-khoi religion, 281.
Brachycephalic tribes, 238.
Brahma, 227.
Brâhmana period, Rig-Veda finished before the, 161.
Brâhmanas, 57, 258.
Brahmanism, 53.
— true, 174.
Brahmans, 9, 27.
— religious books of, 9.
— their view of fire, 164 *note*.
Brahmins at Akbar's court, 226, 227.
Bridges, 105.
— in the Himâlaya, 250 *note*.
Bridgman, Dr., 261.
Brutus, Britons descended from, 46.
Buddha, 18, 22, 72, 73, 79, 148, 152, 169.
— religion of, 18, 59.
— never mentioned at Akbar's conferences, 18.
— teaching of, 190.
Buddhism, 29, 53, 55.
— in China, 63.
— among Turanians, 129.
— expelled the Buriate deities, 135 *note*.
— and Christianity, 169.
— denies a supreme Deity, 171.
Buddhist canon, in different languages, 18.
— miracles forbidden in the, 21.
— legends full of absurdities, 21.
— canon, 60.
— in China, 63.
— parables, 172.
— sermon, a, 172.
— merchant and his young son, 173-175.
Buddhists, 9, 27.
— canon of the, 18, 22.
— history of the, 22.
Buga, supreme god of the Tungusic tribes, 132.
Bulak Museum, hymn to Amon in the, 179.
Bullom dialect, 239.

Bunsen, 147.
— God in History, 166.
Buriates, 135 *note*.
— their idols, 135 *note*.
— displaced by Buddhism, 135 *note*.
Burmese, Buddhist canon in, 18.
Burnaburias, the Accadian king, 122.
Bushman dialect, 98.
— language, 239.
— roots in, 274.
— numerals in, 274.
Bushmen, Bosjesmen, 238, 273.
— despised by the Hottentots, 273.
— tribes, mutually unintelligible, 274.
Byblus, 111.

ÇABÁHÍS, lamp of the, 218.
Çahábah, reviled by Yazídí, 224.
Callaway, Bishop, 41 *note*, 42-44, 65 *note*, 182.
— his story of the Zulu lad, 183.
Calneh, 244.
Çamad, the eternal, 215 *note*.
Can and Ken, 12.
Canaanites, sons of Kush, 243.
Candelabra, found at Malta, dedicated to Baal, 114.
Canny, 12.
Canonical books, not to be trusted implicitly, 24.
— books, 53.
— books, nations without, 63, 64.
Cape Negroes, 239.
Capitol, the, 106.
Carriages, 105.
Carthage, worship of Moloch at, 117.
Caste, system of, 21.
Castrén, the traveller, 130.
— on the Tungusic and Samoyede tribes, 132.
— his derivation of Jumala, 133.
— on Finnish mythology, 133, 140.
— and Samoyede woman, 133.
— on Samoyede deities, 139.
— on the Altaic view of death, 141.
Categories of the understanding, 15.

Y